DEATH

PULP.

CASEY JARMAN

Death

AN ORAL HISTORY

WITH ILLUSTRATIONS
BY BROOKE WEEBER

2443 Fillmore Street, Suite 340, San Francisco, CA 94115 | www.zestbooks.net
Connect with Zest! zestbooks.net/blog | twitter.com/zestbooks | facebook.com/BooksWithATwist

ISBN: 978-1-942186-12-0 | Publisher: Hallie Warshaw | Editor: Daniel Harmon | Marketing: Emma Boyer | Design: Adam Grano

Manufactured in the U.S.A. | 4500614419 | DOC 10 9 8 7 6 5 4 3 2 1

"ALL I KNOW IS WHAT THE
WORDS KNOW, AND THE
DEAD THINGS, AND THAT
MAKES A HANDSOME LITTLE
SUM, WITH A BEGINNING,
A MIDDLE AND AN END AS
IN THE WELL-BUILT PHRASE
AND THE LONG SONATA
OF THE DEAD."

SAMUEL BECKETT, MOLLOY

CONTENTS

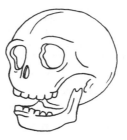

INTRODUCTION

BY THE AUTHOR

I grew up with photographs of my grandparents, but no actual grand-parents. They all died before or shortly after I was born. None of them held me as a baby, or told me about the old days, or passed on family se-crets from a bygone era. My folks told me stories about those mysterious figures from worn old photographs, trying to create some sort of bond between us—but all of the stories just swirled together. "Was it Grandpa Frank who owned a butcher shop? Or was that Mom's dad? Wait, no, he was a preacher, right?" Cue the look of disappointment in my parents' eyes. "I wish you could have known them," they still say.

For my mom and dad, this is all a considerable loss. But the gift of nev-er knowing (and, heaven forbid, loving) someone is that you never mourn them, either. The strongest emotion I can muster from looking at those old photos is a sense of lost history: sort of a skipped beat that I've hardly noticed. After all, whatever your family is like—divorced or together; genetic or adopted; abusive or supportive—becomes your own take on "normal." I always figured my situation was a pretty good trade: Missing out on some vague connection to an older generation was so much bet-ter than the alternative of having a beloved family member die and leave me heartbroken. I watched friends go through that, and for them it was earth-shattering. I counted myself lucky.

Of course, knowing that none of my grandparents stuck around long enough to meet me also left me with the relative certainty that my own parents—both smokers well into my teenage years—wouldn't live to old age, either. I didn't know *how* my mom and dad would croak (lung or liver cancer? heart attack? car crash?), but I was pretty sure I wouldn't make it into my twenties without at least one of them dying. It didn't help that my mom talked about death all the time: "One day I'll be gone, and you'll wish you'd been nicer to me!" That warning echoed in my head three years ago, when her diabetes put her in the emergency room and led to a succession of long hospital stays.

When I was younger, I tried to steel myself for my parents' inevitable deaths, and I put perhaps a bit more distance between us than the average rebellious teenager would find appropriate. This was the best defense I could come up with: Keep them (and death) at arm's length. We weren't a particularly tight family unit to begin with: My parents divorced when I was a kid, and my older brother signed up for the navy before I got to high school. I already struggled to figure out what I had in common with my mom, beyond our love of music; I already called my dad "Mike," a habit I picked up from my brother, whose genetic material (and not much else) came from a guy he barely knows. When I left home for college, which was only an hour away, I didn't make it home or call much. I rarely responded to my mom's lengthy, sentimental letters—even when I could parse her cursive.

I'm thirty-five now, and both my parents are still alive. I've never lost a close friend. Even my uncle John—the closest thing I have to a grandparent—is healthy at eighty-seven years old, despite his decades-long habit of predicting that he isn't long for this world. "If I have a heart attack," he likes to say, "I just want to lay down in my bed and die. I've lived a very full life. I don't want to end up with those fucking doctors."

Over the course of the last decade, though, death has steadily shot up the charts of my preoccupations and displaced the other anxieties of adulthood—earning money, going gray, and making some grand contribution to the world. Why worry about any of that stuff? Why even get up in the morning? Death always wins. The game is rigged.

That's an abbreviated version of the thought spiral I've fallen into a lot over the past few years. That gnawing backdrop of fear—my inability to see the trees for the deep, dark, infinite forest—isn't a brand of depression that I feel comfortable talking about. It doesn't seem special. Every other human lives with the knowledge that they're going to die, and they seem to go about their daily business without too much trouble. So I lock up these questions. Sometimes they sneak out well past midnight with a good friend who'd rather change the subject. Usually they come packaged in desperate little jokes. Occasionally they come out in interviews with artists—who must think I'm a bit goth—in my day-job life as a music writer.

There's one concrete fear that frightens me even more than the existential stuff, though. It goes: What if all my luck in avoiding death so far is just a setup for a truly crushing grand finale? What if, like a gambler who keeps letting it ride, I lose everything (and everyone) at once instead of parting with small sums along the way and hopefully learning *how to lose* in the process? This strikes me as a real and tangible eventuality, one that I'm woefully unprepared for. It's a reality that not only is out to steal my future but is actively souring my present. It begs me to withdraw further from friends and family, so it doesn't hurt too much when they're gone.

Some people write books to try to live past their natural expiration dates. I wrote this one in the hopes of beating death altogether. Talking to people about death for a year seemed like a pretty solid way to combat my own fear of it. Call it exposure therapy. If you have a fear of heights, spend some time in the mountains. If you're scared of physical pain, get yourself into a fistfight. If you're scared of death, what can you do, short of dying? You can spend a year of your life talking about it.

This is not, of course, a definitive oral history of deaths from the dawn of time to present day, as the book's title might suggest. But between the tongue and the cheek of the title, I came to believe in it. There are threads running through these stories that I didn't expect to find: the desire for meaningful ritual; the destructive power of taboo; the search for new perspective via spirituality or drugs; self-expression as a tool for processing grief; the intrinsically bittersweet experience of belonging. Death's history is written by the living, and death affects us in the same ways it always has. So maybe the book's title isn't too far off after all.

That said, somewhere in the middle of collecting these conversations, I realized that I was trying to sneak my own story into the margins. I talked to people whose work and art have inspired me, most of whom reside in the Pacific Northwest, where I live. With apologies to the legendary Studs Terkel—whose own impressive collection of death-centric conversations, *Will the Circle Be Unbroken?*, glares at me from my office bookshelf—I've cut out all of my questions and strung the answers together. But I wonder if you'll still find me in the white spaces between the ink that spells out of these radical, funny, and often heart-wrenching stories. I hope so. I hope you find the part of me that needed to know and that found some real magic in the not-knowing.

Even after finishing this project, I haven't "gotten over" death. I'm pretty sure there's no getting over it. But in talking to people who have found ways through, under, and around it, I'm measurably less terrified than I used to be. I was buoyed by stories of resilience and growth, like Gabe slowly finding self-love in the wake of his twin brother's death, and Andre finding his calling in an entirely unexpected place. I saw positive change manifested in Holly Pruett's quest to create meaningful rituals around death where the old ones no longer sufficed, and Katrina Spade's ambitious plan for a radical alternative to cremation and burial. And I was motivated by the strength and persistence of activists and agitators like Teressa Raiford, Josh Slocum, and Frank Thompson.

Each piece is divided into sections that I hope will function like track titles on an album. Like songs, some sections are connected and some stand alone. Some sections build a subject's story while others are short, esoteric asides. While I edited the interviews for length and clarity, it was important to me to let these conversations roam free. My goal is not to indulge in a cheeky metaphor about the complexity of death itself—which truly will not be compartmentalized—but to subvert the now-ubiquitous TED Talk paradigm of tidy stories fit for on-the-go consumption. The people in this book are more than the sum of their stories and bigger than their bullet points. I'd like you to get to know them.

If finishing this project eased my death anxiety, that relief has come less from specific words of wisdom that are shared in these pages than from finding my own fears and anxieties reflected in the words of so many smart, talented, and brave people. Death is impossible to comprehend, and like everything vast, it becomes an absurd abstraction that can either scare the (living?) shit out of you or reduce you to uncontrollable laughter. Time and time again, when unanswerable questions materialized in front of us, the people in this book smiled and laughed right along with me. I found that incredibly heartening.

The best advice I've ever got from anyone, ever, came from a talented musician and fantastic human being named Rachel Taylor Brown. I was interviewing her about her music, which has a decidedly melancholy streak. The interview sort of turned in my direction after we began discussing depression, and I told her that I felt like death had kept me from caring for people the way I wanted to. She told me what she'd learned from her own battles with depression: "Walk through the darkness with your eyes wide open. *Walk*, don't run." That concept has had a profound impact on my life since. I have tried to face and dissect my fears instead of wishing them away or rushing through them. Some days I'm better at this than others.

It turns out that when you invite friends and strangers to walk through that darkness with you—when you ask them to meditate on death openly, without any particular destination in mind—those people can serve as beacons. In the last eighteen months, I've seen sparks in coffee shops and bars and living rooms, and I've caught glimpses of brilliance in the midst of transcribing long interviews that I sometimes had to rewind multiple times just to soak up. I've found magic in transcendent moments and in little accidents of speech, in weird coincidences and old songs that have taken on new meanings.

On one of the last days of stitching this collection together, I had what felt like a revelation. It came to me in the form of a lucid memory of night swimming with some dear old friends at a lake near my hometown of Florence, on the Oregon coast. This must have been fifteen years ago. I was on top of a sand dune, waiting for the right moment to run down and jump in. My friends were already in the water. I couldn't see them in the darkness, but I could hear them laughing and splashing and hollering that I should join them. I hesitated. Everything seemed so perfect right where I stood.

Our fear of death and our desire for human connection are a package deal. Which is good, the way I see it, because only the latter makes the former bearable.

In other words, it's always worth jumping in—even when the water's cold.

— CASEY JARMAN

JANA DeCRISTOFARO

GRIEF SERVICES COORDINATOR

The Dougy Center for Grieving Children & Families is a low-key place, despite its rather austere name. Headquartered in an oversized two-story house in Portland, Oregon, the center would feel inconspicuous if it weren't for the large artificial tree in the middle of the building. The tree's metal leaves are engraved with the names of donors and foundations who helped pay for this building—and continue to support the work that's done here—after the center's old home burned down.

One might expect a woman with the title of coordinator of children's grief services to be overly serious or walk on eggshells in conversation. Jana DeCristofaro, though, is unfussy and direct. She laughs often and avoids euphemisms when talking about death.

This is a place where people come to talk. Kids talk to other kids. Teens talk to other teens. Parents talk to parents. Some of that talking is about death—the center helps people who have lost parents and siblings—and some of it is just talking. Over thirty thousand children and teens have taken advantage of the Dougy Center's services since it opened in 1982, and Jana DeCristofaro has talked, laughed, and cried with a lot of them over the past fifteen years. The center's services are free to children, teens, young adults, and parents/caretakers who are grieving a death.

After a short tour of the center, Jana and I sit in one of the building's two adult discussion rooms. I ask her, for the record, to introduce herself, and she says she'll give me the introduction she gives when she's in a group with kids.

She leans in to my microphone. "I'm Jana DeCristofaro. I'm forty-one and two-thirds, and my friend Nicole died. She was hit and killed by a car."

THEY HAVE TEDDY BEARS AND THEY CRY

I've been here as an employee since May of 2002. Before that I volunteered for about six months. I've been the coordinator of children's grief services since I got hired. It's a title that doesn't totally capture what I do. I've also been called a wrangler of cats because you can't really coordinate grief. Grief is not very wrangle-able.

I graduated with my Master of Social Work degree in 2001. I went to school thinking I wanted to do traditional outpatient counseling and become a therapist, so I had two different practicums while I was in school—one was doing day-treatment counseling for adolescents who had sexual offending behaviors, and the second one was working at my school's health center. I didn't know why, exactly, but I was a nervous wreck for two years. When I graduated, I said, "Forget it, I'm not good at clinical work. I'm just going to do research because I'm good with numbers." I got a job doing research, and over the course of the year, I was feeling very unfulfilled with that work. I missed working with kids and working with people. A friend of mine was like, "You know, you should check out this place. I don't know, it's called the Doughy Center or Dooey Center? There are kids who go there, they're sad. They have teddy bears and they cry."

I was like, "What are you talking about?"

I looked them up, and they were having a volunteer training a few weeks later. Our volunteer trainings tend to have really long wait-lists, but I happened to write in just after somebody had canceled. They invited me to come to the training. It was held at a small building in North Portland. It was dark and gloomy, in a basement, and we were all squished in there, sitting on colored pillows. I thought, *What have I gotten myself into?*

The person who was leading the training started talking about the Dougy Center's model and their approach. They had a firm belief that people who are going through grief know what they need, and that our job was to facilitate their process, not create a process *for them* or to tell them what they should do or how they should be. I took the biggest breath I'd taken in the two and a half years since starting graduate school. It was like, *Wow, there's a place where people think the way I think, and want to work with others the way I would like to work with them.*

When I was working with families—and I worked with families for a year before I went to grad school—I watched them just really struggling and parents wanting to know how to best support their kids. I thought, *How am I supposed to magically know what this family, which has its own unique culture, needs to do?* I was twenty-four. I didn't know shit.

In particular, working in the sex offender facility was hard. Here were these kids who had harmed others from a place of exerting power over them. They come to this treatment program, and we try to teach them consent and equality. We try to get them to recognize that you can't exert your power over somebody else and harm them.

But these kids were in a treatment facility where we were exerting our power over them all the time. I thought, *Something about this isn't working.* They looked at us and said, "You have power. You get what you want. I need to figure out how to have power so I can get what I want." Meanwhile, we're trying to break down that cycle. I couldn't reconcile those two things.

Coming to the Dougy Center, I realized very early on that the seed of power was not within the people who work here. On some level it's there—if kids are scraping the walls or trying to destroy the place, we have to step in—but the fact is that I don't know what somebody truly needs. They know that. And it's okay.

I mean, I have suggestions and tools that might be helpful for families. But trying to hand those over in a way that is inviting, rather than demanding or coercive or confrontational, makes so much more sense to me.

The places where I was before—especially the sex offender facility—were very confrontational, partly out of necessity. That just doesn't fit very well with my personality. Even though I'm from New York and Connecticut, and I can be very confrontational when I'm riding my bike or in social engagements, I don't want to be that person at work.

WE'RE NOT TRYING TO FIX THEM

I remember being crowded in this tiny basement for volunteer training. I was struck by the wide range of our ages. I was there at twenty-four or twenty-five. There were probably some people who were younger than me, all the way up to a few people who had been retired for many years. And everyone came together around this universal connection of having experienced grief in their life. I was just struck by people coming together and talking about their grief stories, within probably the first twenty minutes of being at the training. I remember feeling so happy to be around other people who had the same sort of approach to wanting to be with people.

At that point the big deaths in my life were three of my grandparents. I shared in one of our activities that my "dad's dad" had died. The facilitator of the training reflected back, which is one of the skills that we use, saying, "Your grandfather died." I said, "Who?" And it struck me: I never knew him as my grandfather. He'd just been my dad's dad. Then I recognized how much early loss really affected my family: not me directly, but the fact that my grandmother's dad had died when she was seven, my dad's dad died when he was fourteen, my grandmother died young, and she had a baby die. There was just a lot of loss—and fear and concern around medical things—in my family, and I suddenly recognized how much that grief really informed how my family interacted.

But all of that is different, I think, from having experienced *my own* loss in that way. You get to know stories, but they're not personal.

Some people will ask, "Do you have a really hard time now? Thinking that everyone's going to die?" I tell them I've always had that. Long before

I started working here. Working here just solidified my anxiety a bit, and perhaps enhanced it.

It seems important to share that with the volunteers because they're going through the same thing, right? They're listening to the kids' stories, they're right there with me. They have to go into their lives, and they have their own grief that's coming out, so we have this hour-long post-meeting after each group. That gives the volunteers a chance to process with one another and share what came up for them during the group. Sometimes it's logistical things for them, but a lot of time it's like, "When that child was talking, it threw me back into my own story, and I'm realizing I have some questions I need to ask my family." I do a lot of helping create that space for them. The purpose is to not have them take home the stories of the children and the families for the next two weeks until we have group again. Because I think that would burn them out really fast.

There are a lot of volunteers who are like, "Oh, I didn't realize how much more there was for me to process." In training that we provide for people—we do a three-day training—there's a lot of emphasis on taking care of yourself. Are you someone who tends to be visual? So when you're hearing stories, you can't help but to transform that into imagery? Here are some things you do to help with that. One method is to take the image in your mind and make it black-and-white rather than color. Or it might help some people to pretend they're watching a movie on the screen, and they're sitting in the back row, or maybe they even go into the projection room, and they have the power to start or stop the movie. Maybe they picture the images moving in reverse. Sometimes that can help bring some distance.

Other people will create an image in their mind of a carrying container, or a vessel of some sort, and will take the story and put it into something. A box, maybe, and then they can put that box in the closet. Maybe you don't want it in your closet. Send it over the ocean, or blow it up, or bury it. Like, let's not stick it under your bed. There are a lot of ways people can think about it.

For verbal people, coming and sharing the words that are bothering them can often diffuse that for them. Or maybe they write it down and rip up that piece of paper. Or maybe it's doing something totally opposite of verbalization. They're so verbal that maybe they need to go for a run.

THEY STAY BECAUSE THEY'RE HELPING OTHERS

After I took the initial training, I got placed in a group working with teens. It was a very small group. There were probably two or three teens that would come at each time. Later I'd have, like, sixteen kids in a group.

I don't know if I remember my first session. I do remember sitting back and thinking, *These kids are grieving. That's why they're here.* But here we are. We're a group of adults who are hanging on their absolute every word about anything they want to talk about. And we're not trying to change their mind, fix them, show them the error of their ways—we just are listening. We're being open to what's true for them.

I thought, *Oh my god. Every teenager could benefit from this situation, where there are adults they're not related to who are not as attached to the outcome, listening and hanging on their every word.* The power of what was happening there was so much bigger than just supporting somebody through his or her grief.

They get to talk with each other, but they also have supportive adults who are listening and able to share from their own experience, too, which I think is the power of the Dougy Center model. The kids are talking with the kids and the teens are talking with the teens and the adults are talking with the adults, but there are also these trained volunteers—and many of them have had their own grief experiences, and many of them had grief experiences when they were the age the children are who they're working with. So they can share, "Yeah, my dad died when I was seven, too, and here's what happened to me." And you see the kids be like, "Oh. So you're an adult. You have a job. You're okay. Maybe I could be okay, too."

I think that a lot of the volunteers come with the expectation of helping other people—they all want to be helpful—and they do, but I think many of them stay because they receive a lot of support and growth and understanding and community themselves. Our model is fantastic because teens see the volunteers as adults, but also as peers in the grief process and people they can learn from and people they can teach. We learn from the teens just as much as we try to show them a variety of ways to be and think. So many of the volunteers come to help, but they stay because they're helped. And so many of the kids come for help and they stay because they're helping others. That ongoing model with the teens. They'll often say, "You know, at one point I realized I didn't really need the group for me and my own grief as much as I just really appreciated being there for the other kids who were going through what I went through."

Our current executive director came here as a teenager, then came as a volunteer, and then came back to work as our program assistant. She worked in many roles, including development director, before becoming our executive director.

DO YOU THINK YOU'RE GOING TO
LIVE LONG ENOUGH TO GO TO PROM?

The Dougy Center was the first program in the country—I think the world, too—to start working with grieving kids in a peer support model. The whole idea is bringing kids together of a similar age who have a common experience of the death of a parent, sibling, primary caregiver, or—in the case of teens—a close friend or a cousin.

There are other programs around the country that work with kids who've had somebody in their life die, but for us it's always been that specific criteria. It's not therapy, it's not counseling, we're not purporting to make any kind of clinical intervention: It's really bringing people together, giving them the opportunity to share with one another and to do so in an environment that's facilitated by trained volunteers and by staff who can help keep the group safe for everybody. That involves creating an environment that's different from what people experience anywhere else. Many people come in and say, "My workplace is trying to be supportive, but people don't quite get it. I try to talk to my friends and they love me, and they are there for me, but it's so hard for them not to try and to put a silver lining on it."

We have over thirty groups for kids and teens that are split up by ages: three to five, four to eight, six to twelve, eleven to fourteen, and thirteen to eighteen. All those groups for the kids and teens have corresponding adult groups for their caregivers, whether that's a surviving parent or foster parent or another relative who's involved in their life. Then there are two groups for young adults—eighteen to twenty-five, twenty-six to thirty-five. Those don't have any corresponding adult groups. There's a paid staff member in every group, along with anywhere from two to twelve trained volunteers.

The groups are ongoing, so the kids can come and stay as long as they want, which is a really important component with our particular approach and philosophy here on grief, that it doesn't follow any kind of timeline. We are really grateful that we can offer our program in an ongoing fashion for families. The other really important part is the groups are free for the families. They never have to pay for their services.

The Dougy Center was started by a woman named Bev Chappell. She'd had a longstanding connection with Elisabeth Kübler-Ross, a pioneer of the death and dying field back in the sixties and seventies. A thirteen-year-old boy named Dougy Turno, who had an inoperable brain tumor, wrote to Kübler-Ross and said, basically, "Hey, how come kids get cancer? And why do we die?" She wrote him back, and it was a long, colorful, illustrated response. It was later turned into a small book called *A Letter to a Child with Cancer*. They created this correspondence. In the late seventies, Dougy came to Portland for some experimental treatment, so Elisabeth reached out to Bev Chappell, who lived here, and was like, "Hey, would you meet up with the family, help them get settled?" Bev did that, and she started visiting Dougy at the hospital. She looked around and noticed that, one, the medical community was not down with telling kids what was going on. Because back in the day, the approach was to not tell them. And not just for kids: I was reading an article recently that said it was not uncommon for doctors to neglect to tell a lot of their patients that they had cancer or they were dying because they didn't have good treatments. For me, that's super upsetting.

The kids weren't being told by the adults that they were dying. But Bev hung out with them long enough to realize that the kids knew. She heard them talking to each other and starting conversations about things like: Do you think you're going to live long enough to go to prom? Have you kissed a girl? Do you think you'll get a chance to do that? What do you think it's like where we're going? You know, all the stuff that the kids talk about in group. They were doing it without adults facilitating the conversations. That's where she got the idea to start a center. She hosted the first group in her basement, and I think there were four boys who came to that group, and from there it has just grown. She's still around. She lives over in East Portland, and was just at our benefit gala a couple of weeks ago. She's still really connected to the Dougy Center. Now we have five hundred children and teens coming through the doors every month at three locations.

WE AVOID HARD CONVERSATIONS ALL THE TIME

Even after almost thirty-five years of the Dougy Center—and our training models have been used by programs all around the country—advocating to tell kids the truth, we still get calls every day from families that say, "I don't want to tell them. What do I do?"

We hear from families that are thinking about coming in, or from families all over the country. They call—"What do I do?" I'm not a parent, but I imagine you have instincts that make you want to protect your children as a parent or adult, and protection oftentimes looks like shielding: "Don't tell them, preserve their innocence." In a weird way, it's protecting yourself as an adult, too, because you don't have to sit down and have that really hard conversation. I think it's natural for so many adults. We avoid hard conversations all the time. We need to tell our roommate to clean their dishes, but we don't want to. We go to great lengths to not say those things because we're fearful of how other people will respond. Here you are as a parent, faced with something heart-wrenching and heartbreaking. "How do I tell my kids? Maybe if I just don't tell them, they won't have to hurt as much as I'm hurting right now."

For the youngest kids, there's obviously a lot of debate about what they can and can't understand. I don't have a lot of experience with babies, but they cry a lot, and it seems like they're experiencing things, including soothing and comforting from their primary caregiver. If their primary caregiver is suddenly not there, I imagine that they would experience quite a bit of agitation. Can they cognitively understand that someone has had a cessation of life function and that they'll never be back again and that they died of leukemia? No, but they can understand that this presence that was comforting is not here anymore. There's definitely a science around cognitive development that says very young kids don't really understand the concept of permanence. You can tell them, "Daddy died," and they say, "Okay, is he coming home for breakfast?" We try to help kids understand that in a more concrete way, but to recognize that that might be a struggle for somebody who's three. I mean, it's a struggle for someone who's twenty-two, right? They just don't come to you and say, "Hey, do you think Dad's going to be home today?" They know Dad's not going to be home. But a lot of people wake up thinking, "Maybe today it won't be real anymore. Maybe today will be the day he comes back from being in the witness protection program, which is where I'm pretty sure he went— even though I know he's dead."

We advocate very strongly when we say, "Don't tell anybody how to grieve." But we also have pretty strong opinions about the importance of telling kids the truth, for a lot of reasons. One of the first ones, for me, is giving kids that foundation from which to experience whatever it is they're going to experience and not have to reserve so much time and energy and cognitive space for trying to figure out where that person went. By telling kids the honest truth about what happened, you can often get in front of a lot of anxiety that can come up for those kids.

Sometimes a parent dies by suicide, and the two youngest kids get one story while the older kid gets a more truthful story. That has happened a few times with families here. That older kid has such a burden now to make sure that their younger sibling doesn't find out the truth. And, you know, those two little kids are asking the older sibling questions all the time. They know they're not getting the straight story from the adults. Then there's a lot of, "Are they in the room? We have to whisper. We have to worry about who overheard what." Then at the big family gatherings over the holidays, it becomes a real challenge identifying who knows and who doesn't know. That is so much energy you have to put into keeping stories straight, and grief takes enough energy.

YOU CAN'T CRY FOREVER. YOU'LL GET DEHYDRATED. YOU'LL RUN OUT OF TEARS.

What I really appreciate about our model is that we follow the same structure kind of no matter what the age range is. There's a lot of reassurance and comfort that comes from having stability, at least in the framework, to talk about things that can make people feel very unmoored. There's always an opening circle. For the adults and for the three-year-olds. People always have a chance to share who they are, share something about the person who died, and how that person died—that last one can seem a little strange in a group if everybody knows everybody. But after a while, out in the world, people start to sense that nobody wants to hear their story anymore. They don't get to share the person's name, or they don't get to tell people about them. There's something really valuable about having the opportunity to say, "Here's who I am. Here's who died." I think for the younger kids, it's just like, "Oh, wow. I'm not alone. This has happened to other people." We always have that opportunity, and what happens next is determined by the group's age range. The littlest kids, they just go "play," and we have a series of creative expression rooms where they go. I say "play" in quotes because we know that for younger kids that's often how they process things and express their emotions and make sense of events—through their play and creative expressions.

There's a music room where they can make a bunch of noise. There's a dress-up room, and a sand tray room, an art room, a hospital play room. Then we've got a couple of areas for some really big energy. A volcano room with pads on the floors and walls where they can throw things and build forts and jump on bears. They can't jump on each other, but they can jump on bears. Then there's outside play, just for like running around and yelling and screaming, or playing basketball. So the youngest kids will spend the most time playing. As the age range goes up, the playtime gets shorter and shorter. Not because of us, but because of them—they get more verbal. In the younger kid groups, the six-to-twelve groups, they oftentimes will do some kind of drawing activity that will focus on all kinds of different things. We don't have a curriculum, but you know, giving kids activities where they can put their feelings into words, or ones where they can access memories that they have. They can express their wishes, express their feelings of regret—things like that.

In one activity, where we're helping kids identify emotions, we give them little address label stickers that they can write on. Then we ask about some of the common emotions people have when they're grieving. Or just in your life. They might say, "Angry, mad, sad, frustrated." And then they write those feelings on the sticker, and they stick them on their body where they feel them the most. Many of the kids have them on their mouths. When I'm angry, it comes out here. When I'm sad, it comes out here. That's an example of one that we've done with the younger kids. Or sometimes it's something seemingly simple as "Draw a picture of your family before, and draw a picture of your family now." Just so we can talk a little about what's different. And then they go play.

In quite a few of the teen groups, all the kids get to write questions that they might not normally feel comfortable asking. They write them anonymously. We put them in a box—it's supposed to be a jar, but I use tissue boxes because it just seems right. One teen will pick out a question for the day, and then all the kids go around and share their story and answer that one particular question. My favorite came out last week. I happened to pick it, and it said, "What's the most BS you've ever had to go through with the person who died?" I had to ask the kids, "What does that mean? What does BS mean to you?" That was an interesting question.

The one we had in group yesterday was, "If the person was alive, what would you say to them?" That's a big one. The teens always have to figure out, like, "Do you mean they've been dead, and now they come back, or they just never died?" I'm just like, "You pick." And they say, "Do I go where they are, or do they come back here? How does all that work?"

One of the interesting questions for me is, "What did you not like about the person who died?" I think so often when someone dies we fall into this place, like, "I can't talk about the full spectrum of who my dad was, and as I get older, I can only remember the good things." Then that person becomes this exalted example of a perfect parent, and the other parent really has a hard time living up to it.

Their children might try to emulate that perfection, too, or rebel against it, or look for it in other people. Whatever. That's a whole other conversation—inviting kids to just talk about the whole range of who that person was. I see a lot of teens feeling really badly that they are living their lives. Yes, they have times when they miss their mom or dad, but they just don't get that sad about it, and they think that they're really weird because they are doing all right. I can't tell you how many times people have come into the young adult group—teens aren't as specific about it—like, "I don't want to feel like this. I don't want to be crying all the time, not being able to work." And then time goes by, and they say, "I feel terrible. I don't cry. I'm going to work all the time." You guys! You are so hard on yourselves!

It's that added layer of "Am I doing this right? Because I don't know how I'm supposed to do it." I had that conversation with the young adult group many years ago—about that question of "Am I even grieving? I don't know what that means. Should I be doing this? Should I be doing that?" You might go back and chastise yourself for all the choices you made after the person died, thinking, *Well, I wish I had grieved harder at the beginning.* I'm like, "Because you think you'll grieve less now? What if that was exactly what you could and needed to do? If you were to grieve more, you would never have gotten out of bed."

It's natural to think that way. Here's this uncontrollable event that happens in your life, and you would like to figure out a way to actually have some control over it, so that you can prevent an event like that from happening in the future. A lot of that is protection: *How can I protect myself from future hurt because this sucks, and I don't like feeling this way. What can I do to make sure it doesn't happen again?*

I also hear that from people saying, you know, "Now I feel like I just can't feel anything." There can be a lot of numbness, especially at the beginning. They might purposefully watch movies that they know are going to evoke the grief because they miss that intensity of longing or absence or happiness—whatever the intensity is—because that reminds them of the time when the person was here. It's almost like a desensitization process. For some people it's so scary to crack that grief open at all. Many people say, "I'm scared to start crying because I feel like it's never going to end." We say, "It really will. I promise. You can't cry forever. You'll get dehydrated. You'll run out of tears." It's still overwhelming.

What I am in total awe of, all the time, is that they come back. Here's somebody who really enjoys looking at pictures and remembering and really delving into the emotional quality of missing their mom, and here's someone for whom, right now, distraction is working a lot better. They come together, and they make space for one another.

Larger society has this vantage point of "Protect kids, don't tell them, it's taboo, don't talk about it." Then there's a newer school of thought that says,

"Distracting yourself is bad. If you don't feel it, you're going to have conse-quences later on." I feel like I live in the middle of that somewhere. There's research out there now that distraction and other ways of coping are ac-tually really effective for some people. When we come up with a universal rule set and apply it to everybody, and we have expectations that everyone should respond the same way, that's where you can get into trouble. It's like saying everybody should wear plaid shirts. Lots of people do, and it's great for them. But for a lot of people, that's not what they want to wear, and it doesn't feel good to them. We try to force people to wear this particular uni-form of emotional expression or processing of loss. I think that's where that can get tricky.

Other cultures might have more explicit and structured rituals for what happens after someone dies, and some of those allow for larger ex-pressions of grief in the moment, but I don't know if this culture or any other continues to talk about death or express feelings for an indefinite period of time. I don't know. But you know, you think back to the days of "You're a widow. You're in mourning. You have to wear black for a full year." That'd probably be constraining for many people, but also reassur-ing for some people, and now there's not a lot of that. Everybody's just kind of got their own weird opinion about what you should or shouldn't be doing, and here you are grieving and navigating everyone's assumptions and expectations of you. It's cliché, but there's no handbook.

RITUALS

Many of the teen groups will spend the whole time talking, but they don't always. Yesterday we had some time for them to go play. They like to go to the foosball room, the art room—they like to go to the kitchen and eat snacks. Then all the groups, no matter what age they are, always come back together and do one to three closing rituals. That's an impor-tant part of the structure. The opening ritual, the open time, and then the closing ritual. There are various closing rituals. In the younger kids' groups, they usually go around and share what they did in group that day. For kids who weren't quite comfortable sharing who their person was or how they died, they'll oftentimes share what games they played because that feels more comfortable, and it helps them to build that comfort and confidence in talking within a group. Some kids are super comfortable right from the start. They talk talk talk, and then over time they might start saying, "I pass," which is interesting. It's unpredictable what they are going to do, depending on what's happening for them that day. Closing circle will look like, "What did I do today at the Dougy Center?" Then most of the groups end with what we call a hand squeeze. We stand up and everybody holds hands—unless it's flu season—then we do some other things. One of my groups is a total ragtag bunch: One kid will squeeze, one kid high fives, one kid hip-bumps. I don't care. Whatever you want to do. The point is to pass it to the next person. The kids get to pick whatever the question is for the hand squeeze. For a long time the questions were things like, "What's your favorite video game? What's your favorite color?" Then something happened this last year. I didn't do it, they did it. Now all the questions are about the people in their lives who died.

The teens also do a candle lighting at the end of every group, so they get a chance to light a candle for anyone or anything that's on their mind. We don't legislate that it has to be for the person who died. Half the time I'd say it is. Other times it's for a friend who's having a hard time, for luck on a math test, for that girl someone asked on a date. Those are things that are important to them.

Then they go around and share something they're looking forward to in the next two weeks. It's a new ritual I started about five years ago. I was running the young adult groups, and I was hearing people talk. They'd crack open their heart-space, light a candle to cry, and I'm like, "Bye! Have fun driving home!" That didn't feel good to me. It's like, *I'm about to get on my bike. I do not want to be on the road with you guys.* We had to do something, so we did that.

It really comes from wanting to help people move from heart space to head space, where you can think cognitively. For some people, this might be the only time where they come and share about the hard things in their life. They need that, but other people in the group can get real anxious if all we share is the hard stuff. When we go around and share one thing we're looking forward to, one person may have just cried for an hour and a half, and they're like, "I'm leaving for a trip to Europe next week. It's going to be great." There can be a lot of laughter all of a sudden. I find it really helpful for people to recognize that not only is there a full spectrum of the person who died, there's a full spectrum of the person who's grieving. It creates a lot of bonding for the group.

Then we meet up with the adults who brought the kids or teens to the center, and we do another hand squeeze. That's always about the person who died, too. It's one of the only times that the adults and the kids are together, asking questions and sharing about the person.

The adult groups do a lot of the same rituals. They just don't have playtime, though many of them wish they did. With the adult groups, I'd say about half of the time is them talking about their grief and half the time is them talking about parenting. *How do I parent my teenager? How in the world do people do this?* You know, it might be something like, "My wife who died was the disciplinarian, and I was always the easy one. Now I have to be the disciplinarian, and I don't know what the hell I'm doing. My kids know that I don't know what I'm doing." They learn from each other. They get a lot of support around the experience of being a solo parent or maybe being a grandparent raising grandkids.

IN A WEIRD WAY, IT'S KIND OF A BEAUTIFUL THING

There's really no fix for bereavement. But talking about it in this kind of setting can be comforting, reassuring, and it provides a lot of solace or inspiration for moving forward in people's lives. For many people, it's the most helpful piece of the puzzle. Then there are people for whom it's helpful, but not the most helpful piece. They're able to go back out in their own lives and access the things that they need that are more helpful for them. There are people who find that talking in a group is not helpful at all, so they don't come to the Dougy Center. We would never suggest that everybody needs to come to a peer-support group. Everyone's different, and for some people talking in a group is too overwhelming. Like, "I'm dealing with my own shit. I don't need to come in here and hear twenty-seven other sad stories. Thank you very much." Or, you know, "I'm an artist, and painting is how I do this. I don't have any words for it, so why would I come to a grief group?"

Then there are people who don't have any words but really appreciate hearing other people talk. They just want to listen. You might ask them, "Is there anything you want to talk about tonight?" They say, "I'm just really connecting to what everyone's saying. Thank you for your stories."

I think that for so many people, there's a huge sense of relief and reassurance in knowing they're not the only person in the room who's going through this. So many people who are grieving experience supreme isolation out in the world. That's perceived isolation or actual isolation, and many people with a strong community of friends still feel isolated because nobody can understand what they're going through. Of course, even in the group, nobody can truly understand what they're going through—but I think it might be the closest they come.

The truth is that everyone's situation is different. Even in the same family, where maybe you've got a mom and teenage kids. Each of those teenage kids had a different relationship with their parent or with the sibling who died. Mary can't really understand what Charlie is missing. They can sort of understand some of the same things from shared experiences, but they had very different relationships with the person who died. In a weird way, it's kind of a beautiful thing that no one can understand that precious connection that you had with that person. Even the person who died could never really understand what you miss about them because it's truly unique to you. What a testament to that relationship, to come and try to articulate it to other people.

I'M GOING TO GIVE YOU A SECRET SIGNAL
WHEN I'VE HAD ENOUGH OF THE HUGS

Half the people I talk to say, "I wish that instead of saying, 'Sorry for your loss,' people would say, 'How did they die?' Then I could tell the story." But then some people think that's rude and intrusive, and they don't want people asking them that. It's tough for the greater society because you don't know what to say when someone dies. But I think those differences can be helpful in our groups. Some people respond to questions the way they think they're supposed to respond, and if they hear someone else feeling differently about it, they're like, "Oh wait. I could maybe feel that way. I could do what you're doing. Maybe I could see my coworkers fumbling around in what to say to me as an honest expression of care, rather than getting irritated."

I can't help you learn the right thing to say. I don't know. In fourteen years, I've learned that everyone wants something different. Overall, I think that saying something is better than not saying anything at all. I think it's ideal to come from a place of humility, and to know that pretty much everything you'll say is going to be the wrong thing to say. Because it's just a wrong *situation*. Somebody just died. Nothing you say is going to make this grieving person feel better. But that's okay: Sometimes being wrong is better than not saying anything at all, and maybe if you reach out from that place of humility, it's the best you can do. "I really wanted to just let you know that I'm here. I have zero idea of what to say. I'm super afraid I'm going to say the wrong thing, so if I do, just, you know, send me a middle finger emoticon or whatever." Then you're being more transparent without putting it on the other person.

Sometimes I've said, "What do you need?" And the person's like, "Uh, I don't know what I need."

What can you do? A lot of it is going to depend on the relationship you have with the person you're trying to support. I think if you're super close friends and you know them and you know their life, you can say, "Is there anything I can do for you right now in this moment?" Then the person might go, "Okay, can you please go pick up my kids?" You know, something really tangible. I think people who want to help don't know what else to say. "Let me know if I can do anything" is an honest question. Of course, for the grieving person on the other end of it, they may hear that as an expectation that they have to come up with something for you to do just so you can feel helpful and useful. Or they might be thinking, "I have no fucking idea what I need, and you probably don't mean it, so, thanks anyway."

Sometimes the mundane things are the most helpful. Providing options: "Can I come over and do your laundry? Can I come clean the dishes?" Some people might not want anybody in their house, but other people are like, "Yes, please come." Things people don't often think about are, like, "Do you need someone to call people? Do you need someone to notify people? Do you need someone to come keep track of the sympathy cards you're getting? Do you need somebody to call a lawyer?" There are so many overwhelming tasks that happen after somebody dies, and having someone who can do them—being the family representative, getting the word out about the funeral—can be really helpful.

If you're close with someone, maybe they want you to be their funeral buffer buddy. That's when you pick someone who maybe is going to the funeral or the memorial service—and like, your family's there, they're all pretty invested in having their own experience—for you, not for themselves. You might say, "I need you to stand by me, and I'm going to give you a secret signal when I've had enough of the hugs, and then you're going to step in front of me, and say, 'She's actually not hugging anymore today.'" Or something to that affect. They might cover you, so you can run off to the bathroom and have ten minutes to yourself to just breathe. Someone to step into the "I'm so sorry's," or whatever's happening. It can be huge just having somebody who's there who will run and fetch something for you, or go outside with you and take a break. That's something we encourage families to do for kids, too: Ensure that they have an adult buddy with them, so if they need to leave and take a break, they don't feel like they are taking their immediate family members out of the experience.

ORIENTATION DAY

When the teens first come in, you can often tell that they do not want to be here. I'm like, "Anyone willing to admit you've been dragged here against your will?" In this last orientation, all five teens raised their hands. I was like, *Wow, I've got my work cut out for me.* But just acknowledging that, it opens up the energy in the room in such a dramatic way. I tell them, "I'm not here to convince you. I won't take it personally if you decide not to come back. My job is to try and show you everything, what we are and what we're not."

I speak to the things that they're concerned about: "Some of you might not want to be here because you're worried we're going to make you talk. We're not going to do that. Some of you might be worried that this is counseling. It's not counseling. Some of you might be worried that everyone just comes in and cries for an hour and a half. That doesn't really happen. Some people cry, some people laugh, some people laugh and cry at the same time. We don't give you any extra credit for crying." That gets a couple laughs out of them.

It doesn't work too well to force people to talk about this stuff against their will. One time, I asked a teen group, "How many people got something for coming to the Dougy Center?" It was like, "Yeah, I got out of school." One kid said, "I got a new MacBook." Everyone was like, "Damnit! We should have asked for more." I thought I was going to start a revolt. It doesn't take long, though, for most of them to realize we aren't in the business of making them do, say, or think anything. They get comfortable being with other grieving teens pretty quickly.

Once I had a group of teens talking about how the death they experienced has affected what they wanted to do with their lives in the future. Many of them were like, "I want to honor my parents by going to their alma mater," or "I really want to become a nurse because the nurses helped my brother so much when he was sick." There are a lot of those sort of more expected answers, and then there were some kids who said, "I hate doing well at things now. I actually don't want to do well. I don't want to have any success with my life because to do it without my person there is too devastating. I'd rather feel like I haven't done anything." I thought, *Wow, what a hole to be in.* We hear so often that kids struggle in school when someone dies. It's hard to concentrate, etcetera. But I never considered that moving forward without this person and having success could mean leaving them behind. That really opened my mind. I always remember to ask about that with the teens now. Anytime somebody says something that surprises me, I always try to remember that there could be someone else in the group going through something similar. My job as a group facilitator, if I'm doing a good job at it, is to speak to what's not being spoken about in the group. Many times there's a sense of, "Yeah, yeah, we all know this is true." And I ask, "Who's had an opposite experience?" Because those people are going to be a little less willing to come forward if 99 percent of the group thinks A, and they think B. My job is to help make that space.

With the younger kids, I think about one boy in particular. We sat quietly and we were talking, and he had so many questions—not for me, necessarily, just questions. He was talking about how it didn't make any sense to him. His mom had died, and he was like, "You know, people say that when your person dies, they are looking out for you, they are watching you from above, and making sure everything's okay. Our roof sprung a leak last night, and, I don't know, don't you think my mom in heaven looking out for me would make sure the roof didn't do that?"

I was like, "Hmm. That's a really interesting question. What do you think?" And then it just went on. We talked for twenty minutes. There were so many questions this little boy was really wrestling with—answers he'd been given from adults in his life that were very black-and-white. He was like, "That doesn't make any sense to me." He wasn't having an opportunity to really muck around in the gray areas. "Well, they say when somebody goes to heaven, they never look back because they're so happy to be in heaven, but don't you think if you were a mom, you'd miss your kids?"

Here's a little boy thinking his mom doesn't miss him. That was really powerful for me because oftentimes we think that developmentally, these kids are concrete thinkers and we tell them concrete answers. But many times they are very wise and have some really deep philosophical questions.

One little kid, their person had died by suicide, and they were like, "I'm just so worried. I hear when people die by suicide, they go . . ." and he pointed down to the ground with his finger. He's like, "But I really think they went . . ." and he pointed up. Just for him to be able to say, "This doesn't work for me" was pretty amazing.

KIDS WITH QUESTIONS

Kids are very curious about the more body-focused details of the story. Like, what's an aneurysm? Does it hurt? Does the person feel it? Did their eyeballs get big? They're just really interested in the body stuff, which makes sense because their bodies are growing and changing. For some of the kids, they're not bothered by that discomfort that other people have, so they'll ask pretty direct questions. For me, my grandmother died when I was fifteen. She was hit and killed by a subway train, and we never found out if it was suicide or an accident or if somebody pushed her. I share that story with the kids every time we have group, and usually they're like, "Yeah, yeah, whatever, teacher lady, let's go play." But one time they just had so many questions for me. They're like, "So, did she trip? Or did she fall?" I'm like, "We don't really know." "Was she drunk? Is that why she fell in front of the train?" I'm like, "I don't know." "Was the driver drunk? Is that why he ran her over? Did it hurt when she got hit? What did her body look like?" They just had so many questions.

Most adults in that situation would be like, "That's not appropriate. I don't want to talk about that." I just say, "I don't know." And sometimes I ask them, "Well, what do you guys think?" "I think it would hurt," or "I don't know. Maybe she got hit by the train so hard that it didn't hurt." You know, they just go along with it. They can really talk about things that other people might be freaked out by.

Kids will ask each other questions, and it's interesting. Some kids don't understand certain words or medical terms like suicide or aneurysm. And then kids try to explain it to each other: "Why did that happen?" They're pretty open and curious. The youngest of the kids talk about it in line at the grocery store, too—"Did you know my dad died? Is your dad dead? Where's my daddy?" And the cashier is like, "Have a nice day!" and the other parents are like, "Come on. Let's go."

FUCK YOU, DEATH

I think I've always been raised to be someone who processes things verbally. I can talk and talk and talk. But when I first started working here, I realized, that's not going to cut it. I'm verbally processing with the people here, but in terms of my self-care, verbal processing is not where it's at for me. I needed to find a lot of alternative avenues that were very body-centered and physical and energetic in nature. That's the only way I was going to be able to really deal with the emotional side of my work.

It used to be that by Friday afternoon I would feel like I gained about twenty pounds of emotions over the course of the week, and many of them were not mine. I needed to do something to metabolize that. There's a woman named Laura van Dernoot Lipsky who wrote a book called *Trauma Stewardship*, and she put into words a lot of what I was feeling for many years in the field. She says that you have to metabolize what you've been exposed to, and that makes a lot of sense to me. I've done a lot of yoga, or running. I ride my bike to work every day, all those things are super helpful.

I find that making sure there's space for my own oxygen bubble to be restored is really, really helpful. My own atmosphere. I think my atmosphere is bumping into other people's atmospheres all the time, and people have a lot of planetary storms going on. So certain times I just gotta spend some time alone.

When I think about my own life, I don't actually fear dying. I fear having a chronic illness, or being dismembered or disfigured in some way. That is way scarier for me. If something serious happened to me, I'm just like, "Let's just call it a night. That was a good run, see you next time." That's how I feel right now. I'm sure if I contracted an illness, that'd probably change. Maybe it wouldn't, but that's kind of a luxury for me to be able to say that. But I've never had that fear of the great unknown, and what happens next.

I ride my bike all over this town. I guess if I was that afraid of dying, I wouldn't do that. It's funny, I'm so careful about safety, but I ride my bike everywhere. I always wear a helmet and an emergency vest, but on some level I do think it's just a defiant "Fuck you, death. I'm riding my bike. I don't care."

I also accept the fact that when I go anywhere, I always have at least two or three stories about how someone has died doing what I'm about to do. That just happens, it's just the way it is. Like, *This river is so beautiful, but there was that brother who fell off that rock over there, and then there was the guy who went mountain biking and hit a pothole and cracked his head open.* But I came that way before I even had this job. My mom's been like that my whole life: "Don't do that, you'll die." I already know all the ways you could die, but now I have particular stories that match up with them. I have to spend a lot of time being, like, "Yes, and we're going to still do that."

It's like going to a career fair when you're in college, and you see all the things you could do in your life. I come here and I see all the ways that grief could affect me when it hits. I'm like, "I don't want that, I don't want that, I don't want that." For years I thought that people, in general, were just too dependent on each other. I spent a lot of years looking around at relationships, friendships, parents, and children, being like, "'Those people are too codependent." Now I'm realizing that those are probably just normal, loving, healthy relationships, that I was just, like, "Uh uh, no way. I'm independent." I'm not. I think it's really just been a preventative measure for me. I do not want to end up feeling the way that person is feeling, so I am not going to let myself get attached.

It took me until this year to be like, "Oh, that's what's going on." I think what sparked a lot of it for me is my parents moved here a year and a half ago. They lived on the other side of the country forever. And I really enjoy having them here, but I also fear it with all of my being because every time we do something together I have so many more things that I'll miss when they die. I do this all the time: I'll be sitting with people and I'll think, *If this person dies tomorrow, what am I going to remember about my conversation with them?* I do it all the time with my family. I think, *This is the moment I'll talk about in their eulogy.*

With the volunteers, I'm there to facilitate their processing of what's happening, and I'll share things from my own life that are instructive, but I don't really go to them with my emotions because I'm there to hold space for theirs. I think everybody that works here kind of has their own slant on how that affects them.

Both of my parents are alive. I haven't been married. I don't have children. I don't have pets. Some part of me steps back and says, "Is there a reason for that, and would it have been different if I didn't have this job?" I don't know. I can't say. But it's interesting for me to think about that. Like, maybe it's that I just don't want the responsibility of all of those things, but then maybe I don't want the heartache that would come when someone or something dies. I probably came this way. I've been this way since I was a little kid: ninety-nine friends, and don't get too close to anybody.

THE HARDEST PIECE

I think one of the hardest things is to sit with people who have deep regret about how their relationship was with the person who died, or people who are questioning things they may have said or done. It's so hard to watch somebody get so upset with themselves, and it takes all of my wherewithal as a facilitator not to rush in and try to fix it for them. That, and the people who say, "This pain is just too much, and I don't know what to do to fix it." As a facilitator, I don't know what to do to fix it, either.

That's not easy to watch or hear. Thankfully, the group is there, so I can say, "What did you guys do when you felt that way?" Then they can get ideas from each other.

The very hardest thing for me is when people are really struggling outside of the group, and there needs to be outside help. We tell the kids that we'll keep their confidentiality unless they're having thoughts of hurting themselves or hurting someone else. When that comes up, as a clinician, that's always the hardest piece for me. I can pretty much sit with anything people want to throw at me, grief-wise. But when there's more that needs to be done to ensure somebody's safety outside of group, that's just really hard for me. I do it, of course, because it's really important. You have to do it, and it's imperative to make sure that someone is safe—but that's agitating to my nervous system in a way that just sitting with the grief is not. I dread that "I'm going to need to talk to your parents" conversation. But thinking about the trust that would be lost if something were to happen is so much worse.

TEXTING

Mother's Day just happened, and I woke up, and my mom is alive, so I did stuff for my mom. Then I spent some time just going through my whole address book for friends who have a dead mom. I texted all those people. Everybody. On Mother's Day. And I try, in my calendar, I have everybody's birthdays in one color, and I have all the anniversaries of death days in another, and then I text the person and reach out to them or call them, even if it's been twenty years. It's often something simple, like, "Thinking of you, thinking of your dad today." I've had people say, "Whoa, I didn't even remember. How'd you remember? Thanks." But I've never had anybody be upset about it.

People come to group and they say, "The first year five people reached out to me, the second year two people reached out to me, and by the third year, nobody remembered—or if they remembered, nobody reached out." I hear a lot of pain in them, so I always take it as my personal inspiration to not be that person. I try and remember. But what's interesting is, in my own family, I can't ever seem to remember the grief dates that I have. I can never remember birthdays, either.

BEING PRESENT

People who come here have an opportunity to talk with each other with a matter-of-factness that they don't often encounter out in the world. Out there, if I share with you that my friend or family member died, and then you feel uncomfortable, and I don't know your history with grief, suddenly we're tiptoeing around that situation. Here, people get to say who died, and everyone listens, and there's a lot of power in knowing that I'm not making you uncomfortable with my story.

For the greater population, anything people can do to present themselves as someone who can be comfortable with the heartache, and comfortable with the discomfort, and comfortable with the not knowing is hugely helpful for people experiencing grief. Being present for someone who's going through something difficult, even if it's not grief or death, it's a big deal. That's what I think most people come in here saying, "I always feel like I have to take care of the other person." It's huge when you can show up and present yourself as a solid person who can handle their story. If you can say, "You're not going to have to take care of me after you share with me what you've experienced."

CONDUCTED APRIL 30, 2015

KATRINA SPADE

FOUNDER OF THE URBAN DEATH PROJECT

Katrina Spade wants to turn dead bodies into compost. That may seem like a pipe dream, but there's a clear precedent for the kind of cultural sea change that her Urban Death Project is looking for. In the last fifty years, cremation has gone from a rare—and for many Americans, seemingly barbaric—phenomenon to the mainstream. In some states, including Spade's backyard of Washington, cremation is now more common than burial. But Spade's modest proposal of building urban facilities for human composting—she hopes to create the first such structure in Seattle, but a best-case scenario still places it years away—still has to overcome a significant "Ew" factor, as well as potential resistance from politicians and the funeral industry.

Lucky for the Urban Death Project, Katrina Spade is a disarming and charismatic frontwoman for the cause. She speaks quickly, like an off-duty auctioneer (a New York Times reporter described Spade as "the opposite of funereal"), but Spade listens with the same intensity. Despite the overwhelming press attention she has received as the project's founder, she's quick to identify friends and colleagues as the sources of even small ideas or phrases. A good idea, regardless of its source, seems to thrill her to no end.

When I meet Spade, at a coffee shop near her office in Seattle's Capitol Hill district, she only has an hour to spare. But in that hour, she touches on her family's story, the history of death in America, and identifies a half-dozen people and organizations that I should look into. She speaks bluntly enough about the composting process that even I flinch once or twice, but I soon realize that Spade has little time for bullshit. After all, the success of the Urban Death Project would actually change the world. Maybe the prospect of changing the world is what makes Spade so visibly, contagiously, energetic. Or maybe she was just born like that.

HIDING AGAINST A HEADSTONE

I grew up on a dead-end dirt road in rural New Hampshire, and we had a cemetery on our property that was mostly really old—gravestones from the 1800s. We didn't think of it as a creepy place. It was beautiful. It had this mausoleum about as big as this room, and square, with a stone wall around it. Everything was mossy and tall. All the stones were so old you could barely read them. We used to play hide-and-seek in there. I remember one time I was hiding against a headstone, and it just cracked. [Laughs.]

I've never had bad feelings about death and all that.

My parents were both in medicine, and they were very frank about disease and death and dying. We talked about that stuff—not confidential stuff, but, "Oh, a patient died." They both did a lot of gardening. We composted and grew all our vegetables. We would always have an animal that we would then slaughter and eat. We lived on what they call a gentleman's farm. Both my parents worked full-time, but they also gardened in their free time. So I think that played into me not being squeamish about decomposition.

I realized the other day, though, I've never been to a conventional funeral at a cemetery before. Most of my family chooses the memorial service and cremation route. Maybe there's something in the genes there.

THE KATRINA SPADE SHOW

The whole thing has been an adventure. Today I was thinking about how it all became real. If I hadn't have gotten the Echoing Green Fellowship, nobody would be talking to me, I don't think. Our Kickstarter raised a lot of money, but it was maybe even better for outreach. The attention really came overnight, and now suddenly everyone wants to speak to me because of other press that's already happened. It's self-fulfilling. The project wasn't any less real or possible or relevant before the press, but now suddenly it's a thing. I get a kick out of that.

I try to not be cynical about it. I ask myself, "What *is* the press?" I wonder who is reading it, and once it's over, it seems like it's just over. But at the same time, it's really helpful.

We are called the Urban Death Project, and we're talking about human composting, so it's something people want to write about. And that's the main outreach tool. For a while I thought, "Why am I doing all this? It feels so weird." But a friend of mine said, "You have to get people to hear about this so many times that they've heard about it, talked about it, accepted it, and got bored of it by the time you want to be breaking ground." I think that's smart, to get people to go from "What the fuck?" to "Oh yeah, I know about that," to "Composting bodies? Aren't we doing that already?"

I guess my timing makes perfect sense. This is a legitimate idea, both on the death side and on the using infrastructure to harness energy side: Whether it's solar or rooftop farms, all of these conversations are happening around the country. Plus climate change awareness and our awareness of death, as baby boomers are aging. It makes sense, this historical moment, but sometimes I just think about the actuality of it as it has gained legs and continues to do so, and I'm amazed.

At first I was a little embarrassed that the whole thing was like the Katrina Spade Show. But, I mean, I made the Urban Death Project up. I'm the one who wants to talk about it all the time, I guess.

Seattle is approachable and accessible. I've met so many people who want to help the project move forward. I've made all these connections, which I think in other cities would take a lot longer to build. If I was in New York, it might take two years to meet people, but here, it's "you should meet this person" and then there's an email from them the next morning. It's really amazing. There's kind of a "we're different and we don't mind" sort of feeling. The environmental ethos is strong here. Also there's a good deal of money here to create the first facility and really get the funds behind it. At least, I hope and think that exists here.

THE CLOSEST THING I HAVE TO SPIRITUALITY

I knew I wanted to look at decomposition and architecture together in my college thesis. Normally those things don't really go together, you know? You want to build a thing and keep it around forever. But I was thinking about that from the beginning.

One inspiration was an installation piece at the Olympic Sculpture Park here in Seattle called *Neukom Vivarium* by an artist named Mark Dion. You never know when it's going to be open, but if you find a gardener outside, they'll let you in. It's a greenhouse, all tinted green to feel like the forest floor. Dion brought a sixty-foot hemlock in from the forest, and there's just a giant nurse log in there decomposing with a lot of stuff growing on it. That's a tree that has fallen in the forest and is nursing new life. A typical tree lives a lot of its useful life, even though it's dead, in decomposition. In my thesis, I got really excited about the symbolic difference between that and the trees at the 9/11 memorial [in New York City], where they picked the ones that grew together, pruned them to look exactly alike, and they dive into the cement and below there's this life support that waters them and gives them nutrients. So they're alive, and the nurse log is dead, but to me it feels like the opposite. It was an inspiration for me.

So I did stuff with dirt. I thought maybe I could design some ground-earth buildings or something. Then I found out about the livestock research that's been happening, and it was just, "Duh. If you can compost livestock, you can compost anything living." I think I was vacationing with my parents when I put it all together, and they said, "Great, sounds great." They're super supportive of the project.

It was always supposed to be a place. It could have branched off at some point and become a system or a small machine that composts people. Each funeral home could own one. You could do that; it's not outside the realm of what could be done, technically speaking. But I never considered that in school because it was about the human experience that we crave and about what would lend itself architecturally—space-wise, but also function-wise—to grieving. I was thinking about that sort of thing. I'm eternally grateful that I was in school and had the luxury of spending two full years, once I decided on the thesis, to design it instead of jumping straight to "What's the business plan?" Because it could have started like that, right? Then it would have been diluted so fast into something else. I don't think our culture needs another type of crematorium or a machine to dispose of bodies. I think we deserve better than that.

It's about the space, but what's happening inside is equally important. It's meaningful, and what happens there should happen as simply as possible.

We talk about this a lot in environmental terms, but someone was asking me recently, "When it comes to climate change, this isn't really the biggest bang for the buck, is it?" It's not. No question. It's important not to be hypocritical. I can't say, "I'd never be caught being cremated because it uses fossil fuels." Please, I drive my car around. I really am happy for people who find conventional burial meaningful, but I think there are fewer and fewer of us who do. There's a really huge gap between it being meaningful and knowing what it really entails. I think people need to know, like, what is embalming? It's terrible. It's pretty gross. I don't want to shove it in people's faces because you may have just lost someone and you're going through so much. But you deserve to know.

It's not as much about the environment as it is about having meaning for people. It just so happens that for many people, like myself, there's meaning in knowing that I'm part of a larger ecosystem and knowing that I could be part of the natural world again. That, to me, is deeply meaning-ful, even though I live in a city, and I only garden a little bit, and I never go camping. Yet it's like the closest thing I have to spirituality. It's somehow tied in with nature. It's not directly about the environment, but it's about finding meaning in nature. I think if I were dying, I'd find solace in that idea. It's pretty easy to find meaning in that simple idea, and I think that's what drives the project.

RITUAL THAT'S BORN
PURELY OUT OF PROCESS

Each facility would function as a funeral home, meaning it could accept a body from the hospital, morgue, or from a home if someone died at home. The facility could refrigerate the body—not embalm it, of course—and also it would have spaces like a welcoming area, offices, space for ceremo-nies and memorial services. The idea is really to let friends and family design their own ceremonies, sort of like people do now, anyway.

The main feature in each of these proposed spaces is the core system. It's an approximately three-story-tall processing core, in which bodies and carbon material are placed. There are about ten feet of wood chips between each body.

The initial reason it became a vertical system is that in our urban cen-ters, it just makes more sense space-wise. Then there became this sort of beautiful concept where the ritual is born purely from the process. Meaning you have this vertical core, and friends and family have to ex-pend their own energy to carry a dead person to the top. I like to think of it as a winding of a watch, so there's this energy, this literal energy used to lay the body into the wood chips, and then over time the body is creating new energy. Then, purely that process of carrying the body, laying it in, and the body decomposing over time, all of that becomes this ritual that's purely born out of process. It's not like, "Let's make a ritual. Let's plant a flower." It's just what it is. I like that. Sometimes I imagine a brass band going up the ramp and having a party, or maybe it's a very solemn and quiet reception.

These facilities are all to be designed by different architects all over the world, and they'll look vastly different depending on their communities. I love to think about, as a design person, the different ways they might look from one neighborhood to the next, or country to the next. There could be a super sleek modern one or a more conventional one. Of course, there should be something growing at each site. If you think, what are the prescriptive things: the core system, gardens, and different types of spaces, that's about it.

Currently, the design has, on the top, a grid of ten bays that go all the way through each story. These bays go through the core. There are multiple bodies per bay, but there's no lateral movement between them. Those bays are also structural, and they provide aeration and exhaust—so they have a purpose besides keeping people separate.

That's stage one, where only natural forces and decomposition are working on the bodies, and they're more or less separated. I think an important aspect of the project is that you can rest assured—when you're saying good-bye to this person—that for the next few weeks as they turn from human into something else, to compost, they'll be doing that in a solitary way.

I'm also proposing that our bodies cease to be human during that first stage. Our molecules literally join other molecules that turn into other molecules. You literally can't always be human. How about that? Somewhere in the system, that's actually happening. Our best guess is that it's about a three-week process. This is another thing that some architect brought up, which I thought was so beautiful. With the composting process, the temperature spikes a few times, from 140 to 160 degrees, just from the natural decomposition at work. It's important that that happens because it kills pathogens, and it also shows you that the process is working. I was talking about this recently, and someone said, "Maybe that spike is the moment when you cease to be human." I don't know, but it's amazing to think about. I thought it was kind of a nice thought.

After the first few weeks of that first stage, there's compost that's not recognizable as human, but not finished in terms of its material. Bones have mostly been broken down. Then there's a second stage, where there's more mechanical aeration, mixing, sorting, and screening—for gold teeth or metal hips or whatever—and also some more human involvement. It won't be purely automated. That's called the curing and finishing of the compost, where you wind up with very consistent material from day-to-day and place-to-place. There will likely be daily testing. That testing might not be necessary to go on forever, but it's certainly going to be something we do for comfort.

My numbers are based on different types of livestock being composted, which is like a week because they're chopping up the pig carcass or whatever, so it goes fast. But if it's a whole cow under wood chips, it might take like nine months or whatever. If you just wanted a really efficient composting machine, and you set human emotion aside, you might do things differently. On one hand, burning a body and chopping a body up is sort of the same thing. Morally speaking, they're both dead already. If you made a machine—it might be like a meat grinder—then a body might be composted in like three days or something. But efficiency, for me, is not the question. It's not like there's a need to do this really quickly. And there's something valuable about the space of time when you say good-bye to someone, and you're grieving for a month, say, and you come back to get the compost. That's special time.

I'm not sure how the compost will be turned over to families yet. It might be interesting to see how different artists and designers think about that, the giving back. When we did some numbers early on, we thought that when you take something like eight cubic yards of carbon material plus a body to start, then by the time it's all cooked down—that's compost parlance—you've got maybe a cubic yard of material per body. Three by three by three feet. It's kind of a lot. But you wouldn't need to take all of that.

The idea is that it's a continual project, and you'll never be finished with that space. I consider it to be more like cremation than burial, even though it has so much to do with earth. I think it's more like cremation because you end up with a different material than you started with, and you can keep feeding bodies into the facility, and it never ends.

Everyone always gets hung up on the idea that there will be more than one person's remains in the compost, and I keep being stubborn and saying, "We're part of the ecosystem whether we like it or not." But this architecture student at a presentation I attended recently raised their hand and said, "What if every person, when they brought their deceased loved one in, brought in like a one-page biography, and when you got your person, you also got the bios of these, like, nine people who are in there with them. It might be kind of a beautiful community thing."

WE'VE HAD SOME HATE MAIL

Natural burial has been around forever, basically. But this is, as I like to call it, accelerated natural decomposition—it happens with the help of carbon. I guess no one else is doing it because natural burial satisfies the same need, but when you start to think about things on a larger scale or an urban scale, it doesn't work. If one person says, "I don't want to be buried the traditional way," then natural burial is enough. But if you want a natural burial, you need space. The problem with cemeteries in cities is that you can't use that land ever again. It's interesting— natural burial people often flip that idea. They'll use a natural burial site to conserve land.

I think cremation has fit the bill for a lot of people, too, and the rise in cremation is so fascinating, how quickly it has happened. If that trajectory is any indication of what is going to happen with the Urban Death

Project, it would be amazing. The Internet really moves ideas along quickly. The fact that I'm proposing building facilities is just going to take a lot of funding. I have a business plan, but it's really about disrupting the for-profit industry.

There haven't been many people against the project yet. We've had some hate mail, but I think that's more about individuals being deeply afraid of death and hearing about it and being like, "This is fucked up." I wouldn't count it as being opposition because it's really just individuals freaking out a little bit.

It sounds weird to say, but what you do with a corpse doesn't really matter. With something like marijuana legalization, there are questions around issues like, "What if someone is fucked up when they are driving?" But there aren't a lot of practical arguments against doing anything to a corpse, so long as the deceased person condones it.

THE CUSTOMER BASE
DOESN'T GROW ANY LARGER

I'm not super worried about the legal and judicial side of things. It's a state-by-state process, which means a lot of small battles. That may be a pain, but at the same time it seems more manageable than a country-wide battle. In Washington, for example, there's a law that says the ways you can dispose of a body are burial, cremation, or donation to science. It's essentially a list of three things. Cremation is defined as disposal by fire. So we either want to add compost to that list—which would technically be an amendment of the law—or we want to alter the definition of cremation as "disposal of a body by turning it into another substance," or something like that. Because in six or eight states now, alkaline hydrolysis* is one of the things you can do with a body. I'd be interested

---

* A disposal process that is currently legal in thirteen US states, which converts human remains to liquid and ash form. Alkaline hydrolysis is increasingly seen as a "green" alternative to cremation.

in whether they're calling it cremation or not. That's usually what they call it in their marketing terminology. It may be that it makes a lot more sense saying, "This is a type of cremation." But it may not matter which one you're changing.

One of the advisors on my advisory board suggested that it might already count as cremation and be absorbed into that definition. I imagine we will have to amend a law, if we have the funeral industry lobby fighting us, and that'll be a big pain in the ass. You know, right now, I'm this wacky person from Seattle. At some point it's not wacky anymore.

Politics is my weak spot. I don't always understand the machine. I'm probably completely naive in thinking this will be straightforward.

So, 2.5 million people die in the US each year. That is the customer base. It doesn't grow any larger. If you're selling cell phones or something, you can say, "Who have we not tapped?" Maybe grandmas don't have cell phones yet. But this is it! There really is no wiggle room to tell the industry, "Hey, don't worry, I'm not taking your customers." They are what they are. And the funeral industry has been going through a real crisis for a few decades, where they can't make enough money through cremation, so they'll like, embalm and then cremate, even though you can just keep a body refrigerated and you don't need to embalm, ever.

The funeral industry is losing money, and even when it's the most wonderful person doing the work, the system is set up so that in order to make a living, you have to sell more, or higher-quality, products. Better caskets, better coffins, better services. The people they are selling to are usually at their most vulnerable. It's a terrible set-up. It's a terrible model to begin with. No matter how good of a person you are, if you're in that industry, you're in a sticky position. It seems wrong to me. I'm saying, let's create a nonprofit model. I haven't spent enough time thinking creatively about the ways it can function, but let's say it's a sliding scale: You've got a baseline number, and you create a culture where people get more for their money and get complete transparency about what's happening.

There's one funeral company, SCI, that owns 25 percent of the funeral homes in the US. People have said, "You should think about how you could collaborate with them." I know I should, and I'm not totally stubborn about it, but I'm not sure I see a way to do that. You know, if you're trying to make money, I'm just not sure our model could work. Maybe, if we are successful, they'll find a way to do something similar for profit. I wouldn't think of that as a failure.

CONDUCTED JUNE 15, 2015

GABRIEL DePIERO

TWIN BROTHER

There weren't really any strangers in my hometown of twelve thousand people, but Tony and Gabe, rosy-cheeked identical twins from a big Italian family, were especially hard to miss. They were affable and outgoing, their family was well-liked, and as one of the community's only sets of twins (there were four, Gabe remembers, but he and his brother were the only identical twins), they were an inherent curiosity. They were special, even from a distance, whether they liked it or not.

Then, at age thirteen, Tony took his father's gun and shot himself. He died instantly.

For the larger community of Florence, Oregon—a scenic coastal tourist trap with crumbling fishing and timber industries—it was a shock. But shock and disbelief gave way to finger-pointing and speculation. Painful rumors flew almost as fast as word of Tony's death. In one version of events, he had left an angry suicide note. He and his middle-school girlfriend had been in a huge fight, according to another. The most malicious rumors were that Tony's twin brother, Gabe, had pulled the trigger. Those rumors always made their way back to the family. It was as if the likeliest culprits—a teenager's failure to grasp the nature of his own mortality; a momentary madness that could never be taken back—were too simple for the community to accept.

Beyond the rumor and blame, Tony's absence in the community was tangible. No one felt it more profoundly than his twin brother. "Every time people looked at me, they thought of Tony," Gabe told me in the living room of his mobile home, his dog, Nix, at his feet. "Every time I look in the mirror, still, I see him."

I'M SURPRISED THAT
WE SURVIVED CHILDHOOD

On the surface, my family life was very Brady Bunch. That's what my dad strove for. He wanted everything to be perfect. It was very traditional small town: Dad worked, mom worked, all of us four kids were into sports, and we played outside and whatnot. Mom worked at the school, so in the summers she stayed at home with us. When she wasn't around, my oldest brother usually babysat us—and tormented us—and we did all the normal shit you go through growing up in a small town. We built forts, we made booby traps, we lit the pitch on the trees on fire, and then, you know, pissed the fire out when our parents drove up—because every time you light anything on fire, your parents show up. I guess in some ways I'm surprised that we survived childhood.

My mom was brought up Presbyterian, and my dad was brought up Catholic, but we weren't raised religious as kids. The only religious thing that ever happened to us as children is when we went to go visit my grandparents on my dad's side. We went to church on Sundays if we were with them, and man, Catholic services suck. There was all this kneeling, standing, sitting, kneeling. Going to church is a workout! Especially when you're a little kid, and you're antsy, and you wanna go do something else.

My mom and her whole family are very open in talking about death. We still, even now, we talk about it. Her father—my grandfather—just recently passed away, and we've talked a lot about that. He was ninety-two years old. Toward the end he was forgetting things, and he called me everything but my own name. He would call me different grandkids' names each time I visited him, but at least he knew that I was his grandkid.

My grandparents on my dad's side had some property near Eugene, with a big garden and orchard, and so we ate vegetables and fruit and played. We had a great time. My grandfather, Jeno, was a woodworker. He taught me how to write in cursive. He died a couple of years prior to Tony. He passed away from cancer, and that affected me because we were close. But when I lost Tony, I lost me, too. I know that I was not the same person afterward that I was before. Because that connection—well, it was weird.

"IF YOU BLINK, IT'S GONNA SNAP!"

Tony and I were the clinical definition of mirrored twins. As a young child I was predominantly left-handed: I wrote left-handed, threw a baseball with my left hand—that kind of stuff. But when I hit school, I got made fun of for writing left-handed because it looked funny. You know, kids are mean. Tony was right-handed. He was into hunting and sports. I was kind of athletic, but the hunting and fishing I could have done without, you know? I didn't want to get up at five in the morning to go kill a bird or a deer, that didn't appeal to me. But it was very big in my family, and since I didn't really hunt, I helped do the cleanup. I remember holding a deer by its legs while my dad gutted it, and he handed me the heart, and there was blood running down my arms. I was a part of the whole process except actually taking the life of the animals. Tony would hunt, but I'd carry a gun for someone. Give me a tag, great. That's kinda how it happened when I was younger. I went through hunting safety classes, I knew how to handle a gun, and I'm still not fearful of guns. Clearly, I know what guns can do.

Tony and I weren't in any sort of "twin bubble." There were always four of us. We had Dominic, who was the oldest by two years, and then Mario, two years younger than him. There are two years between me and Mario, but there were only two minutes between me and Tony. We were the youngest. But whenever we did things as brothers, like when we would play any kind of sports or games, it was always me and Dominic against Mario and Tony. That's how we always matched it up.

We were close. I mean, I was never alone. We shared a bedroom our whole lives. For a long time we shared a queen-sized bed. He had one side, and I had the other. That's just how we were. We got bunk beds when we started getting a little bit older. We were independent, but still had a lot of the same qualities. We never did do the whole "let's wear matching clothes" thing. We never did any of that kind of shit. Tony was into music; he played the drums at school. I played trombone and bass clarinet.

School wasn't easy for Tony. He struggled with it. It was easy for me, in regards to the academic side of things. Tony was really social. He liked to please people and make sure they were happy. I don't give a shit about other people. I'm an asshole. I mean, the mouth I have right now is the mouth I had when I was a child, so my growing up wasn't as peachy-keen as my brothers' was. I stood up for myself where my brothers backed down easily. When Tony got in trouble, I would do things to provoke my dad to take the punishment away from Tony. That was a big thing for me.

My dad's very intelligent. He's got a photographic memory, and he's super smart. But when I was a kid, he didn't know how to be a dad, except "I bring in the money, I put a roof over your head, I bring the food home." Providing was how he showed you that he loved you. I never felt a lot of love, other than that.

Socially, school wasn't the greatest for me because I was overweight. I was made fun of for that. And I was always called *gay*, *fag*, and stuff like that growing up. That started in elementary school. This kid Taylor was a big perpetrator of it. He called me "Gay Gabe." I got that a lot. You've got to love having a name that rhymes with *gay*. I mean, I knew from a young age that I was gay, but living in Florence, and in my family, it was a sign of weakness—and I'm not weak. I'm a strong person. But I was fat, too, and I got a lot of shit for it. I had friends, but I was picked on a lot.

By the time we were teenagers I was two inches taller than Tony. He was more active, so he shed weight and wasn't nearly as rotund as me. I was round. But I always stood up for myself. If someone said something, I said something right back to them. I didn't take it. I wasn't meek. I wasn't shy by any stretch of imagination. When Taylor or whoever would say things, I'd come back with, "Really? I'm that important that you took the time out of your life to insult me?" I was creative, you know?

I was never physically hit or anything because of my size. I was always taller and bigger than the other kids, and I never backed down from an altercation, so no one would try to pick on me in a physical way. As a small child, my dad told me this—and I'll never forget it—he was like, "If you get in a fight at school and I find out you threw the first punch, your ass is grass. If you are defending yourself, and you kick the shit out of them, I will fight tooth and nail to make sure nothing happens to you." I mean, Dominic and Mario picked on us as kids. I remember my parents going off to some function, and my brother setting mouse traps and holding them in front of our faces: "If you blink, it's gonna snap!" Now I can beat anybody in a staring contest. [Laughs.] You know how bad it hurt to have the trap snap your face? It stings.

Like most families, ours looked nice on the surface, but when you scratched just a little bit, it bled like a motherfucker. But when I turned twelve, it was like, *life*. That's when my parents divorced, and it just felt like everything went downhill from there. Tony and I moved out with my mom to a little apartment behind the middle school. My two older brothers stayed with my dad at our childhood home. We moved out in July, prior to sixth grade. So Tony and I went from taking the bus to school to walking across the street.

Tony and I would spend every other weekend at my dad's house. Dominic and Mario mostly chose to live with him because he had less rules and stipulations. They were older, so that was easier for them. Tony and I had just turned thirteen. I remember when they first moved out, one of the first things that Mario told us was, "We eat ice cream after dinner every night." I was like, "Good for you." I mean, my mom struggled, and we worked really hard. That was one thing that my mom did really well—and my dad, as well—is to teach me that you have to earn what you have. Nothing's ever given to you.

IT STARTLED ME AWAKE,
BUT I DIDN'T MOVE

Tony died on spring break during our seventh-grade year. The last time I talked in this kind of detail about it, it was about two years after that. I remember, it was at a football game. My friend McKenzie and a couple of other people started asking questions, so I went into detail and told the whole story. But it has been a while . . . [takes deep breath].

It was just a normal Saturday night. We were staying at my dad's house. Everything was fine. We went to see a movie—*Naked Gun 33 1/3*. Then in the morning, Dad came in and told Tony, "You need to get up. I'm taking Dominic to school." Dominic was going on a field trip with the golf team, and he'd be gone during spring break. Dad was going to come home, and we were going to go to work with him for the day. He was a plumber—he was going to go work on a project or whatever he had going on. So that was the plan.

Tony woke up and I stayed in bed. It was just us in the house. At some point that morning, he came in and said, "Hey, dude, get up," and I was like, "I wanna sleep. I'm still tired, leave me alone." Tony said, "All right," and he walked out.

The next thing I remember is hearing a very loud noise. My dad being a business owner for a plumbing business, he had very large invoice books—I mean like fifty-pound, huge books—and what it sounded like is it came from the dining room–kitchen area. I thought maybe it was one of those falling and slapping against the linoleum floor. So I didn't get out of bed. I just laid there because it startled me awake, but I didn't move.

I went back to sleep. Dad came home and asked, "Is Tony here?" I was like, "Nope." He went down the hallway, looked in Dominic's room, looked in Mario's room, said his name, and then looked in his room and he screamed . . .

The scream is the part that still bothers me. I still have nightmares now about the scream that my dad let out. He said, "Oh my god, Tony, no!" Then he came running down the hallway. At that point I was out of bed, and I remember stomping on a Nintendo system, then on a remote control, and then tripping over the corner of Tony's bed to get out of the door. I come swinging out of the room, into the dining room, and he's on the phone with 911, and I'm like, "What's going on?" My dad says, "My son shot himself, please send an ambulance," and that was pretty much the end of the conversation. He looks me directly in the eyes and says, "If you can see the white of my carpet, you're too close to my room. Don't go near my room." I'm like, "What the fuck's going on?" He's still not telling me what's happening, and he starts just calling people.

I think to myself, *Tony shot himself. What a douche.* You know, he was very accident-prone. He crashed a three-wheeler into a tree and cut open his hand once. I'm thinking he shot himself in the foot—what an idiot. It hadn't occurred to me that he could be dead. Dad called everyone. He called my mom and said, "Call someone to give you a ride. There's been an accident with Tony. You need to get out here now." He called my grandparents and my aunts, and they started calling all the family in Eugene. We had a couple of different uncles, and an aunt who lived in Springfield, and so people started getting these calls.

I went outside and pet the dog on the porch. We had a tree stump across the yard, and I went and sat on that with the dog. I could hear the ambulance, so I walked out to the driveway. Of course, they drove past our driveway, so I ran out to the street and ran after them a little bit to get them to turn around and come to our house. That's when it started to dawn on me that there was something really wrong, because they weren't rushing. I was like, "Hello, the accident's over here." But they weren't in a rush.

Then Mr. L [a local teacher] got there right after the ambulance did. He was the first one to respond. He was at church when he heard a dispatch radio go off, and then that's when all the other police started showing up.

When the police and everyone started showing up, that's when I went back in the house and sat on the couch in the living room. I had to put the dog out because it he kept getting pissed off and barking with all these strangers in the house. I was sitting on the couch, and I remember my mom got there. Chuck, a family friend who got there right after Mr. L, said, "That's the mom." The cops separated, and Chuck grabbed my mom and just lifted her onto our deck. I had stepped out at that point to give my mom a hug, and she just collapsed in my arms. I had to ask the police officer to help me because I was falling over. She didn't know what was going on, so she ran into the house, and that's when Dad came out and said Tony had shot himself, and he was gone. I stayed outside at that point. I don't know if my mom went into the house and saw him or not.

I know that at one point my dad went into the kitchen and got a glass of water. I was sitting on a recliner outside of the kitchen doorway, and he was like, "He hasn't been baptized. Can I baptize him?" That was before anyone showed; the ambulance, the paramedics had just gotten there. They couldn't pronounce him dead until the coroner showed up, which was like two hours later.

The vice-principal brought Dominic back from school after he was dropped off there for his golfing trip. Then he and I went to get my brother Mario from his friend's house, where he had stayed the night. I remember that my necklace had broken somehow, and I was picking up beads from the ground when a family friend came through the door.

My dad was standing there, and the woman was like, "You killed him, motherfucker!" and she pushed him and, like, assaulted my dad. My dad immediately said, "Get this bitch off my property!"

When the police came, they asked me a lot of questions. "Was he unhappy? Was he this or that?" He had a girlfriend at the time, and they asked about her. I was like, "No, there's no indication of anything bad." I mean, come on, it was a seventh-grade romance. What did they do—they passed notes, they held hands. There was nothing going on that I can think of in his life at that point that was so bad that he needed to end it. He had a lot of friends that he was close with, that he socialized with. He wasn't alienated or anything like that. He wasn't ostracized for anything. He wasn't bullied at all. I mean, I can see me pulling the trigger before anyone else. I truly believe in my heart that it wasn't suicide, and I will defend that until I die.

At that point, after I answered those questions, I kind of shut down. I remember saying, "He didn't fucking kill himself. It wasn't suicide." Then I kind of snapped, and Chuck stepped over and told them, "You have to leave him alone." They didn't ask me another question after that.

My Uncle Terry showed up, and he could see I needed to get out of there. He had just got back from a trip to Germany. He took me up the coast just to get away from the house and everyone, and all he did was talk about his trip to Germany. I don't even remember what he said about it because all I did was stare out the window of his truck. I remember staring at the trees. We parked in a parking lot next to the ocean, and I just stared out the window and listened to sound. Then he drove us to Saint Mary's Church, where he got out and said a prayer. I just sat in the back of the church.

When we got back, they took Tony out of the bedroom in a red body bag. They set him behind the ambulance, and our dog went and laid next to the body bag. I had to walk over and take him away because, when they grabbed the body bag to put him in the ambulance, he sort of attacked the paramedic. I had to walk over and grab the dog to walk him away. At that point, I knew I had to leave. That was when I grabbed my mom and was like, "We have to go. I have to go. You have to take me home now." That's when I finally left.

THERE WAS NO FEELING,
THERE WAS NO NOTHING

Tony died on my classmate Matt's birthday. So I went to the birthday party that same day. My mom and her friend Lynette thought that it might take my mind off things. Which was really kind of odd because, when I got there, it put all of them in a very weird place. My friend Spencer—I'll never forget this—he walked into the living room where I was sitting on the couch, and he was like, "I don't know what to say." And I was like, "Neither do I." I said, "How are you doing?" He was like, "I'm okay. How are you?" I said, "It's been a rough day." And that was how the conversation started. Then we all just started talking about normal stuff. Things started feeling normal again. We went to the video store to get a video game to play, and I remember running into a girl from school. I told her, "Tony died this morning." She said, "Nuh uh." I said, "No, he shot himself and died this morning." And she said, "No, he didn't."

We grew up around guns. We had hunters' safety, the whole works. We knew how guns worked: pistols, rifles, shotguns, anything in between. What had happened was that Tony had already cleaned two pistols. He had cleaned two, and he had taken a revolver, and he had all of the shells in his pocket but one. So what they believe he was doing was playing Russian roulette, and he lost. They don't believe it was a suicide thing— that he killed himself that way intentionally—but "I'm the invincible teenager." He was stupid in doing shit, and I could see him being like, "I can win!" And he lost. It was a hollow-point bullet. It went through his right eye and completely removed all of this . . . [motions toward back of his skull].

He didn't know what happened. No, he did not know what happened. It was instant. There was no feeling, there was no nothing. That's the only peace of mind that I get from it, that he didn't know what happened. The click. If he even heard the click of the hammer, he was gone. He was sitting at my dad's bed with his knees under the bed, so when my dad found him, he was partway under the bed. There were two full-door mirrors behind him, with a small section of wall between them that was painted white. I remember after the whole thing, I went in the room, and they had cut the carpet out of my dad's bedroom and torn up everything under it, the base, wood floor, everything. They had completely repainted the wall and cleaned stuff out, so that there was no . . . everything was gone by the time I had seen it. I never saw it or anything. The only time I saw Tony prior to them burying him was we did get to view him in his casket. They reconstructed all of this . . . [motions at back of his head], and he had an eye patch on when I saw him.

THE VOICE

I'm not a religious person, and I wasn't then. I'm somewhat spiritual, but I'm not religious. One thing I do remember and I won't forget, though, is while everyone was at the house—the paramedics and police and neighbors—I went and laid down on my bed, and I remember hearing Tony's voice very clearly telling me, "I'm sorry," and "Everything's going to be okay." There was no one around because I immediately got up like, "Who fucking said that?" I looked out my bedroom door, and no one was around. It was Tony's voice, very clearly. It was Tony's voice telling me it would be okay.

KID GLOVES

Everyone treated me differently after that. Kid gloves. It was like, "I'm a human being. Treat me normal." That was the one thing that drove me crazy. I was so tired. I wasn't a child. I wasn't an adult by any means; I was a teenager. But it was like, "Quit treating me like a baby." I think all teenagers feel like that, but when you throw in the death of your twin brother, it's worse. Family, friends, everyone—everyone took a step back. I felt like I had the plague.

Everyone was kind of looking over their shoulders or side-eyeing me. Like, "Poor him." They wouldn't say anything to me. It was like, "Say something or do something!" I felt very alienated. And everyone, kids, teachers—the teachers were the worst in regards to the baby gloves because it wasn't just me. It was everyone around me, too. When I walked into the room, it was like, "Okay, the plague just got here, so how is everyone else going to respond now that Gabe's in the room?" I wasn't just worried about me. It was the stress of everybody around me. Like, "What's going to happen today?" I had breakdowns at school. I had a couple of them. It was awful. And I had to go to the office and leave because there were a couple of really bad breakdowns that I just couldn't get myself under control. It would come out of nowhere. I would all of a sudden get overwhelmed and couldn't handle it.

It was like standing in a room full of people screaming my head off, and no one responded. That's exactly how I felt. It was like, I was screaming bloody murder for anyone and everyone, but I didn't exist. At the same time it was like everyone was on me, but no one listened. It was all about what was best for *them* in the situation, not what was best for me. It was about what made them comfortable, not what made *me* comfortable.

I'd never felt alone before. I'd always had Tony around. At the end of the day, he was in the same room with me sleeping, too, you know? I never felt alone. After he died, that was the first time. You have all these people around you, trying to support you. Friends' families made our lunches for a month after Tony died. I remember going to school every day, and this girl handing me a lunch because her mom made me a lunch, too.

I felt like such a burden. Like, "Oh god, here comes Gabe." Then, the bullying didn't stop when Tony died. I mean, it didn't get any worse, but didn't get any better. I was still Fat Gabe, Gay Gabe, whatever. That was just part of it. But that was almost better than the fact that most people didn't look at me when I spoke. I just wanted them to acknowledge that I existed.

I mean, if I had had one person who sat there and just looked at me when I spoke, it would have made a world of difference. I didn't have that. I felt so alone. I mean, pluck me and put me in the middle of nowhere, and I think I would have found a friend there before I found one in Florence.

My family had to look at me every day, and it reminded them of Tony. I know how that feels because I look in the mirror and I have to see myself. I mean, I'm thirty-four years old. I'll be thirty-five at the end of this month, and there isn't a day that goes by that Tony doesn't pop into my mind. People say that cliché, but it's true. Every time I look in the mirror, still, I see him. I wonder, *Would we look the same now, or would we look different?* There are all these questions.

It was overwhelming, so I tried to kill myself. I thought, *If I'm this alone, why even be here?* It was so overwhelming, and it drove me nuts. One night I was home alone at my mom's house, and I swallowed a bottle of Tylenol and chugged a bottle of rum out of the liquor cabinet. I woke up in a big pile of puke. That was a few months after Tony died.

The pills seemed like the easy way out. But it wasn't so easy. I felt like shit for like three days afterward.

WE DIDN'T KNOW WHAT TO SAY

I've met a lot of other twins throughout the years. When I was in college, there were like five sets of identical twins living in the dorms. It's difficult, especially when they don't know me from my childhood, and they don't know that I'm a twin. They're like, "Oh, you were a twin." And I say, "Yeah, I'm still a twin. He's just not alive." I'm absolutely a twin. That's who I am. He's my other half.

I met another twin recently, a guy, and he asked, "What is that like? I couldn't imagine that." I said, "Don't." There are certain pains and certain horrible experiences in life that you don't have to go through, and you should never have to imagine. Because you can't. It's not just the loss of that person; it's the aftermath. It was almost like I died with Tony. Then my death happened every day after that for a long time. It's everything after. It's how people treat you.

Looking back now that I'm older I just want to ask everyone, "Why did you do that? Why did you stop talking to me? What was wrong with me that you couldn't talk to me after Tony died?"

We didn't know what to say.

Neither the fuck did I! I was thirteen. You were the adult in the situation! Like, what the fuck!? I mean, I had a lot of rage. I had a lot of anger. Awful rage and anger.

Looking back at it now, I get it. It's a hard situation. But still—why was I punished after he died? What did I do wrong to be treated that way? It still bothers me to this day. Even when I've spoken to people about it, all they can say is, "I didn't know what to say." It's a bullshit excuse. Spencer, at the age of twelve or thirteen, said the same thing, but then the conversation started after that. So, really? You were the adult, and you couldn't do anything? Zip? I mean "fuck you" is better than being ignored. What did I do that you couldn't say, "How do you feel?" or "How are you doing?" Like, why couldn't you ask me that? You asked everyone else that. When Tony died I magically gained the ability to never be asked, "What's up?"

Sometimes I wish my family and friends would have said, "I can't talk to you anymore because Tony died." I would have had closure there. "You're dead to us, too, because Tony died." Yeah, that would've hurt, but I would have had closure. I would have known why. Being ignored, I was left wondering if I was only ever included because Tony was there, too. You know, did people just want to hang out with him? Those were my thoughts as a teenager. Maybe it was because I'm the youngest by two minutes—I'm just the little brother—I felt expendable.

I can talk to anyone now. I don't care. I freak a lot of people out, that's fine. How many people want to put themselves into situations that make them uncomfortable? Or make them feel something fearful or feel something that they don't like? Not many. Not many, if any at all. Journalists, maybe. And gay people! Gay people will talk to you.

THERE WAS NO PAIN

I lost a lot of family and friends when I came out. It's okay. I care about you the way you care about me. Probably in my late twenties, I realized that there were certain things in life that were out of my control—things that I absolutely couldn't do anything about. Why should I stress over those things? If something happens and I can't get over it in three seconds, there's a problem. I need to address that problem and fix it because I don't like feeling that way. I don't want stress in my life. I don't need stress in my life. My home is my sanctuary. I want to be comfortable and relaxed. So things don't bother me. I don't let things bother me anymore.

That took me a lot of years to figure that out. I've been through a lot of therapy. I've had my lows. I was a cutter. I was a drinker. It affected me really bad when I first started college. It was really hard seeing all these sets of twins. That was when my second suicide attempt happened, in college. I was at a very low point. I don't remember doing it. I don't remember how it happened. But when I came to, I had cut my arm twenty-six times with a serrated blade.

I just turned the whole back of my arm into hamburger. I remember looking down, and my whole shirt being covered in blood, and I'm like, "Oh my god, I stabbed myself." I go rushing into the bathroom to find out where the hole is at, what did I do. Remember, I had the knife in my hand. I was wearing a white T-shirt, and it was just hanging heavy with blood. That's when I realized my arm was covered in blood, and I grabbed a washcloth and I wiped it. It was just like, *holy shit*. I had taken the Gerber—it was one of those serrated knives, a Gerber tool—and just sat there.

I had cut myself and burned myself and did those things after Tony had died. I have different scars on me from different incidents, on my hands and legs, wounds that I inflicted on myself. But I hadn't done it in years. I was drinking heavily, and I was living out on my own. My room-mates were gone, and I was watching a movie about Matthew Shepard.* At the end of it his mother went out to where they tied him up to that fence. When she walked up to that, it put me into a crying rage. It made me think of Tony, and it made me think about how I hadn't come out yet. All these different things and all these different feelings, and I just started . . . that's what triggered my crying. That movie. I watched that movie and I remember sitting on my couch. But it put me way in deeper than that. I blacked out. I think when I get put into that situation of total panic and fear and pain and everything, my mind shuts down. My brain doesn't want to do it anymore. It has dealt with it for so much for so long that it hits capacity and it just stops. I don't remember grabbing the knife. I don't remember opening it. I don't remember any of that. To this day I don't remember doing anything. Except I remember I had just sliced the shit out of my arm and it never hurt. That was the weird thing. There was no pain. It was bad, like the scars. There's still certain lines that you can see, different cuts that are still there. A lot of them went away. Some of them I covered up with a tattoo. It was like I went after these veins right here: [points to the inside back of his left forearm].

That one was the worst. I was going to therapy at the time, and I told my therapist that I had cut myself, and he said, "What do you mean?" I pulled up my sleeve and showed him, and he's like, "You know that we

---

* A gay University of Wyoming student who was brutally tortured and murdered in 1998. His death led to significant hate crime legislation.

can put you away for that." I said, "What do you mean?" He said, "You're inflicting pain on yourself. You have to see your doctor about antidepressants right now." I showed my doctor what I did, and that's when the whole world kind of came crashing in on me because, basically, I lost my ability to make my own decisions. It was, *Now that you've inflicted pain upon yourself, we could hospitalize you for three days and put you under surveillance and blah blah blah blah.* You would lose the ability to make the decisions for medications and anything; those decisions would be made by your parents, even as an adult.

I fought taking antidepressants. I was like, "I don't need drugs." I had friends who took different antidepressants, and you could see the change in them. I didn't want that. But my doctor made a really good point. He was like, "You're worried about changing, but what are you in control of right now? This medication is to give you the tools to get things back under control. Then once things are easier, you can start getting off of them. But you're not in control now, so what's the difference?" That made sense. That's when I first started taking antidepressants. I took them for a few years, and then I weaned myself off of them. I haven't taken them since.

The antidepressants made things easier to deal with. After Tony died, I worried about everything. If I wasn't around my mother, I was calling her every hour—"How are you doing? What's going on?" I worried. After Tony died, every nightmare I had, every dream I had, I lost someone close to me. Someone I cared about died. I was so scared that someone else I cared about was going to die. I was always super stressed about that, and I was taking a lot of antacids and stuff. I worried about anything and everything.

Oh, it was awful. If a friend said, "Hey I'm going to call you in a little bit," I'd be like "How long is a little bit?" If they said half an hour, and then they didn't call within that half-hour mark, I was devastated. I'd think they hated me, or I'd be freaked out. I'd think, *Oh my god, their house blew up.* I mean, everything. *Oh my god, they slipped in the shower and strangled themselves with the curtain.* Everything horrible you can think of, that's what I always thought had happened.

I didn't have my childhood ripped away. I had my teenage years ripped away. I got to have a childhood. But as a teenager, you're trying to figure out who you are, and that was all torn away.

MY TURN TO BE SELFISH

I was scared. Everything was built on "I'm not gay." I didn't come out because I was scared that I would lose the family that I had. Because that was a sign of weakness, being gay. They'd all made their comments. I heard all the comments my dad made. It's never been a positive thing in my family. It's not talked about, even now. I was in a relationship for an extended amount of time, and he never met my parents. My mom's comment was always, "I have concerns about the lifestyle." AIDS, and all that, STDs. But I could have sex with women, too, and the same things could happen. I'm not stupid. I use a condom, hello.

I didn't come out until I was twenty-four, but I figured it out in middle school. I remember first changing my status on MySpace from "straight" to "unsure." And the controversy that caused at my job, you wouldn't believe it.

This is me. If you don't like it, kick rocks. Don't let the door hit ya' where the good lord split ya'. I'm not going to stress my life over how you feel. That's been very important to me. When I die, that's one thing I want to be said at my funeral: Gabe cares about every one of you the way you cared about him. Because I know 60 percent of the people in that room didn't give two shits for me, but are there because of the other people that are there. That's how my family is. They're there for show. And that's fine. I know who cares about me, and the rest can kiss my ass. I don't want to worry about everyone else. I want to worry about me. You know what? It's my turn to be selfish. I've earned that right.

In my mid-twenties I was back in Florence, and I was like, "I haven't been to a football game since high school! Let's go to a football game." It's like six years after high school. There were four people there. Three of them I had graduated with [in a class of about 110 people]. I told a girl I'd been friends with that I was gay. She said, "No, you're not." And I'm like, "Yeah, I am." She wouldn't believe me.

I'm your typical guy who grew up in a small town, except I like to be with other men.

Sometimes it's just, "Why was I dealt this hand?" Be a twin, lose your twin. Be gay in a small town. Struggle with your weight. It's like, what the fuck did I do to deserve this? What did I do in a previous life that put me on this path?

At the same time, it has made me a more compassionate person. When someone tells me they lost a loved one, I tell them I'm so sorry for their loss, but I don't stop the conversation there. I know how that kid felt. I wanted someone just to listen, to sit there and stare at me while I talked. No one did any of that kind of stuff. That's what I got out of all this pain—it was compassion. It taught me compassion. Everything else about me is just me. The compassion I have is a direct result of all that horrible shit I went through. I don't want anyone to ever, ever feel like that.

I tell my friends, "If you need anyone, you call me, day or night." I truly mean that. Because you never know when you need someone. I've needed people at 3 am.

MY WHOLE LIFE, IT WAS TONY'S LIFE

I don't think anyone else has been through what I've been through. I know people go through horrific things every day. Is mine any worse or better than theirs? Yes and no. Everyone handles things differently. I mean, I tried to end it twice. It wasn't my time. I feel like I was put here to go through all these horrible, awful things because I can handle it. I've had to.

After Tony died, I had to move on. I had to deal, you know? No one was there to support me. I had to pull up my bootstraps on my own.

People will tell you, "Oh, we were there. We were supportive." I'm like, just because you were in the room doesn't mean you were there. What did you say to me when you were in the room? *Well, nothing.* I'm very vocal when I walk in a room. I say hello; I want people to know I'm there. I don't want anyone to feel that way I felt for a lot of years. It wasn't just that moment after Tony died. It almost felt like my whole life, it was Tony's life. How I felt after all that happened was that everyone wanted Tony, and I was just the tagalong because we shared the embryo at birth. I was expendable, disposable.

There's no guidebook for something like this. The one thing when going through death and mourning is just ask questions. Ask a question. Doesn't matter what that question is—I mean, "What's your favorite color?" Engaging that person in anything no matter what it is or how minute it is could mean the world. I truly believe that. That would have made the world to me, if someone would have just asked me anything, made me feel like they cared about the answer I gave. If someone would have said, "What's your favorite color?" and I told them "Yellow," and they listened to me, that would have meant so much.

I LIKE THE VIEW FROM HERE

When his anniversary comes around, in March, it's rough. My birthday's really hard, too.

It's weird. I went years without going up and seeing his grave. And other times, I just want to go up there and hang out. It's a peaceful place. I like going up there. It's beautiful. It's up at the top of the cemetery, next to that big tree. I signed his casket—"I will always love you. Love, Gabe." I wrote that in black Sharpie on his casket.

It's weird: I'm thirty-four years old, and I have a cemetery plot. I don't own my own home, but I do know where I'm going to be buried. I have a plot right next to Tony's. When he died, my parents chose to buy the plot right next to his. They bought it for me. It's weird knowing I have a cemetery plot. I wouldn't say it's comforting, but—and I know this sounds really morbid—I'm the one who chose where Tony got buried. I sat there, as a kid, and then I laid on the ground. I would lay on the ground in different places and be like, "I like the view from here." I told them that the spot near the tree was where I wanted Tony to be buried. And that's where they put him.

I wanted him to be buried right under the tree, actually, but because of the roots and all that, they don't allow it. Rules. The whole idea of being planted and becoming a tree still interests me. I love that. I think that is the coolest idea. Like, when my dog dies, I will plant her under a tree. My wild fern grows somewhere. I think that is the coolest way to remember someone, to have that. Because the tree can live on forever, you know? It gets its life from you. How cool is that? My energy's all gone because I'm dead, but what's left of me is in this tree.

But I know where I'm going to end up. Saying that out loud, it sounds weird. I've never thought about it much until just the other day, when I was talking to someone and I'm like, "I know where I'm going to be buried when I die." I'm thirty-four years old and I know where I'm going to be buried when I die.

THAT WORLD IS GONE

I remember flipping through channels one day with my mom and landing on *The Jenny Jones Show*. It was an episode about "twinless twins," and my mom was like, "We have to watch this!" I was like, *really?* After Tony died my mom went through this kind of crazy death thing. Twinless twins are networks of people who have lost their twins. I've never contacted one. I've looked into it, but I've never reached out to a twinless twin.

Why would I reach out to another pained soul? I can't answer for what happened then. Back then, I felt worthless. I was the leftover, the remnant. Why would I want to bring another person into that feeling? Or why would I want to surround myself with people who felt that same way? That'd just make me feel even worse. Nothing like a little more death in the room. Ugh, no thanks.

I don't want to reach out to a community where all they're going to do is bitch and moan or talk about the loss of their twin. I lost my twin. I don't want to dwell on it. Your story is your story and my story is my story. I'm not trying to one-up you or any of that stuff with my loss, but then again . . . good luck beating my story.

There's always death. I mean, everyone in the world is going to experience death, close to them, somehow. An animal, a parent, a family member. But there's a certain pain when you lose that other half of you. It's indescribable. I can't put it into words.

I don't want to say it's a special kind of alone because, when you say it's special, it makes it a good thing. It makes it sound positive. It's the worst. There are certain things you don't wish on your worst enemy, and the loss of a twin, that feeling of abandonment and loneliness—I don't wish that on anyone in the world.

At the same time, I'm proud that I've survived all of the things I've gone through. Those experiences have made me a stronger person. They've made me much more of a compassionate person because I know how fragile life is. I know how hurtful words are cause I grew up with bullying my whole life.

My childhood ended when Tony died, and I don't even think about what happened prior to his death because that world is gone. I can't ever get it back, so why dwell on it? I believe your life is a specific path that you're meant to take. I was put on this world to take the path I've taken. I take it full charge. Sometimes I have someone next to me help out. Most times I don't. That's okay. Let's go. I don't know why my path was lined with such awful, horrible things along the way, but I've survived it. And I'm still surviving it, you know?

HERE'S THE NEW PLANET THAT YOU LIVE ON

After Tony died, I was living in that awful negativity. Because one moment everything was—I don't want to say *normal*, I hate using that word—but everything was the way it was supposed to be, and in this one little fraction of a second, my whole world was gone.

Now here's the new planet that you live on. Here's everything new that you're supposed to get used to. Here's the semicolon.

Finally, in my thirties, I was like, "Why am I living in such a horrible, negative world? I want to be happy." I can't say that I've been happy very much in my life. When I met my ex, I remember that feeling, that feeling of happiness. I was like, "Wow. I feel loved." He made me feel cared about. I thought, *This is what being a human feels like. This is what it feels like to be treated with respect and to be cared about.* He showed me what that was like. It was very eye-opening. That's when I was like, *I need to stop doing all this shit. I need to stop letting all these little things bother me. I want to feel like this more often.*

That relationship ended, but I wanted to keep that feeling. I needed to stop worrying, and I needed to stop taking things so personal. Everything that happened, I took so personally. So I just stopped. I mean, it's hard. There are all these what-ifs. My whole world is what-if. But I've finally stopped living the what-if, and that's when I stopped feeling alone. I can't live in a what-if world. I need to live in this world that I have right now.

I'm content right now where I'm at. Ever since I got Nix, it's been a lot better. You know, coming home and being excited for her to be excited that I'm home, and vice-versa. Not coming home to an empty house helps a lot. She has helped me so much, just in the last nine months that I've had her.

It's a day-by-day process. When you lose someone close to you, it doesn't go away. You deal with it on a regular basis. It gets easier to deal with, and some days are just a cakewalk and some days I don't want to get out of bed. I still have those days. But I've got to feed the dog.

I celebrate my birthday. Every year, I'm glad I made it through. I've been on my own since I was thirteen. I truly feel that way. I may not have supported myself financially and stuff, but I've been alone since I was thirteen. Not until I hit my thirties did I feel like I wasn't alone.

It gives me solace that I've lived a life of honesty and I've been myself. I know that one day I'll meet all the people that I care about and have lost. Before my grandfather died a few weeks back, I told him, "Please tell everyone I love them. I'm jealous that you get to see them. I know I'll get to see them one day. Just tell them all hi for me. Give them my love." People are gone, but they're not gone forever. That's what gets me through. There will come a day that I will get to see these people again.

I've always wondered, too: *Is Tony going to be the thirteen-year-old version of him, or am I going to see him as an adult?* Is he going to age along with me? How is that going to work?

\\

CONDUCTED JULY 16, 2015

LOREN RHOADS

FORMER EDITOR, MORBID CURIOSITY

Loren Rhoads started Morbid Curiosity *magazine in the late nineties: before* Death Cafes *where you could share stories and questions about dying with strangers, before Caitlin Doughty's popular "Ask a Mortician" column, and before the advent of endless sub-Reddit holes where the darkly curious could find videos of beheadings and autopsy photos of the rich and famous. Rhoads's concept for the magazine was pretty straightforward: Create a space where any and all topics—no matter how dark or taboo—were fair game. For the three thousand-ish subscribers and fans who found the magazine on newsstands around the world for* Morbid Curiosity's *ten-year run, it was a revelation. That's in large part due to the thoughtful curation of Rhoads herself. Her focus wasn't just on taboo breaking; it was on storytelling.*

In the introduction to her tenth and final issue, Rhoads's stable of writers "attempted suicide, assisted suicide, committed murder, and sat on a jury that sentenced two men to life in prison for killing their parents." It turns out, though, that the pitfalls of editing a magazine about the macabre and the grotesque are the same ones as running any other magazine: lousy pay, a diminished social life, and the occasionally grouchy writer. The perks—satisfying one's own curiosity, networking with an eccentric and talented group of people, getting weird shit in the mail—sound pretty familiar, too.

These days, Rhoads is focused on her own writing. What scandalous subject could the ex-editor of a cult magazine about mass murder, incest, and fetishes possibly have tackled next? She wrote a sci-fi trilogy about time travel and galactic drug dealers. "I was thoroughly amused at one of the first reviews I got that said I was bringing 'dark' to space opera," she says. "I don't think they're that dark, but then again my 'dark' has kind of shifted a bit."

THE CEMETERY

I grew up on a farm in Michigan. Our house was less than a mile down the road from the cemetery where my grandparents were buried, so we drove by the cemetery all the time. My mom was a city girl. We wound up getting farm animals, and she wanted to name all the cows and name all the rabbits. But they were livestock, and they weren't around very long. You kind of got used to not getting attached to things.

At some point, when I was around ten or eleven, Mom decided it'd be a fun thing to do one afternoon to go down to the cemetery and make rubbings on the headstones. That was my first time really hanging out in a graveyard. We'd gone to Washington's grave on vacation, so it wasn't that unusual, but that was the first time I'd been someplace where people I knew were buried. I had a cousin who died shortly after I was born, and her grave was there. Up until that point, I hadn't realized kids could die.

It's a beautiful place. It's not very big, but the stones in that graveyard have the same names as roads around my parent's farm because all the farm families had a plot in the graveyard. It was really familiar once I was in there. A couple of years ago I took my own daughter down there, and we made some rubbings—they haven't been framed; they're still in a closet. But I'm passing it on, I guess.

"YOU'RE NOT OPPOSED TO ANIMAL EXPERIMENTS, ARE YOU?"

I was straight out of college—I was twenty-one, I think—when I got a job at an animal-testing lab. It was kind of by accident. I was supposed to help the professor who ran the lab keep his notes, do his filing, stuff like that—but they didn't warn me that I would be in there while they were experimenting on the animals. After I got the job, they said, "You're not opposed to animal experiments, are you?" At that point I didn't really know.

Because I grew up on a farm, I'm used to animals as part of the food chain, but they were cutting open sheep's skulls and attaching electrodes into their brains to try and find out where the taste buds on the tongue fired in the brain. The ultimate goal was to improve taste for elderly people, so, you know, I guess it's a good thing to help the elderly keep eating. But it was just awful.

I stuck it out for as long as I could, and then in the spring they started experimenting on lambs, and one day they asked me to feed the lambs. That was the final straw. I just couldn't do it. The fact that they tortured sheep seemed like one thing, but feeding the lambs so they could kill them—no. I just couldn't do that.

MODERN PRIMITIVES

It was different back then, you know? This is pre-Internet days. If you were a freak and you wanted to meet freaky people, you made a zine.

My husband's parents used to have a publishing company. They ran a quarterly magazine, like a journal for teachers that taught multicultural education. They published textbooks, basically. They were a very small press, didn't do very big print runs, but I got kind of a sense of the backstage stuff, you know, how you keep a mailing list and how you send things out.

So I started a zine in college that was just science fiction. My friends wrote for it, and we sold it at conventions and all of that. It was Xeroxed and really rudimentary. My husband started a zine on Japanese underground music because he had traveled a lot in Japan and spoke Japanese. People were sending him the greatest stuff in the mail for his zine. I thought, *I've got to do something where I can get strange stuff in the mail from people.*

After we moved to San Francisco, there was an announcement that RE/Search* was going to do a slideshow. The founder, V. Vale, has taken a photograph of everyone he's met for forty years, something like that. He has shoeboxes full of these photographs. So we went to this slideshow, and at the end of it, he and his partner said that they were putting together a new book, and that they were going to need some help packing orders and doing grunt work. That book turned out to be *Modern Primitives*. I don't know if it's well known anymore, but at the time that came out, it was the first book about personalized tattoos, and it was the first book that looked at tattoos as art rather than just Sailor Jerry or whatever. Here in San Francisco, it was huge. All the piercing shops, tattoo shops, everything, traces back to *Modern Primitives*. While the book was in production, but before it had actually come out, we had dinner one night with V. Vale and Andrea Juno, and she had these pages with pictures and layout, and she said, "Come and take a look at this."

One of the things she showed me was labial piercings. I think that was the first one. And she said, "I'm a little afraid because they're having it printed in China." She was worried about it coming in the US—like, was it going to be held as pornography? She said she was going to split the image of a pierced labia over two pages, so it was going to be a split-split-beaver, and she wondered if that seemed okay?

I had never seen anything like that before in my life. I mean, I vaguely knew that there was such a thing as genital piercing, but there it was. I mean, I'm straight off the farm pretty much. Then she showed me a picture of a guy who'd split his penis.

I thought, *If you can publish that, I can publish the thing I want.* And so we did.

---

* A San Francisco-based magazine documenting underground music and culture, published in the 1980s and '90s.

I DON'T SEE THE CREEPY ANYMORE

Just before I published the magazine, I published a book called *Death's Garden*. It was meant to be a collection of my friend's photographs because he had traveled around and visited a lot of cemeteries. But once I mentioned the project to people, everybody had a cemetery story, and it ended up being a big book. That was published in '95, I think.

The first cemetery I went to for the book, it was kind of a life-changing one, and it was totally by accident.

My husband, Mason, is in tech. In '88 there weren't a lot of tech jobs, so San Francisco was the obvious place to move. He started doing sound for this performance art group, Survival Research Laboratories. They were doing research in Barcelona, so we had to get ourselves there. There wasn't any pay involved, but you know, a good excuse to go to Europe.

As we were flying, the First Gulf War started. All the connections got screwed up, and we ended up landing in England, where we had no plans to be. It turns out Survival Research Laboratories lost their venue, and they moved to another venue, and then that one got taken over by the army as they were ramping up for the war—so rather than go to Spain where we didn't speak the language and know our way around, we stayed in London. Over the course of the trip, I picked up this book that was just these exquisite photos of cemeteries that been abandoned and were all overgrown and full of broken statues. Mason said, "You know, I'd rather go see a cemetery than see the Tower of London." So we did. It was a January day, we had the place completely to ourselves, and it was just glorious. It was so beautiful. From London we had planned to go to Paris, and so one of my friends said, "You've got to go to Père Lachaise cemetery and see Jim Morrison's grave." So that was another religious experience. It started out kind of—we'd go to a place and we'd wonder whether they had a cemetery nearby, and eventually I was building trips around cemeteries.

We went to Venice. I knew that Venice had an island that was just a cemetery, and I thought, *That's a bizarre thing, we should go see it.* Stravinski's buried there. When I go somewhere, I want to see how their cemetery is different from the others. A couple of years ago my parents took me up to Niagara Falls. We were in a tourist restaurant, and my mom said, "Hey, do you have any historic cemeteries here?" So I wound up going into one near where one of the battles of 1812 was fought—so it had a bunch of old historical graves. It's also the place where the people that have gone over the falls were buried—the people who've gone over the falls in barrels and not made it. That was a great afternoon, just poking around, taking a bunch of pictures.

I've been doing this so long, I don't see the creepy anymore. I forget that normal people don't like graveyards, and so I'll be dragging a friend along and they'll say, "Oh, I can't wait until I have to go into work on Monday. They'll say, 'What did you do this weekend?' I spent the weekend in a graveyard." But it's so beautiful. The sunshine and the grass and the sense of history and all the stories that are buried there. I mean, there's a lot you can decipher from the shapes of the stones and the iconography and the years of death. I just find it really interesting to take the whole life and kind of boil it down to what you can fit on a headstone.

It's a thing that really gets lost as more and more people are cremated. People will be gone, and there won't be any record. When my friend Blair died, we threw some of his ashes off the bridge, and we threw some in the bay and somewhere in the garden, but he doesn't have a monument anywhere, so I don't have any place to go to talk to him. Everywhere and nowhere. I miss having a place. I go to my family graveyard to talk to my grandma. The rest of the time, I think about her, but I don't feel like she's looking over my shoulder.

THEY STILL DON'T KNOW WHERE
ALL THE DEAD PEOPLE ARE

I want to do a book on the historic cemeteries in the San Francisco Bay Area because San Francisco is such a young community—pretty much everything dates to 1849. Originally all the little towns were different:

One was a logging town, and one was a mining town, and one was farming and ranching, and that's reflected in their graveyards. But they're vanishing. Real estate is so expensive here that once a graveyard is damaged to a certain point, it's a lot cheaper and easier to just pave over it and build houses. In San Francisco itself, we don't have any active graveyards anymore because they tore them all out in the 1940s.

Pretty much every time they open the ground for a certain project, they find bodies that didn't erode. Under the library, under the art museum, the Palace of Fine Arts, a couple of places up on some of the hills—there are bodies under all of those. It amazes me that San Francisco is such a young city, and they still don't know where all the dead people are. Rome is thousands of years old, so it makes sense they've lost their graveyards, but here? A lot of the men who came up here for the Gold Rush were famous people. The guy who invented the cable cars of San Francisco, his grave got smashed up and they threw it in the ocean. Every now and then the sand will shift out in the ocean and headstones come up. One of the parks has rain gutters that are all lined with marked headstones. Most are facedown, but enough are faceup that you can read off the tabs. So, it's weird: I love graveyards and I wound up in a town with no functional graveyards. But there are dead bodies everywhere, so . . .

EVERYTHING IS WORTHY OF BEING LOOKED AT

The first issue of *Morbid Curiosity* was in 1997. Again, this was before the Internet. You couldn't just Google any strange thing that came into your head. I really liked getting stories from strangers. I thought, *What do I want? I want people to tell me their deepest darkest secrets. I'll call the magazine* Morbid Curiosity, *and I'll just open it up to anyone.* It was all first-person true confessions—just all kinds of crazy stuff that people would send to me, and I'd publish. Then I'd do reading events in San Francisco. I'd get up and read them live, and it was so good. I mean, it was really helpful and healing for people to admit to some of this stuff and to process it a little bit.

I'd never been to any reading events where people were so absorbed. They'd get so quiet and listen so intently. And they were long because I'd invite everybody who was local to participate, so it'd be two to three hours of these reading events. It was hard to give that up. I think I miss the reading events the most, just because there was such a sense of community.

I wanted the magazine to be perfect bound, and look serious, because when I'd done zines before they were little stapled Xerox things. In the first issue, I had a guy who was a professor emeritus write me an explanation of what "morbid curiosity" was. I never thought of morbid curiosity as negative in any sense. I think it's really healing and helpful to just be curious about everything. The problems start when we aren't curious and there are topics that we can't talk about. I feel like when you bury something, that's when it has power over you.

Everything is worthy of being looked at. Think about a wedding ceremony. You get a woman in a significantly white dress to go up there, and she hikes up her skirt and takes off her garter and throws it out for all the men. What's the significance of that? People do it all the time, but they don't usually know. It's a ritual, and it means something. It doesn't mean now what it used to mean, but still. The whole throwing a bouquet, where whoever catches it is next to get married—it's creepy, if you think about it. Some of the creepy things, if you think about them, are actually pretty charming. To me, the magazine was for the most part really funny. It had it's touching emotional moments, but the only way through a lot of dark situations is to laugh.

I'm all for fetishes. The more fetishes the merrier. I feel like everyone's fetish is fine in its impact on their lives so long as they're not inflicting it on somebody who's not interested or not in the game, I guess. The thing that interested me in a lot of our stories were the lines that the authors found in themselves, you know? I know people who go to the fetish clubs here, and eventually everybody runs up against the thing that they will not do, the line they will not cross. The fetish is cool, that's fine—but the line is what's interesting to me.

HOW DO YOU REJECT SOMEBODY
WHO'S A MURDERER?

Early on, I got reviewed in *Zine World*, which was read by a lot of prisoners. Some of them started corresponding with me, and some of them were respectful—they were serving their sentences, and they wanted to talk about that a little bit—and some of them were not respectful, so I just didn't answer their letters.

One guy really wanted to tell me his story. He had lived with two guys, and he had met a woman and wanted to impress her. So he ended up killing both his roommates as a way to impress this woman, and he wrote me to say, "I want to write about this for your magazine." And I wrote, "Well, it will depend on how you handle the story. Send it to me, and we'll see." So he did, and it was totally unrepentant. This poor woman had no idea who this guy was. Apparently, he'd never actually spoken to her at the point where he started killing people for her. He went into graphic detail of what it was like to stab his roommates to death, what the sounds were, how the blood flowed and everything.

I thought, *This is morbid. It fits the morbid thing.* But it was so hard for me to read that I couldn't think of publishing it. I couldn't think of putting it out there. I didn't want to hear my readers up. I wanted to give them a taste of things that were dark, but I didn't want to wallow around in it. I knew somebody would publish it. There were a bunch of zines at that point. Some of them were really angry, and others were equally dark. I just couldn't go down that road. We went back and forth a couple of times, and I asked him some more questions. He was on Thorazine or something at that point: medicated, locked up, and he still couldn't really understand what he'd done wrong.

In the end he was nice about it. How do you reject somebody who's a murderer? But he was nice about it and sent me Christmas cards for a while before we lost touch.

LIMITS

When I first published the magazine, I got a lot of drug stories, and a drug story is really hard to tell because kind of by its nature, it's ephemeral, and unless you're taking notes at the time, it's hard to recapture it. Kind of in the middle of the run, I had a whole lot of medical stories. Suddenly people were dealing with pregnancy, or surgery, or accidents. Then I had a lot of serial killer stories: people who had met serial killers, or hitchhiked with serial killers, or somehow interacted with people and got away to tell the tale afterwards.

I have my limits. I went through a period where I was like, "Oh, I can look at anything. I'm tough, I can take it." But I think at a certain point you have to walk in the sunlight. If you decide that you're never going to walk in the sunlight, you're only going to look at the worst things. I think it can warp you, but some of the nicest, funniest people I've met run the Museum of Death in LA. And it's horrific and intense. People walk in there and cry and faint. It's really hardcore. But they are the nicest people, and they deal with death everyday. I mean, I think we're all afraid of not being here and things going on. We're afraid we'll miss stuff because it'll all go on without us. But that's been my experience: People who deal with dark subject matter, they see it as part of life, they see it as a spectrum. The more you look into it, the less there is to be afraid of.

It's possible to wallow in death, and I think you have to ask what's healthy for yourself. If it's making you suicidal to think about death all the time, then go outside, look at some artwork, listen to the birds sing.

I have a friend whose brother taught gross anatomy, and he'd let me come up to the lab and go through a corpse with them. I got to hold a human heart in my hand, and for me that was an intense experience that a horror movie just doesn't capture. I wrote a piece about it for the magazine. You know, I'm not interested in killing people, and I'm not interested in hurting anyone, but I *am* interested in what's inside bodies. I'd go see a medical museum any day, but a horror movie, not so much. For a long while, a lot of horror that was out there was dehumanizing to women—I'm not interested in that. I think there's a lot of ugliness in the world, and I'm more interested in what's beautiful, even if it's kind of dark.

One time I ran a suicide-attempt story. She kind of fetishized a knife, but by the end of the story, she got help. I didn't really think too much about publishing it. I'd never gotten one before, and you know, I wanted descriptive stories. They had to be true, and they had to have dialogue. I was really, really pleased with her story.

The next issue I got seventeen suicide-attempt stories.

The magazine only had around thirty-five stories for every issue, so I couldn't publish them all. And these people, they're fragile, you know? I know already that they're suicidal, and so I don't want to be the one who writes, "No, your work sucks. I can't possibly publish this." It kind of taxed the limits of my diplomacy. How do you tell people no?

The story I did publish was about a woman whose brother committed suicide with a shotgun, and she was the one who had to go and clean up after him. It's horrifying, as you can imagine. There are bits of him everywhere, and she's trying to clean it all up before the family comes and sees the place. That was the story I had to publish, out of all of them.

NOT BEING MEAN

I was really, really conscious of not being mean. It's so easy to be mean and to not really think about how what you're saying is going to be perceived. The Internet proves my point: You can say any cruel thing, and for you it's a joke, but for somebody who's getting piled on, it's horrific. I had a sense with the magazine that I wanted to play between the light and the dark, the funny and the serious. I'd send out postcards every time an issue came out, and people would send me checks, and often letters or fan letters. I had a real sense that there were people on the other end, and they were people that I knew—whose names I saw year after year. I felt like it was a dialogue. They respected me and I respected them, and part of that was not abusing them by showing them gratuitous awful stuff. It was plenty gratuitous, but you know.

On the Internet, stuff goes out and nobody takes responsibility for it. No one stands behind things that get published. It's too easy to be anonymous. Everybody's offended these days, and I think that's because nobody will take responsibility and say, "I understand how you could be sensitive to this, I understand how you could take this wrong, but what I intend by it is this, so let's have a dialogue civilly around that intention rather than whatever hurt you perceive I'm doing you." I mean, I did have a couple people freak out. There was a mom, at some point, who intercepted a postcard to her daughter and did not want me to send the daughter anything else. She couldn't believe I was doing this terrible stuff. I thought, *No wonder your daughter's interested in it. Now you made it forbidden, so you've made it sexy.*

I didn't intend for the magazine to get in the hands of anyone under eighteen, but I didn't require an age statement, either, because why bother? It's so easy to lie about that.

THE LAST STRAW

The last issue came out in 2006. I lost my brother in 2002, suddenly. In 2003 I got pregnant, and my pregnancy was really complicated. Then it got to the point where I had a three-year-old, and I just didn't have the patience to deal with the drama from the magazine anymore. I was done at that point. I wanted to do my own work. By that point, livejournal.com was really big, and everybody who wanted a platform to tell their deep dark secrets could do that. I think kind of the time for *Morbid Curiosity* had passed. I could probably still do it as an e-magazine or something like that, but I think this kind of writing is more easily available now than it used to be.

It was my life for about ten years. I felt so strongly about it, and people's reactions were always really interesting. Every now and then I'll see issue one or two on eBay. Issue two is the one that's really rare. They'll go up to, like, hundreds of dollars. Which is cool, as long as it's going to someone who loves it. Probably a lot of them have been recycled by now.

YOU CAN'T UNSEE ANY OF IT

I'm very anticensorship: I really think everything should be available. For me, when a beheading happens, I think it's important for that to be recorded, but I also don't think it's important for me personally to watch it. I know there's horrible stuff that happens in the world, and I personally do not have to see every horrible thing that happens. It might be easy to find the autopsy photos of John F. Kennedy or Michael Jackson, and that doesn't really worry me. The thing that concerns me is that people don't have empathy, you know? What happened to Kennedy was horrible. It's horrific. But also, Jackie had to sit there and deal with all that. It's brutal and wrong. There were people involved, and that's what's important to me about that story. I think people need to put it in perspective, *why* they're interested—because you can't unsee any of it.

The line for me was seeing the video of small-town politician R. Budd Dwyer, who put the gun to his head on television and blew his brains out. I can't ever get that image out of my head. I don't need to see that kind of stuff. I'd like to lift up the beautiful things, even if it's corpses mummified by time or whatever. I think that's beautiful, but watching someone die is not.

I have a kid, and I do draw a line for her: There are things you can see now, and things you can see later. You know, once you find out about the Nazi death camps, and you see corpses, and they're bulldozing those bodies into ditches, you can't ever forget it. So don't rush to that, I guess. Live with what little innocence you have for a while.

\\

CONDUCTED AUGUST 18, 2015

DAVID BAZAN
SONGWRITER

Stories about leaving one's faith behind hold more appeal for me than stories of conversion. How does a person traverse a chaotic universe where they once saw order? How do you replace that huge absence in your life? Does some small part of you always remain a believer?

The first time I ever saw Seattle-based songwriter David Bazan, it was late afternoon, and he was surrounded by a half-dozen fans outside of the club that his band, Pedro the Lion, was scheduled to play that night. He was deep in conversation, not about records or touring life, but about perhaps the least rock-and-roll subject on earth: the Bible.

David Bazan's shifting faith has always been present on his albums. His early songs work like modern parables; his best albums with Pedro the Lion take a cynical view of modern Christianity while retaining faith in the Bible's teachings. Starting with 2009's Curse Your Branches, *his songs have detailed his creeping disbelief. That album seemed to meditate mournfully over the prospect of losing God, but overall, Bazan's road away from Christianity has largely been a surprisingly hopeful journey.*

Death was not always the focus of discussion when I met Bazan at a dive bar in North Seattle. It lingers, though, behind just about everything else. For Bazan, learning to live without the promise of an afterlife has led to a redis-covery of the entire concept of death. That he has faced that redefinition with open arms is unusual and impressive, but then again, Bazan—who has slowly become one of the finest and most respected songwriters of his generation—has never backed down from confronting difficult subjects.

CHRISTIAN MUSIC ONLY

I didn't know any non-Christians growing up. My next-door neighbors were Christian, and everyone from my Christian school. Everybody who I knew was in that same boat.

I grew up in Phoenix, Arizona. In a conservative country, it's a very conservative state. My dad was a music pastor for at least twenty years. He wasn't a pastor who preached: His ministry was more just relational and into music and people. Then we lived in California for two or three years in junior high and early high school, and we landed in Seattle by tenth grade. My dad had different churches in each city, and then after I got out of the house he went to work doing IT stuff. But his heart is still really in being a music pastor. It's his calling, kinda. If he's honest, that's really what he'd rather be doing.

In some ways my parents were really strict and we were sheltered. We weren't allowed to listen to non-Christian music. But it didn't feel oppressive in that realm of ideas. In a lot of conservative households, wherever your brain goes, at some point, somebody's going to shut it down. In that way it felt really open. My mom's a really strong, vocal woman, so there was a progressive feeling somehow in the house. I think that was because of the battles that ensued from her being herself in a very patriarchal culture. So it was strict and conservative in some ways, but in other ways it was really open-hearted. I remember being encouraged to think our thoughts all the way and to really engage with the world. Except for Christian music only. That was the big one. They were really protective about, like, movies and stuff. They would watch PG movies first to screen them. No boobs.

There were aspects of the Christian culture that really resonated with me as a kid. It was all very natural to go along with. I liked a lot of the people that I grew up with—all the grown-ups were really neat folks. I never questioned any of it.

In high school, though, when I started reading the Bible and interpreting it for myself, I started seeing a lot of discrepancies between what the church was doing and what the Bible called for or strived toward. I had sort of a critical eye for reform. I might not self-describe as a rebel, but there was just a lot of excess and a lot of distortion all around. I never really questioned the fundamental of premise of Christianity. There was always a lot to fight for. I think the world saw that all through Bush's presidency: The country was interested in a particularly ugly expression of Christianity. That was what my focus tended to be. I was just trying to do that better.

A FIRM BOUNDARY

I never thought much about hell. It just seemed like sort of a firm boundary. If you went too far, there was always hell. It was a reason to not question my faith, but that was about it. Hell was just built-in somehow. It was part of the fully formed story. I didn't feel like the fires of hell were licking at my heels. It felt like it was a safe distance away, that I was on the okay side because I was a Christian. It wasn't my favorite aspect of Christianity, especially later in public school, when people always want to dis on Christianity and complain about it.

I thought hell was a bad idea. It might have been my reality, but it was really an uncomfortable one that hurt the brand name of Christianity. I didn't spend a lot of time focusing on the devil, and the pastor at our church didn't preach about the devil.

Hell was distant, but heaven being real was a given. Now it strikes me as a bit of imaginative thinking that took root before I was really in charge of my thoughts. That sounds really condescending, but that's how I tend to think of it now: There's a real, observable world here, and belief often chooses a different explanation than the most observable explanation for things. But back then, it was just a part of the story of humanity. It was built into the fabric of life. I didn't know about evolution: God created human beings. It was this big narrative that, the way that it was administered in the church I grew up with, sought to define the very fabric of the earth and humanity. I wasn't trying to shoehorn heaven into this extremely complex, observable situation. This extremely complex and observable situation, called earth, was just a character in this larger narrative. The nature of reality itself didn't begin with what was observable. It began with the story.

I liked Bible stories and the idealism in those stories. There's a purity, or a really pleasing kind of human fidelity, that was embodied in all of these stories. When I heard them, I wanted to be like the people in them. I remember hearing the story of Enoch when I was five. Enoch was in this long list of begats—just kind of wedged in there—and there are a few sentences that say he walked with God so closely that he went to heaven without dying. With these begats, they always list the ages that the people died, but Enoch never died before he went up to heaven. That's how it's described in the Bible. When I was a kid, I thought, *That's what I want.* But right away, I already felt what they'd call my sinning nature. I already knew that I was a fuckup, and I couldn't please God in that way.

When I think back to things like that, I realize there was a lot of cultural pressure involved. But it was also just the shade of the paint on every wall: There was hegemony all around. There was an inner longing to reach an ideal of some kind. The idea that there was a God and you could be closer to him, and that closeness would give you some juice and make your life better. In a way, I was just on the hook for all that kind of stuff. It really resonated.

MORALITY AND MORTALITY

I feel like the macabre stuff was building in me when I was a kid. In the fifth grade I found some Edgar Allan Poe stories, and they just fucking rocked my world. It was so exciting. I was kinda jittery: There is something about that way of writing about morality and mortality that is still so interesting to me, and fun and funny, that it takes your breath away. Like "The Cask of Amontillado," that's a fucked-up story, and it's so amazing. That's what I'm trying to do with my songs, tell stories like that. There's a beginning and middle and an end, and in the end the guy's fucking walled in forever. Spoiler alert!

AUNT ANNE

The earliest experience with death I can remember was my grandmother's aunt, who I called Aunt Anne. She had moved from New York to Phoenix to retire. We really had a close kind of relationship. She was quite old. When I was in fourth grade, I was in class, and I asked to go get a drink of water at my school. I was out in the hallway and my dad came up the stairs. I was like, "What are you doing here?" And he said, "I have bad news." I was kind of devastated. It wasn't an event that I was expecting to pop up. Like, it didn't occur to me that everybody here is going to die. Like, *really*, not just hypothetically.

That was the first one. We did the open-casket funeral memorial thing, and I thought, *She's so pretty.* She was all made-up. I'm sure it was probably hideous. You know, just seeing a dead body, it was very strange. I was sad, and then I thought, *I'll see her again in heaven.* But it was pretty diffuse, that idea. It wasn't super concrete, that relationship between those two things. There was a gauzy sense of, like, "You're sad, and that's okay. It's okay to cry." My family was good about all that kind of stuff. But it was also like, "We can be grateful because we're going to see Aunt Anne again in heaven when we die. She's with God now." I don't think they really put that fine a point on it, verbally, but that was the assumption underlying everything.

I think religious people are torn between the rhetoric—"They're in a better place," which I think they really feel—and the reality of being in mourning. There's so much about mourning and the physical process of it in the Bible than there is about heaven. Way more. The Old Testament is full of descriptions of mourning. Like, "Mourn with those who mourn." It was a brutal world.

PEDRO THE LION

My band Pedro the Lion started in '95. I was nineteen, right out of high school. We were just playing youth groups. The first club I ever headlined was in '98, down at the Tractor Tavern. It was a youth-group culture, but we were on the progressive edge of that conversation. I mean, I don't know how progressive we actually were, but the world seemed just a little bit bigger to us, and it comes through in all these different ways. It was easy for us to develop a following. There was a pretty thriving Christian music scene underground in Seattle, so we were opening for other bands and playing for a hundred to three hundred people pretty early on.

We played churches and—you know, "Christian coffeehouses." The youth pastor would call it that. It wasn't actually a coffeehouse. The youth group just decided it was going to have more of a coffeehouse vibe than a church vibe. There were also some Christian clubs that were all ages. I had some friends in the independent music scene here, and we started to cross over a little bit, played the Velvet Elvis in Seattle and some other all-ages spaces.

Before too long were playing in front of our own crowds. And slowly, I realized I wanted to not be in the Christian ghetto. I wanted to play rock clubs. I want people to engage with us in the world, buy our record at

Tower. I grew up only having that little shelf space at the Christian bookstore, ten or twenty different tapes to choose from or whatever.

I didn't play music to evangelize. I really believed in this idea that you should sort of live what you believe, and it would come out in the form of your worldview. I also had this fundamental respect for people who weren't Christians. I wasn't assuming I knew how the world worked and they didn't. So I was taking a lot in, but for me, faith had this kind of purity about it. My Christianity was forgiveness and peace, you know?

On the early records, I'm wrestling with ideas. There's a lot of doubt in the music. But it was doubt about this physical manifestation of the belief system. I just thought that honest discussion of these topics in the public discourse, started by me or anybody else, would just be helpful. I don't know where that belief came from, but it was a belief in reason and public discourse. I probably got it from my folks. Music was a way to explore thoughts and ideas, not to convey religious slogans.

Not too long into being a songwriter, too, you start hearing about the old folk singers, Johnny Cash and these guys. A huge chunk of old country folk songs are murder ballads. I think that was in the air somehow. I guess it was just really natural to write about death. It's dramatic. In one sense, it's not something that we tend to deal with very often, but each one of us is going to deal with it, for sure, one way or another.

I'm also naturally just melancholy, and the way that my voice works, it's hard for me to sing fast passages. I guess I'm probably better at words than I am at atmosphere.

Growing up in church, hearing that Christian music, singing those tunes—it's so cheesy. I just felt like, with Pedro the Lion, I was doing a different project that was totally unrelated to Christian music and its aims. I could, in good faith, expose people to my songs and not feel like I was trying to dupe them or take advantage of them or convince them of something. I was just expressing myself, and that would reveal something truer or more powerful.

There were a lot of conversations about God and faith and death and that kind of stuff before and after our shows. It turns out that a lot of Christians, in particular, had a cultural experience where there just wasn't room to talk about the criticisms and ideas that I was going into on our first album, *It's Hard to Find a Friend*. It hit home. They saw me as receptive, as a person who cared about Christianity, but who clearly was not a judgy weirdo or whatever. I was game. It was like our version of free love, you know?

"PRIESTS AND PARAMEDICS"

My mom's brother was a paramedic. I think he was a paramedic for fifteen or twenty years. In the last few years of him being a paramedic, he started a church, so he was a pastor and a paramedic at the same time. And his church was in downtown Phoenix. He would tell us all these stories about being on the job as a paramedic. That was one of those things they were told to do: relay stories to your family as a form of therapy because, if you keep all this stuff inside, you're going to go nuts. It was cool for us. We got to hear the most amazing stories: the most fucked-up, funny, tragic stories.

One of the stories he told at family get-togethers was about a guy who he'd seen a half a dozen times on various calls. He was always hurting himself from being too fucked-up, and this time he had tried his hand at cooking meth, and it blew up. It basically burned him very badly. So they get him into the ambulance, and he's mostly unconscious. Then he comes to, and he's all strapped down, and he says, "I'm going to die."

My uncle said that his first thought was: *We're not supposed to say anything. We're supposed to calm them down. We're not supposed to speak about that.* But he said to himself, *Which is more my responsibility to him? Is it Phoenix firefighter protocol or my responsibility as a pastor?* So he decided to tell him. He said, "Yeah. You are probably going to die in about five or ten minutes. Before we get to the hospital, you're going to be dead. So if you want to take a minute to just get right, think about things, whatever—now's the time." He said the guy, who had been kind of spastic just prior, got really quiet and maybe said thank you. But he got really inside himself, and then he died.

That was a really impactful story on me. I started trying to write that story as "Priests and Paramedics," but I would have had to be doing exposition the whole time. The song I wrote is all exposition, anyway, but it's at least a little cleverly done in some places, I don't know. "Priests and Paramedics" is the song that I could write from that inspiration—it had to be more general. The fact that they're not supposed to say, "You're going to die" is a big part of that song.

"TRANSCONTINENTAL"

When I first started writing songs and playing them for people, the community that I was a part of, all the people who I saw every week and went to shows with were Christian people that were a part of this church in Seattle called Calvary Fellowship. I thought this was unique to Christianity at the time, but it's really just that generally, people are uncomfortable with melancholy. People would just be like, "Man, why are your songs always such a bummer?"

Until people started mentioning that, it didn't ever occur to me that there was any other way to write. I kind of wish that I hadn't heard them. In some ways, because I'm a little bit too much of a people-pleaser, that's when I started writing songs like "Big Trucks" and "When They Really Get to Know You They Will Run," both of which are kind of upbeat in their lyrical outlook—which is because they're satirical, I think. I tended to only able to write about dark shit. If I was going to have a pop song, it was going to have to be about something really dark. Once I did that the first time, juxtaposed the pop song and pop sound with something lyrically sinister, it was very fun. Then I started doing it all the time. "Transcontinental" is one of those.

"Transcontinental" came from trying start doing a freewrite, and the first thing I wrote down on the pad was "Engine severs lower legs." It was kind of apropos of nothing. I looked at and thought, *That sounds cool to me. What is going on here?* I thought, *Well, it's pretty obvious that a guy got his legs got cut off by a train. I assume he was drunk and he passed out on the way home.* Then I realized there was a story there, and I wondered what the story was. Sometimes I don't find out, but sometimes it just comes on out.

I wondered, *What's the difference between a guy who's going to saw off his own legs to get free and me? Would I do that?* I really have no idea. But I just thought, *I don't think this guy pulls it out.* That was my feeling about him from the beginning—that he just laid there, and maybe he couldn't have even done shit if he wanted to, I don't know. Does being run over by a train sever his legs so that it cauterizes the wounds, or is he lying there bleeding out? I have no idea. It's also sort of a dying man's last thoughts. He's just there and he dies, like we're all gonna do. I can only evaluate it after the fact and guess at what it's about.

I think that Wendell Berry talks about how the way that we know what we should and shouldn't do just comes from narratives that are floating around in our culture. In some ways a song like this is a morality play. It's not even a morality play. It's an evolution play. It's a natural-selection play.

THE WORLD JUST GOT BIGGER

On all the Pedro records, I was some shade of Christian. I was Christian through the writing of our last album, *Achilles Heel*. It was that year, 2004, that things started to really shift.

My dad actually kind of put it to me. He was dismayed when he said this, but he told me, "Most people need Christianity because they want to act bad, but I feel like you want to leave Christianity because you want to be better than Christianity allows you to be in your mind." I was like, "Yes, that's exactly how I feel."

The world just got bigger, you know? The possibilities just got wider, and the narrative of Christianity just started to collapse on me, starting with original sin.

I had a daughter, honestly, is what happened. I just looked at this little thing, and I said, "We only kind of intentionally made this." I'm not even as responsible for this being as God theoretically is for the creation of something from nothing. I thought, *There's not a thing in the world that she, in her innocence, could do that would cause me to want to punish her.* And the way the Christian narrative works, that's what happened.

Original sin—as a metaphor or an actual historical event, either way—and the dynamics that it described and the symbolism of this shift, it's such funny stuff. It just didn't make sense to me. It's the equation that branded all human beings as fundamentally sinful. And it just seemed stupid.

In the Garden of Eden, Adam and Eve committed sin in their innocence, their ignorance. They were literally achieving the knowledge of good and evil by the sin. If that's not the definition of innocence, I don't really know what it could be. So, in their innocence, they made that sinful mistake, and God said "At least for the next couple thousand years, I'm not even going to reveal what the plan is." We're *apart* apart. It really does feel like you're fatally separated. People try to describe it as, "Well, he had a plan all along." It doesn't feel like that.

In her innocence, my daughter is unconscious of separation the same way that human beings—even according to that story—really had a difficult time grasping what that separation from God was about. It just hit me: None of this makes sense as what an intelligent being would do. This is just an origin myth. That happened in 2004, when we had our daughter. I was really working through all of that. When original sin left, I just thought, *What is going on? What is this any of this?* There's no question that needed an answer—the answer being that Jesus was crucified as a sort of supernatural event.

"WHAT DO YOU PICTURE AT THE END?"

Most people who are interested in the music didn't know about me losing my faith until 2009, when I put out *Curse Your Branches*. Then, like, thirty thousand people found out about it in a very detailed way, not to mention some innocent bystanders on the bus reading about it. But I had been functionally not a believer since 2005, so in terms of my community and my family, things trickled out slowly for years and years.

It created some anxiety. I still don't talk about it with my parents a lot. I don't know if I ever said to them outright that I'm not a believer. I've said it plenty in public, so they have access to all that stuff, but when *Branches* came out, I didn't know what they knew, either. They are very much "Let sleeping dogs lie" kind of people. So I went to them and I said, "Hey, look, I love how our relationship is going." There had been some conflict earlier, over our daughter. I said, "There are things about me that I don't present to you guys out of respect, but I don't want you to think that I'm doing that to try to hide something from you, to be false in some way." That was a heavy conversation that I felt like a lot was riding on.

My wife and I both stopped going to church for a couple years. Neither of us brought it up. There was no discussion. Then once my wife was pregnant, she was like, "I'm interested in going to church again." I went with her sometimes. But then I lost my faith totally, and I was in sort of shame every time I attended church with her.

Sometimes it was really painful. There were a couple months where I was really wrestling with it, and I experienced, you know—despair. It was like an intense breakup. It was really fundamental.

In that process where she was dabbling in church again, I pushed back and said, "Look, if going to church is really stirring your relationship with the cosmos, great, but I don't think we should do it to conform to tradition." Once our son was born, for some reason, she never went back. It's been six years. She hasn't shown any interest or desire.

At some point I said, "What do you picture at the end?" She goes, "I don't know." I said, "Well, think about it. Take a second." She sat there, and she thought for, like, fully thirty seconds. She said, "Yeah, I think heaven and hell are probably real." I was just curious, so I was like, "When's the next time you think that will cross your mind?" And she said, "The next time you ask me."

That's the difference between us. She doesn't worry about it, and I really hate that there isn't a clear answer. I sit and trip balls over it. Just, *What is this? What the fuck is going on?*

THAT COULD ALL JUST BE
WORLDS AND WORLDS OF PEOPLE

The universe wasn't just this collection of data in my mind growing up. It was this very elegant set of characters: It was divine, transcendent. It was this struggle, this fantasy battle. Going from that to, like, "It's just raw data"—that's a big mental shift. But it was freeing in a way. I wanted to be able to come to my own conclusions. Or rather, I was already coming to my own conclusions, and it was causing problems. I needed to be able to do that without it being so disruptive to my psyche.

My wife and I were definitely of the mind that you weren't supposed to have sex until you got married. Even as we got closer to being married I realized, *Wait a minute. What? It's absurd. To what point, to what end, and where is this coming from?* We started realizing that it was just up to us. And that's the thing with Christianity: It's tough to pin down because of the forms that it takes, even within a particular person. It's not super consistent, and it changes from denomination to denomination. They try to make you think there's one way to do it, but they all do it differently.

To me that just said, "You gotta think for yourself how to act." There are consequences that are not beneficial, so avoid those. That was how I thought of Christianity as I got deeper in deeper in it. That's what led me having a really progressive view. The one thing that I was unsure of how to resolve was homosexuality. I was enough of a literal Bible guy that it was sticky. I knew how I felt, which was that it was not a sin. But I couldn't reconcile that with what I thought I was supposed to believe. It was one of the rare instances where there was a party line that I needed to tow that I didn't. It was sort of a relief realizing that the Bible was not infallible. It was like, "Okay, cool. And I'm off the hook."

Toward the end of my believing, heaven just seemed kind of crazy, considering the size of the universe and quantum physics. That could all just be worlds and worlds of people. When heaven disappeared completely for me, everything just made more sense. The entire project of life is trying to make sense of the data that's in front of me. *What is this? What explains its existence? What's happening next? Is there a next?* There's a natural flow to life: Why would we get an afterlife? Where did the idea that this isn't all there is come from? Was it a way to scare people into believing that things would go badly in the afterlife if they didn't behave in this one?

We are conscious, inexplicably, and then we die. To me, there's symmetry and elegance to that. To me that makes sense. The idea that we come online to perceive certain aspects of this life, but, more importantly, to learn about what's coming next? That doesn't' make sense to me. Why not just be what it is, rather than a precursor to something else? There's no orientation to consciousness, obviously. You don't go into some room and people tell you, "Here's what to expect." It's, like, you just come online, and you're here doing this thing. That's what it is. That just seems real. It seems true.

"YEAH! WE'RE DONE WITH THE DEATH TALK!"

I have a reasonable expectation for myself as a good actor in the world. I make mistakes, but time and time again, I have an ethical, humane, sort of unselfish set of responses that are fundamental to how I act in the world. My perception is that it came from the somewhat rigorous philosophical framework of Christianity. Just thinking about goodness and my behavior—those were things I took seriously, and I thought about it a lot. I want that for my kids, and I don't know where it will come from. I assume that there are other ways people just have that innately, or maybe I have that because of my family. Maybe the culture was just coincidental, and I would have emerged somewhat similarly in terms of my fundamental framework.

Those are things I think about, and I wonder how it's going to be for my kids. Do they have reasons to act right? I think for me the reason didn't have anything to do with God. I think people who insist that morality flows from God—like, "Well, if there's no God, I'm just going to shoot up and fucking kill you right now." Yeah, but what about the consequences? Do you want to die? If there's no God, and you just want to die, then I understand that. But there are consequences that you're going to be super bummed about. You'll go to jail. You'll have withdrawals from heroin.

I'm not worried about my kids in that way. I think that morality flows from consciousness. You find equilibrium with your surroundings. You find your place in the world, and you think about your effect on it and take stock of the destruction that you created before you even started caring or knowing that you needed to look. I give a shit, and they live in the culture of our home. What's that going to yield? What role did church play for me? Mostly, I'm not worried enough to make a major shift and take them to church.

When my daughter was four, we were driving. I pulled into this parking place real quickly, and my wife goes, "Oh, God." I made fun of her overreaction, joking, "We're all going to die!" And my daughter goes, "Wait a minute. We're not all going to die." Then she goes, "Oh, we *are* all going to die—just probably not today." She was like four years old, and that was what she said about it. I was like, "Yeah! We're done with the death talk!" She already gets it. She already knows what's up.

Then just recently, within the last two months, our dog died. She was the love of our family, really a particularly special animal. We went to the vet because she'd kind of collapsed, and it turned out she had a tumor in her belly that we didn't know about. We were all there when they told us the prognosis, which was not good. We said, "All right, let's do this." We were all pretty broken up. We went to another room, and they brought her in. She was still alive, and kind of wagging her tail. She was pretty cold because she had lost all her blood flow. We were all there when they put her to sleep. We walked through that, which is truly not the same as human death, but it was training wheels for death in the most profound way. I think my kids understand it more now. They have both sets of grandparents still alive. They're going to start experiencing a lot of death in a very short amount of time. Our parents are getting to the age where they're five years away from life expectancy, so they're about to get a pretty heavy dose. Because of that, I think they understand that when someone dies, they're gone. You don't have access to them anymore.

Have you read *The Road?* Cormac McCarthy's book? It's one of my favorite books. Toward the end, the kid in the book is sort of adopted by this family. They're Christians, and the mom tries to teach him to pray, which he's never done. He tries, but praying to God doesn't do anything for him at all. So he starts praying to his dad. My take on it is that he doesn't believe that his dad is actually in spirit form up above him somewhere, but that he is just sort of interrogating the memory of his dad. When I read that, I was deeply moved, and I thought, *That is so much more meaningful than any concept of heaven had ever been for me.* The idea that the things and the people who you've lost, you have the opportunity to honor and interact with them by interrogating their memory by a form of prayer or meditation or whatever. That's real. It's not magic. You have all these memories and you really get to interrogate them, and you create new modes of thinking and interpreting your experience.

For all intents and purposes, if there is a God, there isn't a God that we have access to. We just try to make sense of all the stimuli we have.

We're really interrogating the notion of the characteristics as you expect them or believe them to exist. That's become a big part of death to me and a comfort that I take in my own death. I don't really like the feeling of wanting to be remembered for it's own sake. But I'd like my memory to exist for the comfort of my kids, just the way that I would do with them if things were flipped. You just get to sit and talk about funny things that have happened. "Wasn't it amazing when they did this?" Or, "It really hurt me the way that he was always dot dot dot."

To me, that's a really meaningful kind of afterlife. Only the conscious beings who are alive are experiencing it, but you're still available to people because there's a narrative that they can interrogate. You're available because you existed. My kids have got data on me. They know about me. *The Road* occupied a somewhat biblical place in my life for a while.

As time goes on, I get more comfortable with not knowing. I feel like there's enough data around to make sense of existence. You plant tomato seeds, and tomatoes grow: This is the kind of data that exists that you can understand.

I still come back to the biggest questions. There doesn't seem to be a substitute for heaven, but death is real, and the blow could stand to be softened a little bit. It's kind of harsh. In some cases it's especially harsh. To me, little things that are demonstrably real, that aren't some sort of superstitious wishful thinking, but real mechanisms like interrogating the memory of your loved one—to me that takes the sting out of it just a touch. I can make peace with this.

THERE'S NO BIRD'S-EYE VIEW

If you had any consciousness to evaluate the moment after death, it just seems like it would be so boring. That's something that I would worry about or lament. But you don't get that opportunity, I assume. Once the lights go out, I always think, "That will be so boring." But it won't be boring. It won't be anything.

There's no bird's-eye view. That Radiohead song "Videotape" plays around with a lot of stuff. Every Christian has a different picture of what it's going to be like in heaven, what they hope for. Do you watch it from a videotape? Are there highlights? Do you get to understand from the bird's-eye view what it all was?

It's almost intoxicating. It makes me giddy to think about: There's no bird's-eye view. There's just the subjective viewpoint that you have. Your little window on the world is your consciousness, and your eyeballs and skin are what it is. Of course, that's what it is! That makes more sense! Why would it have been any other way?

I don't regret growing up Christian. I feel like this experience has been pretty rich. Especially given this time in the world and in American history, this shift that I had is at the crux of all human turmoil: How do we relate with dogmatic religion? Almost all human conflict is about this thing. To me, it's a front-row seat to this conflict in humanity. It wasn't always fun, but sometimes a bad trip is still better than being sober.

CURSE YOUR BRANCHES

The *Curse Your Branches* album* works like an argument against Christianity, but it's open-ended. When I put that record out, tons of Christians came up to me and they said that it gives them the space to doubt almost as a devotional exercise and retain their faith. It was one of the ten or twelve best records in 2009 at *Christianity Today*. In the review it said that my record was more obsessed with God and relating to God than any record that they could think of, Christian or not. In that sense it's a very Christian record.

It's not propaganda. It really is exploration. That's the difference. I don't even call myself an atheist. It's not important to me to call myself anything. Because I sit and contemplate the possibility of the existence of

---

* Bazan's 2009 debut under his own name, a collection of songs largely about Bazan losing his faith.

God in a way that is not an atheist exercise. I'm still crunching the numbers and saying, "Is it possible?" I don't know if I want it to be possible, as time goes on.

This consciousness is a crazy thing. It feels so meaningful. That doesn't mean that it *is* meaningful. MLK said, "The arc of the moral universe is long, but it bends toward justice."* You can just barely see the curve if you look at it on a large-enough scale. It really does feel meaningful. As I'm pondering that, I haven't stopped trying to work the equation out where God is part of it. I also try to work the equation out where God is not part of it. Just anything that could jive with reality.

IT'S GOT TO BE MUCH HARDER
FOR THEM THAN IT IS FOR ME

Technically speaking, I'm going to hell, in some cases. My grandmother will tell me that I'm a Christian even when I say I'm not. "No, you are. You just don't know it." She thinks I'm going through a phase.

If I said to my grandma and family, "This is what I think happens when you die," outright, they would be kind of horrified. A couple of my cousins—who are my age, and we're like buddies, and they're Christians—we have deeper philosophical conversations, you know? But with the older generation, they still won't look directly at it. It's gotta be tough. It's got to be much harder for them than it is for me.

My dad has always been a little bit more open to sort of kicking the tires of his existential model. We still do that in our conversations. We're able to talk about certain things. My mom's not capable of that. It's way more tense with her. Some of that has to do with me. She probably is like, "Where did we go wrong?" She's probably actively feeling shame, and it's heavy for her.

---

* While often attributed to Martin Luther King, Jr, this line was originally delivered by a New England abolitionist named Theodore Parker (August 24, 1810–May 10, 1860).

It's faith driving that wedge between us, but it doesn't have to. That's my message. There are a lot of things that we have in common. You want social justice, I want social justice. You call it kingdom-building, I call it social justice. But we can go to the same rallies. You value hard work, I value hard work. You value the environment—you know, leaving a campsite better than you found it—I have that same value. We're not going to disagree about anything but the existential. In some cases, the existential informs political things, but even then I think there's common ground. Like, if you look at it from a neutral perspective, Black Lives Matter is right down the middle of your values. Not even a hair off: right down the middle. But you have these massive obstacles. All of the rest of the people that believe the way you do—or the vast majority of vocal ones—are trying to have you see that in a different light.

I think that a lot of the identity of Christianity in America now is so intertwined with politics that the fact that I'm not a political conservative is definitely a strike against me. But when it comes to the fundamental way that you treat people, I still think there's deep wisdom in very unstrained interpretations of Jesus's teaching. You don't have to strain his teaching to get some really troubling, counterintuitive shit. Love your enemy; turn the other cheek. These are not easy. They cut right against human nature, I think.

My mom and I will sit at dinner, and I'll try to illustrate the things that we have in common. In doing so, sometimes we end up getting in arguments, because I'm a little overzealous—I just think this is basic shit. "Of course you don't think Mike Huckabee is reasonable or good." But she does, on the surface. And then I've just hurt her feelings. Or I say something like, "All media is biased, for sure, but it's more a laziness bias than a liberal bias. You can't say Fox News is biased to the same degree as everything else. It is actually performance art, it's a prank. It's theater."

So we talk about that, and I insist on talking about it, and then she cries. And then I've made my mom cry. What's wrong with me? It doesn't happen every single time we get together, but you know, it happens twice a year.

ANY LOOPHOLE

My mom is searching for any loophole that her system accepts for me to not go to hell. She is, I'm sure, actively trying to sort it out because it's just too uncomfortable, the idea that I'll burn in hell for eternity.

I understand the power that that idea has. The amount of leverage that it has is really out of proportion with anything else. I mean it really poisons everything. It poisons all of Christianity. It poisons every reaction. It really makes free thought unrealistic because it'll always put you in danger at some point. I see the power it has over her, and I empathize with her. I'm crushed for her. For me, it's an unnecessary stressor. It's a source of profound stress, and it doesn't need to be there.

I wrote about it on *Curse Your Branches*:

> *If my mother cries when I tell her what I have discovered*
> *Then I hope she remembers she taught me to follow my heart*
> *And if you bully her like you've done me with fear of damnation*
> *Then I hope she can see you for what you are*

I wrote the song, and the lines came out, and they felt potent to me. Then I thought, *Fuck, I can't put this on here. She's going to hear it.* As soon as I recorded the demo, I emailed it to my parents and said, "Hey, here's a song I just wrote. I don't have any plans to put it out yet, but before I even broach that, I just wanted you guys to hear it." They understood what I meant, that I asking for permission in a way. They said, "This is a great song. You should definitely put it out. But it's perplexing to us, the way that you see the world."

That was over email. That was definitely a moment of candor and openly facing the conflict that we were having. But they were very supportive. They've always been very supportive. My mom has definitely struggled with whether or not she is right to be supporting me playing music. She has said that if I was only singing about girls or superficial stuff, it'd be one thing, but I'm singing about these things that she is concerned will influence other people to be in hell for all eternity. She's really torn.

After that song came out—the record was doing well, the press was good—I was telling my family how excited I was. They were excited, too; they had been following it all. And my mom said, "I need to tell you something. The only reason why I taught you to follow your heart is that I thought Jesus lived in there." I said, "I know, Mom. But the thing is, I feel like I'm doing the right thing." And she said, "I know. It's so strange. I also kind of have that feeling some of the time, but I just can't reconcile it with what I actually believe." That was a very sweet moment where we saw that we have this thing in common, but the dogma that we both frame it in is disruptive and not in a good way.

She's one of my favorite people. She's so intelligent and really passionate about justice. All of her stories from being a kid are about sticking up for this kid and that kid at school—really taking up the cause for the underdog. That was her role as a kid. She did it in church while we were growing up. We watched her do it. She's a revolutionary who, if the things in her life were a different way, might subscribe to *Sojourners* or something like that rather than Pat Robertson's magazine. I really have huge respect for her. I call her for advice, still. Some situation will come up, and I'll be like, *This is so hairy. I don't know what to do here.* And I'll call her. Nine times out of ten she gives me amazing advice. One time out of ten she gets insecure, and she says, "Well, if you just put Jesus at the center . . ." I'll say, "Mom. Stop. You know that I'm calling you for specific practical advice because you're so good at it." It's rare when that comes up. She's so brilliant. I really like her.

YOU CAN'T LEAVE STONES UNTURNED

Occasionally, I'll come to a topic or idea that seems like I should consider it off-limits, but in every case, I just think, *No, I can't.* You can't leave stones unturned. Or I can't, anyway. That's just not how my brain works.

It seems like we could all do with more data about what it is to be human. I will say that when you think of the Mark Linkouses and Vic Chesnutts of the world—all these brilliant artists who make the choice to take their own lives, you wonder, *Is it just a trick of genetics, or is it that they're flipping over page after page, learning about everything, and finally they flip to that one page where they are just like, fuck, and that's it?* You think about that. But I don't think it's inevitable.

If you go down the rabbit hole too far, does it lead to ending your life? That's the sort of thing that I suppose one would be afraid of where you'd say, "Maybe I should back away from this precipice, existentially or philosophically." But I don't think I'm gonna back away from the precipice. I don't feel like I'm in mortal danger from it. It's painful, and it's challenging, but I think that just understanding our place here more and more, whatever that might mean, is really important.

I know that for some people, the well just runs dry—or apparently that's what happens—and they choose to end it. But I just feel like that's just one of the outcomes. There's nothing that I've come up against where I think, *No, I'm gonna save this for later.* There's a morbid fascination that probably propels me. You know, like loving Edgar Allan Poe's, "The Pit and the Pendulum" when I was a kid. Just like, what the fuck is this? It blew my mind.

I aspire to be an artist. Maybe that's a little juvenile to say it that way, but whatever. I don't think of it as a negative thing to really face down all this existential garbage. It strikes me as a positive, you know? It strikes me as one of the perks of this endeavor, that I actually have time to think on it. Somebody else would have to call in sick from work if they were having a super heavy existential day, and that's my job. I feel like that's what getting to be an artist is, if you get to do that as a vocation. You moonlight as somebody without a horse in the race and take everything in.

I feel like I'm just beginning. I feel like I'm in beta mode, and 1.0 is not going to be less engaged; it's going to be the most engaged. If I get there, it'll be scary. You know what I'm saying? It won't be like, "Oh, the new Bazan record is pretty good." It'll be like, "Holy fucking shit, someone send an ambulance." That's what I think. For some musicians and performers and writers, there's a period in their career where they're working at such a level that it feels like a perpetual-motion machine for a minute. I'd like to do that, if I can, even if it's just for a couple months. I wouldn't mind squeezing five or ten years out of it, either.

I don't feel like I'll want to slow down. I just need to see my kids a little bit more, that's all.

CONDUCTED SEPTEMBER 10, 2015

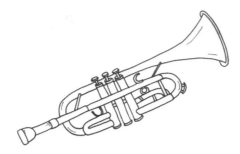

WENDE JARMAN
BARBER, AUTHOR'S MOTHER

As one of the few barbers in the small town I grew up in, Wende Jarman is known—usually as "Red," for the name of her barbershop and her dyed hair—by everyone. I'd go so far as to say that my mom is beloved, though there are certainly conservative townsfolk who can't stand her progressive politics or her tendency to speak her mind, at great length, on just about every subject.

When I was a teenager, Mom would try and scare me from driving with friends by giving dire warnings of "black ice on the roads" or "ninety-mile-per-hour winds." When I moved to Portland after college, she'd call to tell me about job openings at the local paper. "You can always come home," she'd say.

I never knew the grandmother that my mom speaks of in saintly terms, but the truth is that Mom never met her, either. Not as an adult, anyway. The only relationship they had was of doting mother and youngest child. In a lot of ways I think that informs Mom's overprotective relationship with me. She is a wonderful and caring human being. She's intuitive and self-sufficient. She has good taste in music, and she's a strong writer who has been penning letters to the editor for as long as I can remember. She's also stubborn, eccentric, and a bit hard of hearing. We fight about the most mundane things imaginable. I am trying, as an adult, to dig at the roots of all of this, and to see my mother as objectively as possible. Instead, this interview—conducted over beers in her cozy one-bedroom home just off Highway 101 in Florence, Oregon—reminded me that we have an awful lot in common. Our biggest difference might just be that I've never lost a parent.

GET OFF THAT COUCH
AND BE MY MOMMA AGAIN

In the Baptist church that I was raised in, they always dwelled on what was going to happen when you died. You'd better be baptized, you'd better be saved, because otherwise you were going to be up in big trouble. You can't have eternal life unless you're saved.

My mother sang in the choir. My father did, too. My father's brother was a minister, and he actually knew the reverend Billy Graham. My dad sort of hung around him because he really liked Billy Graham.

Even with all that talking about death and all that talking about the afterworld, all that "you have a soul," no one ever told me that my mother was so ill that she was going to leave. Nobody prepared me for that at all.

It seemed like she was lying on the couch probably for six to eight months. I was eleven; it's hard to think back and tell how long she was like that, but it wasn't fast. She had pancreatic cancer. All I knew was that she wasn't as fun as she used to be anymore, you know? I had to fetch a lot of things for her. She was weak and tired. I think I just saw my beautiful mother. I don't know if I noticed that she was getting thinner and weaker. One day I had a little temper tantrum and suggested that she just get over this and get up and *get off that couch and be my momma again.* Because I wanted to go play with my friends. I was the only one home with her sometimes, until my father came back from work.

My older sister, Barb, already had her first child. She got pregnant really young, so at eighteen she was out of the house. My brother was at that age—fifteen or sixteen—where he was just trying to act like nothing mattered. He hung out with his buddies and learned to drink beer. He was in denial. I'm sure he knew more than I did. I know Barb knew.

The thing is that my mother and I, because I was the youngest, we'd been home alone all of my years. I was her shadow. We were attached. I adored her, and I looked like her—everybody said so—and everywhere she went she took me with her. She cared for me very, very much. That's the most dreadful thing I think there must be about dying. I know how difficult it must have been for her to leave me. Not placing importance on me, but knowing the relationship we had, that must have just torn her apart. Once, right in front of me, she told my father, "Watch over this one. She's different." In fact, those are the last words I can recall out of my mother's mouth.

phone rang one day when my brother was playing pool down in our basement. I picked it up and said hello, and it was the church secretary, who was also the organ player. She said, "Wende, your mommy's gone to be with Jesus. Go say your prayers." I think my father was there at the church with her. I don't think anybody cared whether I was all alone when I heard that news.

Of course, right away I ran down to my brother and said, "Mommy's gone away and she's not coming back anymore! Marge so-and-so said she's gone to live with Jesus!" I was so confused and so heartbroken, and really the thought of her really being gone hadn't even set in. My brother just went back to playing pool. I was scared and shaken up, and no adult was there to hold me or hug me. I had to deal with that by myself.

My father came home later that day, and I think there was a little hug and a "Don't worry, Princess, everything's gonna be okay," but my father didn't really know how to listen very well. I had a lot of questions and things I wanted to say, but he probably turned on some football or something and avoided talking about it. I know he was heartbroken, too—maybe even more about me being without a mother than about losing his wife.

I WAS SO EMBARRASSED TO NOT HAVE A MOTHER

It was an open-casket funeral, and I don't remember that vision of her lying in that casket. I didn't want to see it, so I shielded myself. I do remember the cold Fort Snelling military burial ground, I remember they had her plot dug and ready and kind of roped off, and then I remember the casket. I remember the machine that slowly took her down, after some words were said, and I just remember the ground was so cold, I didn't know how they could have dug it up. They get a pretty hard freeze in September there.

For a while, I couldn't go to school. I was so embarrassed to not have a mother. That's a strange thing. I felt so really different from all the kids my age because they all had families, and a family wasn't complete without a mother. I felt awkward; I felt like hiding. And later, I did. I skipped school a lot and hid in the woods and tried to make sense of it all with my poor little brain.

One day I brought home paper and pens from school. I decided to write about it. I didn't get to it right away. I put the paper by my bedside, and then one night I wrote. In the morning I looked to see what I had written because it was almost like a dream. It was very final and sad and almost morbid for such a little girl. I know it was absolutely connected to how I felt and the loss of my mother, not knowing where she was or if I'd ever see her. "Oh, she's in heaven," everybody kept saying. That really made no sense to me. It didn't help at all, you know?

I cried myself to sleep every night. I was in pain and anguish all of the time, and one night I actually—I swear this is true—I felt a weight on the edge of my bed, and it was the weight of my mother. It was so familiar. Then I heard her voice. This is the only time in my life I have ever heard voices. And it was Alice, my mother. She just said, "Oh honey, don't you cry another tear, sweetheart. I'm singing and I'm dancing, and it's lovely here. I'm happy and I'm well." And I knew it was true. I knew that was true.

I'd been going down to check the mail ever since she'd died, to see if she'd write me a card and tell me to come with her to some exotic island or some faraway place. But when that experience happened to me, I think it was just a teensy bit of healing that began, you know? Then I didn't cry so much. I think I started pondering that there might be another place that's better than here, for the first time.

I wasn't healed for the long run. It took years and years and years. I had a dark teenage year. I'd just be so moody, and sometimes I'd just hide from everybody. Got really average grades. I could have done a lot better, but I wasn't very interested. It just kind of stole my enthusiasm away.

For the rest of my developing years, I had that wound. I carried that wound, and I had to talk about it with friends. Every new friend I made, I had to bring it up. It was almost like I didn't want to believe it, still, even into my eighteenth, nineteenth year. Then I ran as far from Minnesota as I could get, all the way to Oregon, to get away from her absence. It really was a catalyst, her death, in my life. I wouldn't be here if my mother were alive. I never would have left Minnesota. You wouldn't be here. Everything would have been different. I never could have left her. In a way, I think I was searching for her out here. She talked about the sea sometimes. She'd been to the ocean. I just think I was still searching for her.

OUR SOULS ARE IN SCHOOL

I was still "Daddy's little girl" until I'd had enough of sitting in church looking at the vacant spot where my mother used to sing in the choir. I began getting rebellious about that. The more rebellious I got, the more he tightened up and wanted to make sure I was in that church. I usually had to go no matter how I felt about it. But then, when I was about thirteen, I moved in with my sister. She lived about fifteen minutes away. I won't say I was better off, but she tried. I helped her raise the kids. I didn't want to leave my dad and my brother, but my dad worked a lot and didn't want me home with my brother and all his friends, and my sister thought it would be better. My dad still came to take me to church on Sunday mornings. [Laughs.]

When my mother was gone, the church didn't seem like a family anymore. I didn't really feel I belonged there. I wasn't looking to find a religion. I was just sure that all that stuff about one way and absolutism could not be. I needed to understand, "What's at the root of all this? What's at the root of man's seeking?" It put me on that path, and I read and read. I read about Bahá'í, I read about Hindu, I read about Buddhism, I even read the Koran. In all of them I noticed that there was something common, a common thread. And there is. It doesn't really matter, as long as you study. Study love, because that's all anything really is. That's what it all is. That's the force that I think gives birth to the entire universe. You don't have to call it anything. It just is. That's what we all come from.

In a way, I've come to believe strongly in reincarnation. I haven't been to séances. I haven't needed to go that extent or anything, but in the tilling of the soil within me, I've come to the conclusion that we do go on and on. That everybody has, in a way, eternal life. Our souls are in school, that's what I believe.

I would talk to my father about this stuff, too. He'd usually just say, "I don't know where you get these ideas." I don't think he ever dared to delve himself, but he'd listen. I was the one kid in the family that he would give an ear to. He so desperately wanted to just keep believing in his little princess. He never said, "You're full of crap," and slammed the door. "You ought to be ashamed of yourself." He never said those things to me.

Once I said to him, "Dad, your religion gives you a message from God, you believe." I said, "If you believe that God created everything, and God created me, why would he create someone with such a curious mind that had to understand all these religions?" My dad just looked at me and said, "Well, you've got a point there." Somewhere in the good book it does say we are all different but on the same path. I think my father stretched his mind, accepted more, and was more balanced with me than he was with anybody. He allowed me to help him open the door a little bit.

A LINE THAT I SHOULDN'T HAVE CROSSED

Your father and I both took Belladonna* before we knew each other. I don't know why we did it. It was the generation. That's what people were

---

* A highly toxic plant also known as "Deadly Nightshade." Elements of the plant are still used in various medicines, though I couldn't pinpoint the canned asthma product that my mom mentioned. (I asked Art Spiegelman about the drug after he described his own psychedelic experiences. "Belladonna was on my forbidden list," he said.)

doing. It was an ingredient in a medicine for asthma sufferers. You were supposed to burn it and breathe it in, not ingest it. There was a skull and crossbones on the side of the can.

This was during my searching years. I was sixteen. I was really miserable from losing my mother, and I just was trying to forget about that. So I took it only one time. My friend Charlie said it was really fun. He talked to a big bowl of strawberries all night long. I said, "Wow, that sounds like fun!" To be sure that I'd have as good an experience, I took a little more than Charlie took, and that "more" was pretty much a line that I shouldn't have crossed.

I didn't know whether I was having a good trip or a bad trip because I was all the way gone. I'd make little appearances; I'd come back and know where I was for a few minutes, but then I'd go back into it. Total hallucination. I wasn't analyzing things as they were happening. I just accepted them like an infant would.

My sister was horrified. She came home and found me sitting on the kitchen floor playing with pots and pans in a pool of urine. But I was sure having a good time. I knew no fear or guilt. I remember her looking at me going . . . [imitates senseless yelling]. I had no idea why she was doing that. I couldn't connect anything.

My sister didn't want to deal with me, and she called my dad, then she took me to the hospital. I suppose I was on the floor where people who are on stuff go. I don't know. It was like the eighteenth floor of the hospital, and I saw a little spotted dog running along the ledge outside my window. I kept saying, "Somebody let that poor dog in before he falls!" The black telephone in the bed next to me kept turning into a woman's hair—she had it up in rollers. There was a little couple sitting at the foot of the bed every time they were there. I thought it was a little Mexican lady and her husband, and he was smoking little stogies while she was crocheting. She had fruit on her straw hat. It made me feel safe, having them there.

You want to see yourself in that state, but you can't see yourself. You don't even have any sense of self. You know, your dad saw grizzly bears climbing up the buildings in downtown Los Angeles—and it was very real when he saw them.

My father even thought it was funny listening to my hallucinations, although I scared him to death when the doctors told him they didn't know if I'd ever be normal again.

WE DIDN'T LIKE HIM VERY MUCH, BUT WE LOVED HIM

After my dad married Irene, my stepmother, I would go out there sometimes on weekends and stay with them. I had my own room that they kept up for me. It was comfortable there. Irene had . . . I think it was six kids. Only one, the youngest, lived with them. I actually went back home, just for the last six months of high school. My dad made me. [Laughs.] "Come home or we're not going to give you an open house—and you'll get money at the open house," he said. That did it. I really enjoyed my six months there in his house. I graduated high school, and my dad was at my graduation.

After graduation, my friend Arlene said she was going to go to Eugene, Oregon, where her sister was in college. I said, "Oh, I wanna go!" And she said, "Get your things!" So we drove out west. I told my dad I was going, but I didn't know I was going to stay out here. He hated to see me go, but he was supportive. "You let me know if you need anything, honey. Be careful out there." He thought Oregon was a lawless place where the women didn't wear bras. What could be more dangerous?

I always kept in touch with him. We loved each other. He was so strict when we were younger. We didn't like him very much, but we loved him. He was pretty hard on my brother, but he wasn't a bad man. Frustrated, more than anything.

Years later I went back to Minnesota to go to barber school, and I built a wonderful relationship with my father. We had so much fun. We went out to dinner all the time, and I cooked for him in my apartment. He just loved my cooking.

My dad fell ill—there were some terrible heart attacks—before I moved out to Florence, where your dad was living. I think I knew that my dad was dying the whole time he was in the hospital. Four chambers of his heart blew one at a time. He thought he was going to live after each heart attack, and so did all the nurses and doctors. I would talk to him on the phone, and he'd say, "Oh honey, don't you dare take a plane back here. I'm going to be fine. This summer we'll have a good time. You'll come then." Repeatedly, this is what he said. I asked my sister, and she said, "It's pretty bad, Wende. He just doesn't want you to see him like this, with tubes all over him, and weak."

So I didn't go see him. But the reason I didn't is that there was no unfinished business between me and my father. His illness had lasted for almost a month, so I knew to expect that he might go. It wasn't like when I lost my mother. Then he died, and I went back there for the funeral. Then we went to England. My dad never met your father. I think I did say I was dating somebody, but that's it. He said, "Be sure he's saved!" That wasn't ever gonna happen.

So I was orphaned. I was twenty-eight years old. It was scary and a bit frightening because my father was always there. I never asked him for money, but he always offered. He always said, "You know if you ever need anything you can have it. Just tell me." That was some security that I lost. And I had some regrets about not having gone home more. There's nothing he could have done to keep me from living my life exactly as I did, but I wish he could've been there during my divorce. That was the roughest time, other than my mother's death. Very rough.

EVERY DAY IT WAS *LIFE*

Both of your dad's parents died shortly after we got back from our trip to England. We'd just been with them. It was terrible. His mother died first, and then his dad, Frank.

So we both were orphaned within a year.

Frank was alive when you were born. He so wanted to see you. But for me, from the day you were born, every day it was *life*.

I was so busy. I totally threw myself into motherhood, all of it. Made homemade baby food; made it myself, froze it. I was a good mum.

I think I found the love that I lost in my mother through my children. Through the act of loving, she taught me how to love. I was too little to realize that she was teaching me, but she told all her sisters that by the time she had me, she was really ready to be a good mother, and she was. She put me right alongside her in the kitchen and taught me to bake, and I'd have flour all over me from head to toe. She'd laugh and giggle. We had a family cabin. She loved to go swimming with me there. We were always, *always* together—and she was so attentive. She made me all my little taffeta and chiffon dresses, my nightgowns. She sewed my entire wardrobe. I was her little doll.

I found that same love through being a mother. I was able to find my security, knowing that you boys were mine to love and care for. Most of the time, I felt you loved me, too. Sometimes I wondered about it.

THERE WAS A BEGINNING

When I went through my divorce—I must have been nearing forty—I fell into clinical depression, and it was really a lot like those years after my mother died. I knew something wasn't right, but I didn't know what was happening for a while there. Then, after months and months of crying—just crying, no signal telling me I was going to cry or particular thoughts that necessarily made me cry—I would have these visions of myself lying dead somewhere. Walking across the icy little bridge up the North Fork, I saw myself lying on the ground like I'd hit my head on the rock and died. Stuff like that.

I ended up talking with a female psychologist. I guess my doctor sent me to talk with her. She said, "I want you to talk with this woman. You'll really like her." I did like her, and I started working through all that. She took me through inner-child therapy, which I needed when I was a little girl. She put me in touch with my most tender self, my most childlike self, so I could nurture her. That was an important lesson in life to learn—that my momma was gone and now my husband is gone, but that I needed to really value myself and to nurture myself and to listen to my inner self. To hear those thoughts of sadness and dismay and grief.

There was a beginning, really, when I went through that therapy. My therapist said, "What you're going through is clinical depression that you suffered when you were a child. All these years that you didn't know what was eating you, what you were seeking, what it was. It was comfort, because you never had the help to face that when you were a little girl." And it all rang really true.

MAYBE THEY WERE THERE
FOR US IN OUR LAST LIFETIME

A lot of the old customers from the barbershop have come and gone. I used to go to their funerals in the early years, but there just really got to be too many. Their spouses, most of the time, would come and tell me that they'd passed.

I've had the experience of being the main hospice personality for a few people's last days—like Helen. I met her when she'd just found out she was terminal with lung cancer. We just formed a bond. I was able to be real helpful in her going out on a good note. I think sometimes we're meant to be in that honorable position with people. Maybe they were there for us in our last lifetime.

I benefited in many ways through knowing her—through not being afraid to sit with her in the wee hours and hold her hand while she was dying. I helped get her out of the nursing home that she hated, and we rented a house a block from ours. Through becoming Helen's daughter, I experienced a lot of healing of that pain from losing my own mother. She looked like my mother. She had real thick, brown hair, and her hair was soft like my mother's. She adored me. She helped me get a loan to open my barbershop. She gave me all of her clothes, which were very nice. Lots of professional working clothes. We were really close, and I was with her the moment she died.

I went in and sat on her bed. I'd always go over there in the evening when her boys were at the bar or something, and we'd laugh and talk, just like she was my own mother. And we'd hold hands. That last evening, I went in there and sat on the bed. I touched her hand, and she made a grimace. Then when she opened her eyes she looked at me, and this natural, delighted look came over her face for a fleeting moment, but she went right back into her pre-death coma. But I had that moment with her. She seemed comfortable. I checked her bedding and fluffed her pillow up and went into the living room, and I was watching the evening news. Then, about twenty minutes later, I just had this urge to go check on her again.

Even from the doorway, I could see something different about the light around her and the light *of* her. I went over and sat closer, and then the stillness told me that she was gone. I didn't have to listen for her breath. You know, I got misty, but I was happy for her. She'd been suffering badly.

I called the bar to get her son home. He came home and just fell apart. He might as well have been six years old. What a mess. He shook his mother and yelled, "Momma! Momma!"—trying to get her to come back. I said, "No, no, don't you see how her body is worn and tired? You don't want to call her back here. Who would call anyone back for more of this suffering?" Then he just broke down and cried. Then he broke down again in the backyard, crying on the ground and pulling up the grass. I went and got his brother, then stayed with them until the mortuary came to take her away.

HE'S NOT GONE, BUT
HE'S NOT HERE, EITHER

A good friend and client of mine, John, went into the nursing home long after his wife, Amy, died. I'd go cut his hair in the nursing home, just to make him feel special. He really liked that. We'd laugh and talk, and he paid me very well. Then he got weaker and weaker, and I knew something was fundamentally wrong.

One day I went to see him, around Christmas time, and brought cookies. The nurse's aid in the hallway said, "You don't want to go in there." I said, "Yes, I do. I have cookies for John." I looked at her face, and I said, "Oh." She said, "He's not gone, but he's not here, either." I knew what that meant. I said, "I want to go in. Is that all right?" She said yes.

I sat by his bed and talked to him and ran my fingers through his wavy hair. This was after I'd lost my brother, and my sister had described to me being with my brother in Minnesota while he was dying—running her fingers through his wavy hair. So that's what I did. I might have sang him a song. I don't remember what song it was. I told him, "You're a good man, John. You don't owe anyone anything here. There's no tie. Everybody who ever knew you is proud to have known you. You should go. You should let go." He died the next day.

I WAS STRANGELY POSSESSED BY THIS THOUGHT OF JOHN WAYNE

A couple years ago, I thought I was coming down with something. That turned into the nightmare. My blood sugar surged to 750, and I passed out and hit my head on the wall and crawled on my back, inch by inch, for three and a half hours to my cell phone, and almost collapsed. I had a lot of funny experiences on the way, like—you can find a sense of humor when you're on the edge of dying, you know? I was strangely possessed by this thought of John Wayne. I pretended he was in the room with me as I crawled along, wondering if I'd make it. I couldn't get to my knees because my legs were dead, so I just had to inch with my back and pull my lower body along.

I was about four feet away from the cell phone and the bedside table, and I just went weak. I felt things were getting dark all of a sudden, and I think that was the moment I would have died, if I hadn't seen my beautiful granddaughter's golden face and blue eyes just come right floating along in my mind. That was the moment of determination. I just felt something change, and I was going to make it to that phone. So I did and got out of that one. My heart stopped in the ambulance right as they were taking me away, but they got it started again. I nearly died, and then I did die momentarily in that van. Everything went white, and I laugh because as I came out of that one moment, I saw that it was a very foggy day in Florence, and it looked like white—you know, I think I was looking mainly at the fog, but I did have kind of a white light experience. I was too weak to be frightened. I'd been through so much; I'd fallen many times in the past weeks.

Then there was the ICU and the hospital stays. Then off to the nursing home, which was a nightmare in itself. People were being wheeled out of there every day that died, and my roommate was dying.

But I made it out of there, and I got to go home. I didn't die. I kept waiting to get stronger over the next few weeks, and the strength wasn't coming. I thought I was just lazy. I couldn't get my legs to be strong enough to support me. After a couple weeks of that, my belly button opened up, and all this poisonous, infectious liquid that had built itself in an abscess and wrapped itself around my body let loose. So, off to the hospital again and emergency rooms. I went to the hospital in Eugene, where the surgeons were all baffled. It was such a rare thing, they said. They hadn't seen anything like it, but they knew they had to get it out of me.

That whole time I was on opioids and had weird dreams and did a lot of thinking that *this could be it*. I felt like I had a lot of unfinished stuff, and I would cry when nobody was around. I wanted to get rid of some things and go through photographs so my kids don't have to go through it. That's on everybody's thoughts when they prepare themselves to die. They just don't want to hand down all kinds of stuff that their kids won't understand. I wasn't a nervous wreck over it; I just had some regrets. My writing: I wished I'd gone through that and taken out what might be okay. You know, thoughts like that. Because you prepare yourself. That might have been it.

I'VE FALLEN IN LOVE WITH THE MYSTERY

It's true, I've been telling you your whole life: "You're gonna regret what you just said to me! You'll think about it when I'm dead." [Laughs.]

Well, I didn't think I'd be alive this late. Sixty-five years old. No, you don't know when you have a family history. I didn't think I would be alive. I didn't think I'd be a grandmother. It's just because I look a lot like my mom, so I always identified with her dying young, too. It's probably going to be me, too. But I'm still here, determined as ever to experience every day like a new day and to be grateful for every day I am. I'm tired some days, but I'm grateful. Grateful to whatever holds it all. The infinite. I'm grateful to the infinite, and I'm blessed. I love the mystery. I don't have to seek answers anymore. I've fallen in love with the mystery, and I wouldn't count out any possibilities.

That's why I can't be an atheist. I think they're very sad people in a way because they won't allow themselves to consider the possibilities. They think it's all just fantasy silly stuff, but there's always—as long as man has existed—been a yearning in every heart to find some light of hope. And that's all it is! I think you decide to have it, period, and then that's your grace. You get that comfort of having made the decision to believe that all is well and there is a power. You let yourself believe that there's a sensibility to all this—and you sure can't find it sometimes, but it's there. I truly believe that.

There's way more than we can see. This is just the tip of the pin, you know? Infinity! Think about it! I love to think about it. Nobody could ever tell me that there's nothing beyond this experience. I wouldn't believe it for a second. I don't seek spiritual experiences like that anymore, but sometimes when I'm just sitting in the sunlight, I get lost in that same world that meditation gives you. I do start my mornings by lighting a candle, usually, and reading a little something inspiring. Then I just hope that inspiration holds with me all day long.

I studied a lot of different religions, and there is a golden thread. I don't have to dissect it anymore. I'm not a holy roller. I don't even go to church. My church is right here.

As you lose more and more friends, you certainly want to believe that there's a cycle, like there seems to be in everything. I just think life is that way, too; that we live life after life after life. Nature and the whole plan of things was kind to let us forget each time we live. I think tiny babies come into this world with a little bit of an understanding. They do remember, but the minute they breathe and see the bright lights and people and everything, they forget about their last life. I'm sure of it.

IT'S BETTER TO BELIEVE IN EVERYTHING

Somebody asked me what I believed in a little while back, and I said, "Everything." I think it's better to believe in everything. Everything! You know? Like a child.

But as I get older, and I know it's coming, once in awhile I have momentary fears that I won't be ready when my time comes. I think, *Oh god, it'll be scary, like jumping off a cliff!* You know? Jumping into the void! Driving a car off a cliff into the ocean. But that's one thing I work on in meditation, is trying to remember not to be so attached to this body. I've astral projected. I've done it! I wouldn't say I did it if I hadn't. I left my body, and I went out and counted the street lights, probably for six miles altogether. Then that's all I wanted of that. I always said to myself, *You're here, you don't need to be out there. You're here to live your life here, the way your momma didn't get to.* But I have had that experience.

I think what frightens me the most is my own horrific sadness about leaving my loved ones. That will be very difficult. I don't think there's any way for you to prepare yourself for that. You'd have to try to not love them all, you know, try to push them all away. Go somewhere all alone. I used to think, *I'll go up Big Creek* and sit under a tree and die.* But you don't wanna be all alone. I don't need to have people filing in a room to pay their respects.

---

* A country road where our family once lived.

You already know what I want. I want the guy in Reedsport to cremate me. And then I want you to carry my ashes up Bay Street. I want Ian to play his saxophone just for one block on Bay Street, and I want you to bring your trumpet. Brush up a little, and you could just play a few of the notes of "When the Saints Go Marching In." You don't have to play the whole song, but just accompany whatever your brother is doing. One block! And I don't need it in the paper. Just you guys can do it, you know? Walk on the riverside, from the gazebo down to the boat basin. You don't have to play the whole way. You know, and scatter my ashes where all my friends went, into the Siuslaw River. I used to kind of want to be transported back home to the St. Croix River, but the Siuslaw River is fine.

Then you could rent a cabin the next Christmas up in the mountains or something. And I'll be there! You'll see me in the snowflakes.

Life's too short, though. I know that.

＼

CONDUCTED OCTOBER 10, 2015

ANNA URQUHART

SOCIAL WORKER, AUTHOR'S FRIEND

Anna is a friend who often does everything she can to crack me up at parties. Sometimes she'll linger in my peripheral vision, making desperate or pitying facial expressions at me until I finally notice. Other times she might make outlandish accusations about passing acquaintances just within their earshot. I try my best to keep up but seldom do. She is relentlessly and inappropriately hilarious.

About a month before this interview, I shared drinks with Anna at a mutual friend's birthday party. I told her about this book-in-progress, and she proposed a foreword, which she herself would write. It was to be penned in a sort of caveman vernacular, be vulgar in the extreme, and have only a tangential relationship to the topic at hand. I told her I'd get back to her.

I immediately thought of that ridiculous conversation weeks later, when I heard that Anna's mom had been stricken with a sudden, terminal illness. Anna's greatest coping mechanism must be completely overwhelmed, I thought. There was no way that her sense of humor could hold up.

I was half-right. A few weeks after her mother's death, I met Anna on her front porch, and she seemed torn between despondency and earnestness. She was searching herself, and occasionally grilling me, for anything that might help make sense of her loss. There were tears, sobs, and pregnant pauses throughout our interview, but they were punctuated by sharp bouts of gallows humor. "Is this all you can do to get off right now?" she asked. "Listen to girls cry?"

I asked Anna repeatedly if she felt comfortable talking while still in the midst of the emotional chaos of grief. She said she was, and I knew Anna would be honest with me about what she was going through. She's never been one to avoid talking about grim or personal subjects. I asked if she saw a light at the end of the tunnel. "No," she said. "I don't know how I'm ever going to be happy again."

LETTER FROM A FRIEND

Mandy, she's an old soul. She processes things very kindly. Her card meant a lot.

Dear Anna,

I do wish you peace, and peace will come with the consoling power of the passage of time. But now is the time of tears and anger and weeping. Now is the darkness, now is the heartbreak, now is the gut-wrenching loss, the chaotic reeling of shock. My best advice is to let it all in, and feel it. Be true to your grief. It is a reflection of your love. But in your grief, don't forget to feel your love. Give into your love, for your mother, and love for your family and friends who remain alive with you. Let us in. Give us the gift of your honest emotion and allow us to be there for you whenever you need it. We love you deeply and we long to be able to show it. Please be good to yourself. I wish you lights in the darkness, I wish you moments of beauty and grace. I hope you feel your mom's energy, I hope you feel all of your friends' and your family's love.

—Mandy

She's one of the only people who has been comforting to me, really. I mean, I've had lots of friends who have been incredibly kind, but if you haven't gone through it, it doesn't really mean a whole lot.

DRINKING HELPS

Mandy spent like six months with her mom, not knowing. I had two days of that, and it was awful.

One thing that Mandy told me was, "You'll find that you aren't listening to anything." People keep talking to me about things that I just don't fucking care about. I don't give a fuck what's going on. With friends, social groups, people having arguments. I just completely check out. It's just not what I'm thinking about. All I have been talking and thinking about is my mom. Thankfully, I've had friends to talk about it with. My husband, Mike, has been amazing—I think he's trying to cheer me up. But it's pretty much fucking daily that I just, like, burst into tears out of nowhere. Drinking helps. A lot.

CRUDER THAN MOST OF THE GUYS

I probably have a closer relationship . . . [Anna pauses when she realizes she's using present tense]. It hasn't even been a fucking month.

My parents were still married. And they were in love. I had a closer relationship to them than any of my friends did with their parents. Some of my friends spent more time with my parents than they did with their own. They lived twenty minutes away. I mean, my dad's still alive. He has his own pain. I would see them two or three times a month. I'd go out to lunch with my mom two or three times a month. We would always go to the Indian buffet.

We made each other laugh. My mom's favorite joke was about the hairlip midget with a lisp who goes to buy a horse. This was my mom. It was also really weird because she was an attorney, and she worked for police unions. A bunch of cops and firefighters showed up to her funeral. She worked all over eastern Washington, in these tiny little towns where she was assigned to be their legal rep. She would show up, and the shit that would come out of her mouth would just make them gasp. Like, I can't believe you're talking cruder than most of the guys. But anyway, I'll tell the joke.

So the hairlip midget goes to buy a horse from this old Texan. He has an appointment already, and he wanders into the stables and the Texan's just kind of taken aback, like, "Huh, oh, hi there." The midget, who has a pretty serious lisp, is like, "Hello, thir. I'm very intherethted in the horth that you have for thale." And the Texan's like, "All right." The midget says "May I athk you a favor? May I pleath athk you a favor? Will you pleath lift me up so I can look in ith ears?" The Texan is old and frail, but he gently lifts the midget up to the horse's ears. And he looks around in his ears like, "Very good, Very good, okay." And the Texan just sits the midget back and down, and the midget is like, "May I athk you to pleath pick me up again so I can look at ith teeth?" And the Texan is kind of exhausted, but he says okay. He reaches down and lifts the guy up, and the midget inspects the horse's teeth and gums. The Texan sets him back down. The midget is like, "Oh, thee's very good. Very very beautiful. Uhm, one latht thing: May I see ith twat?" And the Texan's like, "You dirty fucking asshole." He picks the midget up and just shoves his head into the horse's ass, and the horse kicks the midget onto the ground. The midget sits up, spits out some horse shit and hay and collects himself, and says, "Let me rephrathe that: May I thee it gallop?"

WE WEREN'T REALLY LISTENING TO WHAT THE DOCTORS WERE SAYING

I've been going through photos. Stacks of them. [Hands me the photos to look through.] She was awesome. Most of these are just like family photos. Mostly of my brother and I. She was usually behind the camera. We were cute kids, huh? That's my dad. We were really, like, the whole family, incredibly close. And we traveled together a lot.

We never talked about death. My mom didn't really even talk about it with my dad. She was very stubborn. My parents had conversations about, if there were to be an accident, how they wanted finances to take care of things. Like, clearly, if I'm brain dead, I don't want you to keep me on life support, those sort of conversations—but that was it. We never talked about how we felt about death, what we thought of it.

My dad's a drinker. He's been smoking since he was maybe eleven. And I think, in her head, she was probably prepared to comfort my brother and me at some point. Losing my dad early because of that stuff seemed like a possibility. He's also just done stupid reckless shit in his life, and she was the one who never smoked, and would get buzzed off of two drinks, and that was it. She didn't do anything to excess.

The week before she died, hospice came in to the conversation, and she was just like, "Nope. Too soon. Not talking about this. We're not talking about this." And at that point we weren't ready, either. We weren't really listening to what the doctors were saying.

It was Mike and my anniversary. The twenty-third of August. I was supposed to go get fucking Indian food with my mom the day before and I canceled. Which drives me insane. Because I can't have that back.

Sunday it was our anniversary, and there was a knock on our door at eight on Monday morning. Mike answered the door, and it was my dad. He said they'd gone to the emergency room because she'd been having back pain that wouldn't go away, even with pain meds.

They took her to the ER at Providence, and they did a scan. They found tumors on her spine and took her into surgery thirty minutes later. That was on Sunday. They had to do massive spinal surgery, but she wouldn't let my dad call me about it because it was our fucking anniversary. She didn't want to spoil it. So Monday, he came here and said, "Mom's in the hospital. They found cancer." By the time I got to the hospital that morning at, like, nine, they'd done more scans and it had spread. They'd found lesions in her brain and lungs and liver. But we were still like . . . there's treatment. There are things that we can do. Let's just wait. Melanoma— they didn't even know if it was melanoma, but they assumed, from the tumors they removed, that it was—is treatable, so there was still hope. There was treatment available.

They did radiation when they removed the tumors. They did radiation on her spine. She was in the hospital for two weeks. We basically needed to get her up and moving because she couldn't walk. She had to have this crazy brace on, and we were trying to get her strength up because, if she had to be able to be up and moving, then they would let her continue the treatment. They don't let you get radiation if you're not healthy enough to do it.

We took her home for a weekend, and my brother had to go back home to New York, so it was just my dad and me taking care of her. She couldn't hold any food down. She couldn't hold any of the medication down. We had to call an ambulance to get her back to a hospital. We were in the hospital for three or four weeks altogether, and we got her home two different times, overnight.

The idea was that once she was home, she might be more comfortable, and she'd start eating, and she'd get a good night's sleep. In the hospital you're woken up every moment. But the hospital kind of fucked up with pain management. They were not very good about telling us what to expect. And we didn't have any remedies. After the second time we brought her back, they were like, "Oh, we should have sent you home with liquid morphine." My dad was maniacally writing down and keeping track of what we were giving her, and we couldn't stay on top of it. She was just in excruciating pain and couldn't walk. So, my dad and I are there, but just getting her to be able to sit down on the toilet to try and go to the bathroom was a fucking nightmare.

It wasn't really awkward for me caring for her in that way, that just felt necessary. But she was so physically weak. And her hair was—she had really fine hair—and just from being in bed for days, it was a huge dreadlock. I tried to fix it: I went and bought detangler, and tried doing it in bed, but it was just like, *fuck*. I had hair down to my ass as a kid. And I remember my mom working on it and getting all the knots out. My family's very naked. I'm not, I think, because they were so naked. I think I have body shame because they were too naked. My parents' shower didn't have curtains on it, so there was no weirdness with my mom's body or seeing her body. I'd seen her naked body a thousand times.

But, I mean, cleaning your mom's vagina and wiping her ass and like lifting her boobs to clean under them, is, yeah, it sucks. She was apologetic about it. She just kept saying things like, "I'm sorry I'm ruining your weekend."

I remember one evening we had this really bitchy nurse who was going to get us set up to take a shower. My mom was hooked up to all sorts of wires, and she had a catheter, and she couldn't move without this crazy brace. So it was getting her up, standing with a walker, and getting her in the shower somehow. This nurse who was just coming on her shift didn't know she was going to have to do that and was kind of bitchy about it.

The nurse was just telling me, you know, "when you're cleaning the vagina, be really careful, and try to just gently rinse off the catheter and tube." I'm just like, "Okay. My eyes are going to be closed, and I'm going to be dry heaving violently at that point, so is there—can I just like, feel, where it is?" And the nurse just gasped, and my mom and I just burst out laughing. The nurse was like, "Wow, I love you guys. I seriously thought that your daughter was a total asshole."

It was tough, but my mom was still there. Her brain was there. That was the easiest of any of it, was caring for her, physically.

I don't know if that's because we were close or because she was my mom. I'm pretty positive that, like, in a second I would do the same thing for my dad, but I'm sure there would be an element that would be much different in that situation. It didn't phase me or my dad.

She was exhausted, but she was *there*. She was drugged up and weak. But she also didn't want to—none of us wanted to talk about it. It was devastating, and it wasn't actually very treatable, but there were still treatments. The focus was not going to be on anything negative, like whether or not the treatments would work. The focus was just on getting her the treatment. That was it.

I WISH I'D KEPT THAT MESSAGE

My dad does not know how to use iPhones at all, and he butt-dialed me with his phone one morning. We had planned this trip to Mexico. It was going to be my brother, Mike, me, and my parents. So my dad butt-dialed, and it went to voicemail. It was right after they had talked to the oncologist. He was mumbling, and all I could hear was her. She was clear as day: "I don't fucking care what they're saying. We're going to Mexico. I really don't give a fuck what they're saying. We're going to fight this. We're going to Mexico. It's going to be fine." I wish I'd kept that message.

At that point it was like, "This is going to be a shitty fucking year 'cause my mom's going to be going through this." When we got Mom home, my brother flew back to New York where he lives, and then when my dad and I had to bring her back to the hospital, he flew back out again. He was gone for maybe three days.

We are still going to go to Mexico in November for Thanksgiving. I'm not looking forward to it at all anymore.

THE CODE TO THE SAFE

I was trying to go back to work, unsuccessfully. I went back for two days when my brother and my dad were at the hospital. One of those nights my brother came to me and said, "Why are you and Dad not listening to what the doctors are saying?" I said, "What are you talking about?" He said, "You guys are not fucking listening to what the doctors are saying. Mom's dying. Why won't you guys fucking listen to that?"

I said, "What the fuck are you talking about? They're telling us that she needs to get stronger in order to do the treatment." The treatment itself had an 11 percent success rate, and then with a trial they wanted to put her in, it was supposed to up the success rate. My brother said, "She's not strong enough to do it. You guys are not listening." I said, "But we can get her strong enough. That's the whole point. She just had major fucking spinal surgery. Let's give her time. She's in recovery." We had to get her eating again. She hadn't eaten in, like, weeks. We're going to get her strong. That's what we were there for.

My friend Darcy, who had cancer and had her treatments at the same hospital, got in touch with her doctor, who referred us to another oncologist. He came in and looked at her charts, and he said, "The doctors you're working with are doing what they can, but there's really nothing to do at this point."

That was the first time anyone put it that way, but the doctors had been telling us to do hospice for about two weeks. It was one of those things where it's like, "Okay, we'll do hospice if we have to, but we'll get her strong enough for the trial." With hospice, you have to really say that you're not seeking treatment. It's end-of-life stuff. My dad and I decided we'd lie to them if we had to—to get extra support, to get her home and get her healthy—but no. We were going to pursue the treatment.

My mom didn't want to talk about it. She listened to us fight for her, and she just got weaker and weaker. I lost it one night. Just fucking lost it and couldn't go back to the hospital. I was spending all days there, and we'd go get dinner and then come back. My brother spent the night there that night. In the morning, he called and told me, "Mom just really wants to talk to you. Just you." I went in, and I could tell that she was fighting everything to break out of wherever her head was. We held each other and said I love you and said how scared we were and—I got that with her. There wasn't anything to hash out. That was pretty fucking amazing. We didn't have anything to apologize for—we just loved each other. All we had was a moment to just hold each other and cry and love each other. We didn't say anything, but she understood. We had, like, three minutes before she started drifting off into other things that didn't make any sense. I think she was struggling to have that moment with me, and we didn't have to spend it doing anything other than holding each other and telling each other how lucky we were. Then she said, "I should probably give you the code to the safe." [Laughs.]

I said, "Fuck you, mom! That's the last fucking thing I want! I don't give a fuck about that!"

And now we don't have the code to the safe.

She was trying so hard to have that moment with me. But it was excruciating. She knew at that point that it wasn't okay, and she was drugged up, but she was listening to what the doctors were saying more than we were. She was listening to us fight with the doctors. But I also think that she never liked having those conversations, and she went into her head. She went into her head and just shut off. I don't know what I would've done. She was diagnosed on the twenty-third of August, and she died on the eighteenth of September.

THE LAST PAGE OF THE BOOK

Toward the end she started drifting off again. She didn't handle narcotics very well. She would mostly get sleepy. She'd get out of it a little bit, but she wasn't delusional. Anyway, one day I knew that something was not right. They found lesions in her brain, but at first, the doctor said that they could very well be naturally occurring, noncancerous lesions. They just did a full MRI and those were there, so I think that that was another one of our reasons for hoping she could pull out of all of this. Like, maybe there was nothing in her brain. We knew it was all over her lungs and her liver and spine and bones, but maybe it wasn't in her brain. But that day, she was just not tracking things. We had odd little conversations. Then, suddenly, she said, "Just remember the last page of the book we're reading right now." I was like, "I don't know what book we're reading right now, Mom." She said, "Remember the last line of it. Always remember the last line. Be kind to one another."

EVERYTHING HURTS

All this shit just plays out in my head all fucking day. I want my mom back. I don't know where she is. That really bothers me. I'd love to be religious right now. I don't know where she is. I see her in everything. Everything. And I don't know where the fuck she is I don't know if she's watching. I just know she did not wanna fucking die.

My mom's mom died really suddenly when she was twenty-seven, and I don't know if she ever got over it. It was kind of similar to how my mom went. I talked to her about it a little, and it was incredibly painful. She just didn't like talking about that stuff. My dad and I are much more emotional than my mom and my brother. My dad calls it the blue- and the brown-eye thing.

Anyway, she didn't like talking about it. She wasn't close with her dad or her brother, but she was really close to her mom. She died of cervical cancer, I think. Basically, she started bleeding really heavily at like sixty, after she'd gone through menopause, and they went to the hospital, and at the time they didn't tell people when they were really close to death. They heavily sedated her, and she died a week and a half later. It was sudden, and it was out of nowhere. Which was like my mom. She thought she had pinched a nerve in her back.

Melanoma is awful. My mom loved being in the sun, and they told us that it's one of those things if you get really bad sunburns when you're a kid, or in your teenager years, your body absorbs it because you're healthy. So you'll get melanoma cells but your body will absorb those cells, but they can just stay there dormant. My mom continued to be out in the sun her entire life. She loved it. She loved Mexico. That's where we're taking her ashes after this.

We used to go every year, or every other year, when I was a kid. She and my dad went every single year. She really wanted to go on this trip. They were going to go like a week before Mike and I got there, and stay a week after. Now my dad's going to be there by himself, and he doesn't want to be there by himself. And I don't want to go back there without her.

I've told Mike, "I don't know how I'm ever going to be happy again." Everything's just fucking rough. My dad wants to sell the house. I mean, it's just everything. I can't even be there. I hate being there. It's so sad. It was a rundown log cabin that they spent years and years and years making into this beautiful home, and every inch of it is her. I don't want her to be gone. I don't want him to sell it—but I also don't have to live there everyday. I don't have to sleep in a bed where she used to sleep.

My dad and my brother and I talk every day. Every day. And there's nothing to say, some days. I'll just call my dad and say, "How are you doing?" And he'll say, "Not good." We'll cry on the phone, and then it'll be quiet for a while. And I'll be like, "I was just calling to say I love you. I have nothing to say to you. I love you."

He'd been retired for a while, but she was still working. She was looking at her emails to clients a week before she died. She was sending out emails to clients saying, "I'm sorry it's taken me so long to get back to you. I've been down with a bit of a bug." My dad had to make all those phone calls.

There's an overwhelming amount of love and support from people right when you don't want to be around anybody. Then that goes away and it's—my brother's not here and my dad's alone all week long, and so I want to go and see him over the weekend, but it's so painful going over there. Everything hurts. Everything. You go pee and get another roll of toilet paper, and it's like, "I was with you when you bought that!" Everything in the house is my mom. It's the same for my dad. He says, "I give myself two things to do every day."

I went over there last weekend. The place is a huge log cabin, and he felt like it was too big for them when it was just the two of them. Now there's dust on the windows and cobwebs and things. I'm going to come over next weekend and clean. He's unshaven. I know a couple of times I've gone over that it's very clear that he's hung over.

Having to work doesn't help, but I also feel like I would be fucking miserable here by myself otherwise. If I wasn't working, I would probably be in bed. I just want to drink. A lot. I want to be drunk. I want to be fucked-up drunk. I want to not have to deal with this.

I don't know what to do. I have no idea what would make me feel better right now. Other than having my mom back. I have no fucking idea what to do.

Losing a parent is a nightmare, especially when it just seems like it's too soon. It was too fucking soon. It shouldn't have happened that way. If we had had time to start treatments, and have a couple of months, even, of treatments not working. Just enough time for her to be able to go through her shit and have those conversations, and to even have a second to process what was going on. But now I'm looking at her jewelry, just looking at the stuff in the house that might have been valuable for her. I want to know, like, *These were passed down, or these are really, really special to me—please hold onto these things.* And now I don't know.

THE BEST-CASE SCENARIO

Objectively, I am so fucking lucky. I am so lucky for even what I have now. I have a brother and dad who are mourning the loss of my mom with me, and we can talk to each other. Any time, I can talk to them about it. And I don't have any regrets about my relationship with my mom. There are so many things—it was so incredibly rare and wonderful. Absolutely.

But I'm not grateful. I'm angry. I'm pissed. I don't know where the fuck she is. I'm pissed that she's gone. I'm pissed that it went this way. I'm pissed that it's not how she would have wanted it to play out. She was so active. Her and my dad had so many plans. She relished getting older, and now I'm pissed that my dad's alone. I'm pissed because it was too fast. She never would have been okay with dying. But there were people she wanted to say good-bye to. There were things she wanted to do. There was control of the situation that she didn't get to have. She spent those last weeks in a hospital. And that pisses me off. But I also know that she spent it in a fucking hospital surrounded by people that loved her and wanted to be around her—people who were grieving just as much as she was, probably, in her head, when she wasn't talking about it. I think that's rare.

I think about what Louis CK says, when he talks about the ideal, the best possible situation. He says that the best possible situation is that you find somebody you really care about and really love, you spend your life and have all these experiences with them, and even the things you hate about them become things you love, and then one of you dies. That is the best-case scenario. And I look at all these pictures, and I look at all the memories we have, and I think of my parents' life together. Oh my god, they fought like fucking dogs. They could fight each other. But they loved each other dearly and traveled the world together.

THE DONKEY

I brought this little creature outside. [Opens her cupped hands to reveal a small, ugly, one-eyed donkey figurine with a miniature broom for a tail. It is hideous-looking.] It's very beautiful.

We think he was a part of a desk set from the thirties or forties. You should take a picture of its winky eye. Because this one eye has a gemstone in it. The other one fell out. So we think this was like a pencil eraser.

My mom's mom and her mom—as a running joke—would trade this back and forth. My mom and I have been trading this thing back and forth since I was a little kid. Sometimes one of us would have it for a while and forget about it, and it'd be in a drawer for a year. But usually—maybe twice a year, birthdays and Christmas—this was given as a present, and it was, like, the big gift. It was usually intricately wrapped in a much larger package. Sometimes it was buried within several boxes, or it was the one thing that you could save, like, "Oh, you still have one present under the tree."

I remember thinking, as a kid, "Oh, I have something really cool coming because there's still this present that's under the tree." Then it would be like, "Oh, thanks, Mom, for giving this back to me." This started when I was like eight.

Maybe she would have given it to me earlier, but she and my grandmother did the same thing with each other. I needed to be old enough to understand the importance of it. There were certain times that I lost it. I lost it in college in whatever shit-show place I was living. I'd just get totally frantic, and then I'd find it again. And it did used to have the other eye, it just fell out somewhere.

One day while Mom was in the hospital, I was home taking a shower, and I got really frantic. I was like, "Where the fuck is the donkey?" I finally found it and brought it to the hospital. She laughed about it a lot. I put it in her bag because she didn't want someone stealing it or for some nurse to throw it away. She had it with her in the hospital when she died.

THE LAST THING THAT GOES

Back on Mike and my anniversary, before we knew about Mom, Mike surprised me with a massage and spa treatment. It was steam, saunas, whatever. We just hung out in the sauna. It was great. We had breakfast and went there and hung out in the sauna for about three hours. I got a massage, and we went and got dinner. At dinner, my back, my lower back, started really killing me. Lower fucking back. And I was sleeping on it weird. I couldn't sleep, I was twitchy. I thought, *Oh, maybe the massage did something, maybe they tweaked it.* Then my dad came and woke us up at 8 am. And where my back hurt was exactly where mom's tumors were.

Later, my brother was spending the night at the hospital and I was at home. I had been wide awake for an hour, just laying in bed, staring at the ceiling, with a massive headache. My brother called at three in the morning. I immediately answered because I was wide awake, and he said, "Something happened to Mom. They're taking her down to surgery. She's unresponsive." She had been coughing a lot because it was in her lungs. She woke up and was coughing and woke my brother up. She sat up and let out a huge gasp.

The lesions on her brain had spread all over and bled out.

Then it was two days of her being unresponsive. Her hands were still warm. I was grabbing her hands really tightly. Her heart was still crazy strong. It took two full days. It would be nothing and then these huge gasping noises. It was her body trying to keep going. But any time any of us left to go smoke a cigarette, or go walk, it was just these frantic calls. I don't want to remember her like that.

People told us, "The last thing that goes is the hearing." Nurses were saying, "Just talk to her. Tell her how you're feeling. Play her the kind of music that she likes." Then the doctor told us that she had no brain function, and that removing the oxygen would speed up the process if we wanted. But they'd just told us that she was still in there, listening to us. It was this back-and-forth. We wanted to sit there and hold her hands. She was warm, and she was breathing, and we thought, *This needs to be on her terms.* But then it was thirty-six hours later, and family members started showing up to stare at us grieving.

Where I am right now, nothing is funny or happy. Wait, let's talk about something funny or happy. You've heard the story of me doing the little deaf girl thing, right?

ANNA-BUG, THE LITTLE DEAF GIRL

I was probably ten. The whole family was going to a movie in downtown Portland, and I think we got there early. It was like, "Oh, it doesn't start for forty-five minutes." So we went to Nordstrom's. My mom was looking at clothes, and I was looking at something in the girl-lady department. My mom checked the time and said, "Anna-bug, we gotta go." She called me Anna-bug. She called me Anna-bug in public until she died. And I would always say, "Mom, I'm thirty-five. My name is not Anna-bug."

She said, "Anna, Anna! Anna-bug!" Then she saw me, and I was just like looking at some clothes and ignoring her. She said, "Anna, we gotta go. Your brother and dad are waiting for us. We gotta go." I kept ignoring her, and she was like, "Anna! We have to leave! We need to leave! Don't pull the little deaf girl routine!" I think it was around Christmastime, and the place was packed. So I looked at her and said: [impersonates the speech of a deaf person and does mock sign language with her hands] "But—but Mom. I'm sorry. Did you call for me?" And every mom in the store was just glaring at her because they'd heard her yell, "Don't play that little deaf girl routine." I was like: [again impersonates the speech of a deaf person] "I didn't hear you call my name."

So then it was a running joke, but she was also pissed about it. We went back and forth with cruel jokes from there on, but she won in the end.

During my adolescence, she embarrassed me in public so many times. The best one was at Lloyd Center mall. I was like fourteen. I was awkward and in my body and just like—my sleeves pulled down, and I just felt weird in my own skin. I went in the bathroom with my mom once at Lloyd Center, and there were all these hot high school girls—popular cool high school girls—doing their makeup in the mirror. I didn't have to go to the bathroom, so I just stood there, and my mom went into one of the stalls. So I'm just leaning against the wall, and I hear "Anna-bug!" I said, "Yeah?" She said, "You stay against the wall. We don't get down, and we don't look under the stalls. That makes people uncomfortable. We stay against the wall when Mom's in the bathroom. We stay against the wall, and we don't get down on our knees, and we don't watch people while they go to the bathroom." There was just no way to respond to it. There's no way of coming across as cool in that situation, and then having a bunch of sixteen-year-old, seventeen-year-old girls there laughing.

Another time, we were going down the escalator at Pioneer Place mall. I think I was probably like fifteen, and there was a group of hot dudes in front of me that were probably a year or two older. My mom must have seen me making eyes at one of them because she said—totally out of nowhere—"I understand that you're mad, Anna-bug, but they do not make footed pajamas for girls your size. We can't find them!"

DO NOT SEND FLOWERS

Sympathy is weird. The way people feel like showing it is fucking weird. I mean, I get it, there's no right way to show it. But people make the pouty face and say, "I'm so sorry for you." My closest girlfriends have basically said, "I'm so sorry, please tell me what I can do." And when I haven't written to them in a few days, they have texted me to check in. That's perfect because it allows me to not respond when I can't, and I also know that they're thinking about me—but there's no obligation. I don't feel like I'm obligated to get back to anybody, and that's been great. Because I just don't always have the energy. But with some people it's just this nonstop: "I'm thinking about you. What can I do? What can I do? What can I do?" I don't want to talk to anybody. I don't want to talk to my closest friends right now, so I'm certainly not going to reach out to strangers or distant family members. But it's also just, like, people sharing their grief.

I don't post personal shit on Facebook. I just don't. I would much rather get drunk by myself and stew in my own shit than be like, "Hey guys, I'm sad today. Give me feedback." I'm also not in a position where I feel like I need to stop what I'm doing and write back to you to make you feel comfortable about what I'm going through.

If you're going to say something, just say, "Hey dude, just found out about this. Love you and I'm thinking about you. If you need me, please let me know." If you're not sure what to say, just say, "Hey, thinking about you."

Another old friend's response to the obituary was perfect. "Hey Anna, I'm so sorry you're going through this, please know that you have a ton of people, a ton of friends that love you and care about you—even old friends who you haven't seen for years." Just the fact that he took a second to write that, it was thoughtful and kind and really touching.

I have tons of fucking flowers, and they just die. Send a fucking plant. Like seriously. If anybody wants a good tip, do not fucking send flowers. Send a plant. I was at my parents' house—my dad's house—last weekend, and there were ten huge vases of dead flowers. He just didn't have the energy to deal with them. My dad can't even shave. And his house is filled with bouquets of dead flowers that he doesn't have the energy to take outside. My mom would be shitting herself right now if she saw all these dead, molding water flowers. Everywhere. So give some plants. Plants are easy. They live. You water them, they live.

TOO MANY PRAYERS

When I told my mom that there were so many people praying for her, my mom said, "I think there are too many people praying for me, and it's disrupting the balance of me getting better." But my dad and I were all for it. Any positive energy was great. My boss asked, "What's your mother's name?" I told her and she said, "I've been praying for you, and we have a whole prayer circle that's been praying for you for the last few weeks, and we'll be praying for your mom, too." I was all for it. Like, why the fuck not?

I think that's the hardest thing about this, not being religious. My dad and my brother and I sat on my parents' porch the day after my mom died, just drinking beers. Getting drunk and crying. Exhausted, and talking about just that. My dad was raised Catholic, and my mom was raised Lutheran, and my brother and I were not raised that way. We were raised with those values, absolutely. We went to church with my grandparents, and the religious values were definitely ingrained in us. Like, "Be kind to each other." But during this time, I just think faith would be the most comforting thing.

We were sitting on the porch, and we came to the conclusion that nobody fucking knows. But then again, right now, we get to believe whatever we want to believe. Whatever's comforting to us right now is what we get to believe. That in itself is comforting, but it's also a little too open-ended. I feel like if I had been raised with religion and was faithful to a religion— if I just knew in my heart that my mom was watching me, that she was someplace good—this would be so much easier. My mom was good. That would feel so good to me right now.

I know she's not in any place bad, though. I saw my dad last week and just burst into tears and said, "I miss her so fucking much." My dad was like, "She's not in the back bedroom, crying in pain right now."

She never hurt anybody, and she was kind to other human beings. There's no way in hell she's in any place bad. My biggest fear is that she's not anywhere. People say, "But she's in all your memories." But she's not *here*, so it doesn't help. I can't sleep at night because I'm thinking about her. I'll wake up in the middle of the night and be talking to a doctor. Or I'll see her at the hospital. Or replaying something in my head, or be thinking about her cremation. I have to snap myself out of it. She's not here.

A PAIN I'VE NEVER FELT BEFORE

Maybe it's the fact that we don't talk about it enough. As a society, we don't talk about death. It's kind of a private thing. How does this happen to people? How do people go through this every day? It's amazing to me and horrifying.

It's just the fact that people lose people every day in the world. There's nothing comforting to me about that. How do people move on? 'Cause right now I don't . . . and I'm not saying this in a weird, "I'm going to kill myself" way because I'm not. I promise. This isn't a cry for help, but I've been terrified of death and kind of obsessed with it since my friend Darcy got sick. I kind of don't care if I die right now. That's how shitty I feel, right now. I don't really want to be here dealing with this.

My mom would kill me for saying that. Again, I'm not threatening anything. I'm just saying that the pain of being here without her . . . I would give fucking anything to be with her again, and it's a pain I've never felt before. The people I've lost have been, like, grandparents who were in their eighties and had been sick for a really long time, or friends that overdosed, or friends that intentionally killed themselves. That's its own sort of pain. But it's not your mom. I feel physically ill. And I don't know when that passes.

About every other day, I stare up at the sky and burst into tears and say, "Where the fuck are you?" I wake up almost every morning thinking, *Oh wait, my mom's not here.*

EVERYTHING IS RELATED

I'm a depressive person already. But I never ever felt the kind of pain that I'm feeling right now. Ever. It's just every day, getting up. It just feels painful and shitty. It has been eighteen days. I don't like counting it down, but I do. Some days I wake up and I just think, *Why am I not better?* I was looking at the picture of my mom at my wedding today at work, and I broke down. So, yeah, I do that all the time, too.

Everything is related to it. There was a dying fly that was walking across my computer at work, and I was just staring at it like, "Maybe that's my mom." I kept pushing it away. I would never kill it because I have weird Buddhist tendencies, just like my mom did. It kept walking across the top of the monitor, and I was just thinking, *Maybe it's my mom trying to tell me something from some place.* It makes me feel like I'm insane.

One friend sent me a really nice, thoughtful message, and I replied, "Really, the lesson in all of this is never ever to be close to anyone, ever." Don't let anyone in.

JUST A LITTLE BIT OF HOPE

This is what religion is for. I want comfort. I want to know. Even if it's some dude telling me, "Anna, this is what happens after you die." I want that. That, to me, would be comforting right now.

What's weird is that my fear of death is gone. I never thought I would get to that point. I've always been very interested in death. I've always been fascinated by it. But it's always scared the shit out of me. And whatever it is that's keeping me going believes that there's some comfort in it—and I think that it's the level of grief that I'm at right now, where I kind of don't give a fuck. Which is sad, but I don't really recognize that fear I used to have.

There's just a little bit of hope in my head that maybe I could say hi to my mom and hold her for a second before I go off to wherever we go? I really don't like the idea of cremation. I don't like the idea of being burnt up. I like the idea of being buried, in the ground, in like a cardboard box filled with flowers under a beautiful tree. I like the idea of my body falling apart and nourishing a tree. That's comforting to me, way more than being cremated. Maybe there could still be a gravestone. Who knows? When you go to the cemetery and there are wooden boxes under the ground, that seems weird. But if your body is down there growing some sort of beautiful bush? It's so hard to do natural burials right now. I watched a whole long documentary about it.

THE END

You know, death is not fun. It's fucking gruesome. I have this picture of my mom in my head, taking her last breath and turning gray. It's miserable. But I would rather be there holding her hand and experiencing that than to have her mouth glued shut afterward and have makeup applied to her body to make her look normal. That's pretty fucked up.

My grandmother died when I was in college. I think I was twenty-one or twenty-two. I was there when she died. And all her kids were there. She was sick for a really long time, and she was very meticulous—there were things that she wanted to be in the room, she was wearing a particular nightgown. She helped pick out her casket, and there were items she wanted in there with her. She'd been in the hospital a long time and had tubes and wires attached to her. When she passed away, all of the women detached her from this stuff, and all of us cleaned her with her favorite soap, and dressed her. We washed her hair and put it up the way that she wanted it before she was taken away. There was a beauty in being delicate and kind and caring for her body after she died. It was a respect thing. There was something lovely about it.

Before my mom died, there were too many people in there. People just started showing up. There were people sitting around in chairs, and my mom's gasping, barely breathing. Every time I'm holding my mom, I look up and there's somebody just standing there. When she died, my cousin and my aunt and I were going to do the same thing. Her hair was a terrible mess. She had a catheter and a pick line and tubes everywhere.

I could not do it. She had a whisker on her chin, and I went and got tweezers and plucked it out. My mom would be so pissed if she knew there was this black whisker on her chin. It would drive her insane. So we're cleaning her to be cremated. I tried to stay in there, and I couldn't. My aunt and my cousin stayed in there, and they gently cleaned her body and took her out of the hospital gown, and put her in her nightgown that she loved. They took the rats' nest out of her hair. They did it gently and lovingly. I would do it in a second for anybody else, who I could be there for. But it was too close. I couldn't.

I was also incredibly comforted knowing that some random person wasn't pulling tubes out of my mom and throwing a blanket over her. It was people who cared for her, and they were gentle and they moved her limbs awkwardly into the nightgown. They made her look more like herself, so that we could say good-bye.

I came into the room one more time after that.

She was gray. She was gone.

Ever since my friend Darcy got sick, when I drive past that hospital I am the most patient driver in the world—because I remember going there to see my friend. I remember crying in the car and I remember everything. When my mom was there, it was the same thing. People come in and out of that parking lot, and they're not driving fast enough, or they're not using their blinker—they're not in a good spot. I will always know how that feels.

\\

CONDUCTED OCTOBER 15, 2015

KATHERINE MacLEAN
PSYCHEDELIC SCIENTIST

A friend introduced Katherine MacLean to me as a woman who lived on a farm in rural Connecticut, studied psychedelic mushrooms, and had been brainstorming about something called "the psychedelic hospice" after her sister's death. I knew immediately that I had to talk to her.

The psychedelic hospice turns out to be a relatively modest proposal, albeit an idea that's still in its infancy. Psychedelic drugs could play a role, but the meat of the concept is in respecting a dying person's wishes, and perhaps guiding them into death rather than encouraging them to fight like hell for a little more life. There's a sort of magic in hearing MacLean speak about this hypothetical dying place, which is so transformative and life affirming that even healthy people would want to visit.

MacLean occupies a space somewhere between science and activism. She's aware of this, and often, after stating a deeply held belief about the healing potential of psychedelics, her scientist side finds her playing devil's advocate and suggesting sobering alternate theories. This trait is incredibly endearing, but it also prompted a question: Aren't those scientists who study psychedelics, but have never taken them, just as potentially biased as someone who has, like MacLean?

That tension—along with her sister's unexpected death—was one of the things that led MacLean away from the lab-based studies she worked on at Johns Hopkins University. "I just found that there were limits to where science could answer my most meaningful personal questions," she says. "There's always some subjectivity. But for me, that line has been a lot more blurred."

THE CLASSIC BAD TRIP

If I trace my interest in death back, it kind of parallels my experiences with psychedelics. I had my own recreational experiences with psychedelics in college, and then after college I moved to California. I took mushrooms at this party, and it was kind of a bad idea. Everyone else was drinking; I was the only one on mushrooms. I remember putting myself in a bedroom and shutting the door. It was kind of intense. At one point I looked in the mirror, and it felt like an arrow that went straight through my brain. It was something about existential truth, or the truth about life and death. At first it was really cool. I was like, *Self-inquiry can lead me to the truth.* That's what came through. Then it was terrifying because I knew that I'd have to confront death.

The rest of the night was just terrible: the classic bad trip. I felt like I was physically going to die. I was apologizing to my boyfriend—my now-husband. It was such a bad idea. I was like, "If I die in my sleep, tell all these people I love them." It was totally dramatic and over the top. Of course, I was fine, but every time I've encountered psychedelics since then, that idea has been in the background: that this is not fun and games, that this is connected to the real importance of life and death and the truth about reality—and that no matter what I did, it was going to keep calling me back. That was kinda scary.

After that, I was just captivated by this question of "What is the truth of reality?" I also got into meditation. I did some retreats.

All in all, I think I'm probably naturally more into the philosophical side of things than the scientific side. Science is really compelling because I like things to be organized, and I like solving problems. With philosophy, you can never completely solve a problem that you're faced with. At least with science, you can get answers. So I found that part of science very compelling. I still do. If there's a problem in my life that I'm trying to solve, I will experiment with what works and what doesn't and keep track.

I kept studying the things that I found the most compelling, so I was studying meditation and then I studied psilocybin. I wanted to study psychedelics in grad school, but no one was really doing it at that time. So I studied a really boring version of vigilance, or sustained attention, as a way of getting my dissertation. I was also helping out with a new meditation project, which is still ongoing. We took sixty people and studied them for three months of retreat. They were full-time monastics for three months, but they were Westerners, normal people. We lived at the retreat center and studied them basically around the clock. It was kind of the closest thing I could get to doing the psychedelic work.

In the middle of that project, in 2006, the Johns Hopkins study was published that linked psilocybin and mystical experiences, and I was like, "Oh, that's definitely where I'm going next." I'm kind of happy I had the background in meditation first.

THE JOHNS HOPKINS STUDY

The day-to-day work at Hopkins was a mix of sitting at a desk in front of a computer, writing and analyzing data, and having meetings. But the other end of the extreme was having these all-day sessions with volunteers.

Our volunteers would get assigned two guides: one head guide and an assistant. Ideally, the head guide was someone who had facilitated a bunch of sessions before and had been trained. The assistant could be a research assistant or a postdoc student. You'd meet with the volunteer a few times, for an hour or two each meeting, and the idea was to get a full life history from that person and also cover the basics of what they should expect during the session.

We were dealing mostly with healthy people. It could take more preparation if someone had a trauma history or something. But we would go through this whole life review and preparation. Then, in the morning before each session, there was a little ritual that we'd do to offer the capsule—which had psilocybin in it that was prepared at the pharmacy—to the volunteer.

It was double-blind, so we didn't really know what was in the capsule. Everyone was getting some amount of psilocybin, but it might have been so little that there'd be no effect. In the study that I was a part of, it ended up being that some people got almost nothing. Basically you either got almost nothing or a substantial amount. People will claim that the blinding doesn't work with psychedelics—because how could you not know—but I found that the blinding actually works well. Sometimes people had effects that looked really strong, and there was nothing at all going on, and vice versa. Sometimes people got a very high dose, and it didn't seem to have much effect.

They would take the capsule, and the effects would start in about an hour. Most of the day they were laying on a couch with eyeshades and headphones, listening to a classical music soundtrack. If things were going fine, we would just check in every half hour or hour. There was a break in the middle of the day, where they could go to the bathroom, and then we'd end about seven hours later. But if things were really tough, there were all sorts of methods we would use: reassuring them that they had taken psilocybin, that we were with them, that they were safe, and also just holding their hand and being with them physically. Sometimes it took a lot more than that, depending on whether or not effects were really strong, and it was hard for people to orient themselves. Then it was a lot of just physically keeping them safe.

The head guide at Hopkins, Bill Richards, was involved in the original psychedelic studies in the sixties, and a lot of it is run on the apprenticeship model of continually passing on the techniques that worked the best. For the most part, the methods come from the kind of humanistic and trans-personal methods of the sixties, and positive psychology.

Every single person's experience was really different, which I found really cool, because it's the same drug, same setting, and the same preparation. And I was the same person from session to session, as much as I could be. But the experiences were wildly different. Almost universally positive, in the long run: even people who had a really tough time during the session, it was universally a positive thing once they integrated back into their life. The results were very clear: No matter what happens during the session, the effects afterward are positive. That's compelling for people who are in pain or people who are dying.

A PROFOUND EXPERIENCE
OF YOUR OWN DEATH

We had a question, "Did you have a profound experience of your own death?" People could rate it zero to five. When I went back into the data and looked at just the people who said four or five, it was only about 30 percent of all the study volunteers. But almost 70 percent of the people I had guided rated that question a 4 or 5. So it was like, "Okay, I'm seeing something here that's a real phenomenon. Maybe they haven't focused on it in previous research because it's not as common as what I'm seeing."

I was processing this death stuff, and just thinking about the interactive nature of what the person's going through and what I'm bringing into the room. I mostly worked with young people, so it could just be that the young people who were in the study had these big life-and-death questions as well. It wasn't totally random. If a new volunteer came in, they would assign them to the best guide that they felt could support them. So I ended up mostly guiding young people.

Some people described feeling like they were kind of traveling through past lives that they'd had, taking on different identities, experiencing things that were either a long time ago in history or far into the future, or somewhere not on earth. I certainly had people who felt like they were out of their bodies, or that their bodies completely dissolved, especially at the peak of the session. I had people who were completely quiet and calm and peaceful the entire time, who had really profound spiritual experiences that just—they were completely disconnected from this world while they were having them.

I did not see many people have classic encounters with religious figures or deities or anything. But there was one guy who, during this Indian chanting music, was chanting along with the music, and then all of the sudden, his voice shifted, and I don't know what was coming out of his mouth. It wasn't the chant, and it didn't sound like him.

I didn't experience this, but I know that some volunteers encountered dead family members, had reconciliation with people who were no longer living.

For the most part, if people had a really intense dissolving or death-like experience, and their ego-resistance was low enough, then they just kind of had the experience and then felt really good about it afterward. In a way it was kind of a relief. But one volunteer in particular was really terrified, and most of the session was helping coach him to be okay with dying, basically. We tell them this ahead of time, that they might feel like they're dying or dissolving or whatever, and we will encourage them to do that. We're not encouraging them to physically die, but we're encouraging them to let go to that experience, and that we promise to keep them physically safe. We tell them that ahead of time, so that when they're going through it, and we say, "You can just die," or "You can let go," there's no confusion.

I don't know how I feel about this, but I know there are some elder psychedelic folks who are convinced that if you really will yourself to die on a psychedelic, you can just die. There's one woman in California— do you know Sasha Shulgin, who developed all those new psychedelic chemicals? His wife, Ann, had people agree to a verbal contract that said, "I promise not to die or harm myself during this session." Because she really believed it was up to you whether you stayed or went. It sometimes happens in Iboga ceremonies, which is a really intense kind of initiation in West Africa. People die sometimes, and there's some debate over whether there's something about the drug that's potentially lethal to people with certain heart conditions. But when I hear those stories, I wonder, *Maybe if your spirit isn't ready to be initiated then it will just leave?*

A SEETHING FORCE FIELD
OF ENERGY WITHOUT FORM

I think I realized by the time I had been at Johns Hopkins for a few years that I didn't really want to do science so much as I wanted to study these compelling questions around life and death and the mind.

I was like, *Oh, I don't want to be a career academic scientist. I want to keep solving this life-and-death riddle, or whatever it is.* It was really cool to work with other people in pursuit of that truth, but ultimately when it really comes down to it, I was more concerned about my own state of reality. "How do I exist? What does it mean to exist?"

Two things happened toward the end of my tenure at Hopkins.

One was I had a very unusual experience in meditation. In Buddhism, it's something about a realization of emptiness, where I was shown that the nature of reality is a seething force field of energy without form. Some people experience it as really blissful or freeing, and for other people it's really terrifying. For me it was terrifying. It launched me into a several-month period where even just to maintain stability, I had to constantly be asking myself, "Where am I? Where is my mind?" It was very powerful because it forced me into the present moment, for months at a time.

Right after the experience, I started having major breathing difficulties. I had a history of asthma, but it was never something that just came on out of nowhere. This was months and months of deep chest pain, coughing, and asthma. I went on a daily medication that usually only emphysema sufferers take. I was still active, but I could feel this thing in my lungs. So I'd been paying attention to my lungs.

Shortly after that, in this totally strange twist of fate, my sister went into the hospital with metastatic breast cancer. And where my sister's cancer eventually came back was throughout her lungs. I had felt like I was on the edge of death for six or seven months, and then I was literally on the edge of death with my sister, who was basically every single day less and less able to breathe.

All of a sudden, I knew that I had been preparing for this moment my entire life. How could I have known, taking shrooms at a party, that a few years later I would be helping my sister die at the age of twenty-nine?

I FELT LIKE WE HAD DONE THIS BEFORE

So much came together for me in her hospital room that I felt like that's why I had been so well prepared. I thought these experiences I'd had were just about me, and then I realized that I was being prepared to help my sister when no one else could really do that for her. It's like all of a sudden my life became much weirder and much more important.

I don't know how I feel about it now as I say this, but at the time, with my sister I felt—I'll just say the words: I felt like we had done this before. In some capacity, we had both done what we were doing at that time before. I don't know what I mean by that now. What would it mean for there to be some past incarnation of us practicing her death? Or what would it mean for us to incarnate as sisters so that she could die in this way?

It felt completely planned. It wasn't random. Something about her life was being sacrificed as an example, so that then I could take that and teach others and kind of change how people die. This, again, kind of loops back to psychedelics because people will have an experience on psychedelics and then create a story around it—and no one ever really knows if the story was the real experience or if it was just added on later. I don't know, maybe our minds are just that fast. This thing happens, it sucks, it's crazy, and so we create a nice story around it so that afterward we have something we can do with it.

I guess I should emphasize again that at the time of the weird meditation experience I had, during the six or seven months before she went in the hospital, she was completely healthy. Completely. The doctors were like, "You're in remission, there's no cancer, you're good to go." She moved her family to Connecticut, where I live now. She was thinking about having another child. It wasn't even on the horizon that her cancer could come back, and things were going so well for me at Hopkins at the time. Everything was totally fine, and then these two experiences—the meditation experience and her death—just blindsided me.

SHE WANTED TO GO, AND SHE GOT THE RIGHT GUIDE

The doctors were saying she had months, at least, and I was looking at her thinking, *She's got maybe a week.* I think she held on up until the point when she realized her quality of life was going to plummet, and then she was like, "That's it, I'm out." From that moment, it only took two or three days, and I was continually guiding her to let go. I think that she was able to die as quickly as she did because she wanted to. Not that she didn't want to live anymore, but the calculus was just like, "I'm not going to ever be able to breathe better. I'm in horrible pain. My four-year-old daughter is going to see me like this for months instead of weeks."

The doctors were shocked. This was at Memorial Sloan Kettering in New York City. They see cancer patients all the time. They literally were just like, "What happened? How did this happen so quickly?" For me, it was obvious. She wanted to go, and she got the right guide. You know? I don't know how many people in that scenario have that combination of the intention and a person there saying, "It's totally okay to die."

Her doctor was focused on survival, and he wasn't focused on what she actually needed, which was mostly palliative care. My dad was definitely on the side of "Fight this." I remember a couple times, he said, "I hope someone is always in the room telling her she's gonna make it." When he was in the room, it was "You can do this," and "You're strong."

I think my mom was really supportive of her letting go, once she realized what was happening. My sister's husband, I think, was really conflicted. He obviously didn't want her to die, and he kind of felt similar to the doctors; he was shocked to see how quickly she deteriorated. In the last two days of her life, though, I told him that basically we were going to make this as good as possible for her. He's told me since that, at that moment, he was all in. Whatever it took.

I think I was on board the earliest, and then I slowly brought people on board who were ready. My dad never really got to the point of being ready, until probably the last day. By the end, what my sister had was essentially a whole team of people who loved her the most, saying, "It's totally okay."

BEING LIBERATED FROM HER BODY WAS GOING TO BE AN ECSTATIC THING

The thing about my sister's death is that she didn't want to take psychedelics. She wanted to die in the hospital. She wanted all the pain released. She wanted to basically try as much as she could until she couldn't anymore. But I really wanted my sister to be at home. I wanted to get her out of the hospital. I even entertained this fantasy that maybe it would help for her to do MDMA or something. The only thing she wanted was pain relief.

I kind of came away from that feeling like maybe the hard push for psychedelics in death, or psychedelics in cancer patients, ignores the segment of the population who has no interest in taking a different kind of drug—but they still want the same type of support. When we give someone a high dose of psilocybin, there are only two people there in the room. Your guide is the most important person in the world at that moment. I feel like we could get maybe 80 percent of the improvement in death and dying if we just modeled the experience after that, rather than adding a new drug on top of it.

I had gone through what felt like death practice myself, through that weird meditation experience and through the daily practice that I was doing. I had a meditation teacher who shows people, basically, how to die: how to dissolve your own ego. He had been coaching me the entire time, leading up to her death. This teacher seemed very happy. I had confidence that this path leads to more happiness, not to more pain. I had also just been on a silent Zen retreat with Joan Halifax, who is a big death and dying person in the Zen community. The experience I had there was so uplifting and positive and liberating that I just felt that what I was guiding my sister into was not this oblivion, but that I was guiding her toward something that was going to be liberating and blissful.

I don't know, maybe I was wrong, but I was convinced that I was helping her out of a situation that was very painful, and into something that was much better than that. Whether there was an afterlife or not, simply being liberated from her body was going to be an ecstatic thing.

I was with her, and since I didn't know what else to try, I just started trying a lot of things I had been trained to do. At each step I kept being surprised by how well it worked and how appropriate it was. There would be moments where I'd just be like, *Is this a weird thing to say?* And I would just try it, and it would help her. So it was more that I just kind of learned as I went, because there was really nothing else I needed to do.

When I wasn't interacting with her directly, I was sitting in meditation. I kind of drew on the two things I knew how to do—meditate and sit with people who are on psychedelics—and if those two things didn't work, I probably wouldn't have been very helpful—but they worked.

Mostly I was paying attention to my sister's breath, and my breath, and just doing really basic things that she needed done, like dealing with the clothes she was wearing or the oxygen or the food or the water—all that minutiae. It was very ordinary. It was like, just deal with what's coming up right now. The nights were really tough. Once I left the hospital, everything would kind of flood back, and I would be really upset and scared and kind of projecting out into the future and worrying. But when I was there with her, all of that just kind of went away. It wasn't like I had no fear at all, but when I was with her, I knew that it was the right thing to do. It was very easy to be in the present moment because all of my other life concerns were just irrelevant compared to that.

I think that's been a question for me: I want to help other people in the same way, but will I ever be as motivated as I was to help my sister? How can I call upon that same motivation for a stranger, and can you fake it enough to help someone? Does it have to be completely real?

"I'M YOUR SISTER, AND I'M DYING,
BUT I'M ALSO THIS GOD"

My sister died on a Monday night. This was Sunday night. Sunday was very chaotic, and Sunday morning was the first time that she had said, "I'm ready to go." Most of the day Sunday, she just kept asking me, "Why am I not dead yet? I've made up my mind. Why can't I just die?" Most of Sunday was a lot of visits with family and me trying to help her understand that it wasn't just a matter of deciding to die—that her body had to die, and that that was different from her mind. She was kind of coming in and out of consciousness, and it was very chaotic and confusing, but it was very clear to me and the family that she wanted to die.

By Sunday night, we'd all kind of come to terms with this. We just didn't know how long there was left. It felt like her death was imminent. That night, it was just me, my husband, and my mom in her room with her. I think that was the first night they put her on a steady morphine drip, so as much as she wanted, basically. It was the first night that she'd had relief in a while. She was sedated. It was probably two in the morning or something. I remember my mom was sleeping on this pull-out couch bed in the corner, and my husband and I were sitting with my sister, holding her hands. Later on, my husband told me that what he was doing was breathing in sync with her, just to try to ground himself and to keep supporting her.

She was totally sedated, and without opening her eyes, she pulled her leg up so that she was in this strange kind of position, and she put her hands out. It was a very specific kind of body mudra, and she had the oxygen hose coming off of her face. So, for a moment, I was like, "She looks like an elephant."

And then she was this god, Ganesha.

It wasn't like I was trying to see this thing in her—that I was filling in the gaps. I was just suddenly in the presence of this god. The room and everything around me took on the feeling of psilocybin. I didn't hear her voice say this, but—I'll call it "telepathically"—she said something like, "I'm your sister, and I'm dying, but I'm also this god who has been meditating in bliss for eternity, so it's cool. Don't worry about it."

I'd never, ever had anything like that happen to me before.

Now I know a ton about Ganesha because, obviously, I was compelled after that experience to learn more. But when I was there with my sister, I didn't know much at all. I just knew that there was this elephant-headed god. But afterward, that Ganesha symbol became a total point of orientation throughout everything that happened after my sister died.

Ganesha is known in Hinduism as the remover of obstacles. An American friend living in Nepal told me that he's one of the gods who hangs out in the dying grounds, the cremation grounds, to help people navigate the path between life and death. And the elephant is also all about having this perfect memory, right? You never forget. I took it as this total spiritual package and the last thing that my sister was going to give to me before she was out of here.

It was like, *This is going to last the rest of your life. Here's this mysterious package. Go with it.* And still now, I can kind of see it in my mind's eye. I have an altar. I have Ganesha on the altar. I have my sister's ashes.

Psychedelics and meditation were never really a focus for my sister, and she was generally kind of interested in what I did, but not that into it. She would probably hear me tell this story and be like, "That's fucking strange." She was very practical about her life. It was awesome to see because—compared to a lot of people who meditate and are allegedly religious and are actually jerks—she lived her entire life helping people. She was really effective at everything she did, and she didn't do any of the stuff that people claim to need to do to be enlightened.

It feels a little bit like a kind of cosmic joke from her, that she was going to give me this last little bit to live with, knowing that in real life she would never be into it.

I WOKE UP, AND I WAS SOBBING

I still remember waking up the night after she died—we were staying in one of those crappy patient hotel rooms that's right near the hospital; me, my husband, and my mom. I woke up, and I was sobbing, and I just kept saying, "I feel like there's more I could have done," or "I just don't know if I did the right thing." I was kind of plagued by that afterward. I felt like maybe I hadn't listened closely enough, or I had interjected my own ideas too much.

One thing is that I really felt like I had screwed up by leaving her body in the hospital. I felt like it was not the right thing to do, but I didn't know what else to do. It was so strange to help shepherd her all the way up until that moment and then just leave her. I felt that something about her spirit was a little confused or wandering for a week or two until she was cremated because we had left her body unattended. That kind of haunted me.

I think that came from my understanding of Tibetan Buddhism. In that tradition, you attend the body for a certain amount of time after the physical death. They believe that there's certain subtle energies that exist after physical death, and the spirit can even hang out until the spirit knows that the person is clearly dead. They'll kind of hang around and be confused. That's also why they do cremation and other means of completely returning the body to the natural world because anything that's left over could be confusing to getting that person to reincarnate or to keep going.

THE PSYCHEDELIC HOSPICE

The entire time I was with my sister in the hospital, my focus was on her. Then, as soon as she died, my mind was like, *What are you going to do with this experience?* The answers that came were: *You're leaving your job at Hopkins, you're going to write a book about this*—I still don't know what "this" means—*and you're going to help people die.* I was so impressed by my sister's palliative care doctors that I immediately thought, *This is what I want to do. I finally know what I want to be when I grow up!*

Leaving my job at Hopkins was the easiest thing to do, and it was still pretty hard. I've kind of been stuck on the other two humongous tasks, and I think the psychedelic hospice concept came out of that: *How do I talk about this in a way that people will understand? How do I write about it? If I do write about it, is it going to be beneficial to anyone other than my family? And how do I help people die if I don't want to go back to med school?*

I started thinking about how my sister's experience itself seemed psychedelic, and how it could have been a lot better if she wasn't in a hospital. I think the first time I spoke publicly about what I had gone through, that's when people started coming up to me and saying, "Have you thought about using your sister's death as a model and working that into something like a psychedelic dying center or something?" I can't fully take credit for the idea of a psychedelic hospice. It was kind of developed over time, and it seemed like every time I talked about my sister and my experience at Hopkins and my hope for the future, people kept coming up, like, "What about psychedelic hospice?" A lot of people think it's a good idea, but no one really knows what it means.

DEATH ITSELF AS THE SACRAMENTAL RITUAL

In my mind, "psychedelic hospice" means a manner of helping people die that doesn't necessarily involve different drugs. It's just a manner of holding space and guiding them through the experience that is modeled after the way we are trained to guide people through psychedelics. What I did with my sister was exactly what I used to do with people at Hopkins.

I think there are some Catholic and Zen hospices that do the kinds of practices I did with my sister, but I think standard hospices are still more institutional. It's still more a lot about pain relief and the physical stuff, rather than these existential or spiritual concerns.

A good friend of mine who was a shamanic practitioner and knowledgeable about psychedelics used to work in hospice, and he tried to use drumming and singing, which are really effective in helping pain. He would get in trouble with the hospice. "That's not our protocol. You're not allowed to do that." He would resist. Sometimes they would say, "We need to give this person more morphine because a family member is really upset that they're in pain." He'd be like, "Well, maybe we should give the family member some morphine because this person doesn't want it. I'm sorry it's distressing to people around them, but this isn't what they want for their death experience." He eventually retired from hospice, and he said he would want to do something like what I'm talking about, with psychedelic hospice, but include all these other modalities, too.

Esalen is this gorgeous spa near these natural hot springs on the cliffs of the Pacific in California. They've got a garden there, they've got delicious food, there's massage. It's beautiful. There are little hiking trails. What if you had a place like that where people died? That's totally a place that healthy people already really wanna go. They'll pay huge amounts of money to go there for a few nights. It doesn't take too much for me to imagine a place like Esalen that revolves around dying people. Add some animals so that there's an interactive component for either kids or teenagers or whatever—I could see families wanting to spend a restorative time there with their dying family member. I don't know what the price tag on something like that is, but we already have these kind of retreat spa environments that people are paying to go to. The question is, how do you make it so that it's not just another elite, New Age thing?

How do you create a space—and how do you support people—so that death itself can be this transformative, psychedelic experience for the person who is dying and for their close family and friends who are there with them? Because if everything we've found is true about psychedelics, then the experience itself—not just the drug—should help people in their life.

Rather than sign a young woman up for a high-dose psilocybin experience, where she just has it and no one else really gets to benefit directly, what if you assign a young person to attend to someone who's dying? And what if that experience is just as powerful or more powerful, and then it propels them into a life of meaning and service? Then we're not talking about taking mushrooms as the sacrament, or MDMA, we're talking about death itself as the sacramental ritual that everyone participates in.

Of course, the other, trickier side is, how do you actually administer psychedelic drugs in a hospice setting? When do you do it, what doses, what drugs, and how do you not screw up the process for someone? I think the assumption is it's just going to make it better, but what if it doesn't? One of my concerns is that we set up a hospice where psilocybin becomes the next morphine. That it helps people, but everyone thinks, *Oh, this is my only option. I better take it.* Some people aren't looking to dredge up every single thing from their past before they die and share it with their families. My concern would be if things are going pretty well, then a high-dose session could stir up all of this old stuff that may be really difficult to work through in the time that's remaining.

I think psychedelics are great for anyone who has existential concerns, whether that's a healthy person who has anxiety, a person who is aging and is wondering what's coming next, or someone who is actually ill. They can be very helpful during the active dying process, but not exclusively in the last few days. When the physical body is really starting to break down, there's something that starts shifting in consciousness that is already psychedelic. It would be ideal to time it so that people have a few months left—it's almost like a practice session for death. A psychedelic can help people move into that space, and then they still have a few months to work through the actual physical process. During that time, I think it would also be great to include family members. Not necessarily have them *taking* the psychedelic, but at least being there with the person so that there's a bridge and it's not just a professional person coming in and administering this thing and then leaving.

That's what I really want to do: work with young people and their families. That's not the primary clientele in most hospices. I just feel that I have the most help to offer young people. It's one thing to convince an eighty-year-old person with metastatic cancer that it's okay to die; it's a totally different thing to convince a twenty-nine-year-old with a young daughter and a family. I feel like the bigger message is that it can be a really positive experience, even when there's so much to live for. That it's not just, "Oh, you've had a great life, and now the only next thing to do is die." I feel like that will take a lot of fear out of the equation for some people, if we can normalize even those kind of tragic, young deaths.

When I've asked people I know who aren't into drugs, just ordinary people, "Would you take a high dose of psilocybin at this point in your life?" Most of them say, "No, I don't have any need for it." But if I ask them would they take it if they were dying, almost everyone says yes. Either "Yes, I'd consider it," or "Yes, definitely, I would do it." That seems to me to be a shift in how people are thinking about it.

THE CIRCLE

The Zen teacher I was learning from said that if I'm enlightened, I should be happy with how I'm caring for every single living being. If I'm not at that point, of being happy with how I'm treating everyone and everything, then I'm not enlightened, and I've still got work to do.

For me, maybe these last few years of experiences were enough to just shake me out of this very self-centered, selfish mode of achievement and living a life that makes me happy. Finally, I had to care for my sister in a totally selfless way, as much as I could, and now I try to do that for my daughter.

My circle, I hope, is continually widening. There are all sorts of people who I don't treat nearly as well as I treated my sister or I treat my daughter. That circle should be a lot wider than just your immediate family. Death has a way of either totally making you focus only on your own pain and grief or, if you work on it with intention, you can widen your circle.

CONDUCTED NOVEMBER 3, 2015

HOLLY PRUETT
LIFE-CYCLE CELEBRANT

Holly Pruett officiates ceremonies from cradle to grave—think baby bless-ings, weddings, retirement rituals, and so on—but her interest in funeral rites has made her one of the central figures of Portland, Oregon's burgeoning DIY death scene. Through the Death Talk Project, she plays an important role in organizing Death Cafes—conversational gatherings where strangers come to talk about death— along with symposiums and public ceremonies with a focus on death and grieving. She also hosts a monthly death-themed movie night at a local theater, and she organized a sold-out conference in 2015 called Death:OK.

It's easy to see why she's had success as a facilitator and organizer. Before we'd even begun our interview—in Pruett's quiet, two-story house in Northeast Portland—she had asked me a handful of questions about my project. I explained that death was still more of an academic concept to me than a cold reality. "I still think your experience is crucial," she told me, undeterred. "You're a generational representative: A lot of people your age are starting to ask these same questions. And your experience is really unique. People are going to want to read about that."

So I'll share. Talking with Holly really sort of rattled me. I have always looked at cherished social conventions like weddings and funerals as old-fashioned relics. But I never spent much time thinking about what, if anything, they ought to be replaced with. That's Holly's line of work. She is a certified Life-Cycle Celebrant, and while that term may elicit images of tree-people wearing white dresses and daisy chains, praising "the goddess," Holly is clear-eyed about the need for ritual in our lives. Ever since our talk, I've been keenly aware of its absence.

CONVERGENCE

I was a history major. One of those programs that qualifies you for everything and nothing. During my senior year, I saw an ad for volunteer training for the Portland Women's Crisis Line.

The women who I had the good fortune to be trained under were the founders of these institutions that came out of the seventies. They had, out of nothing, created rape hotlines and battered women's shelters and established the first real laws pushing for equal opportunities and protections for women.

I saw myself as a part of a social justice movement, but the Crisis Line also exposed me to all the social services that make up the safety net, and political advocacy. I worked on violence against women and children for ten years, for a series of organizations. During that time, I'd come out as a lesbian. I became involved in fighting Measure 8 in 1988,* and then Measure 9 in '92.**

After a two-year, super intense battle, Measure 9 lost, but the group behind it—the Oregon Citizens' Alliance—basically said, "Thanks for helping us edit the most inflammatory language out of this measure, we're filing tomorrow to come back in two years." So we had stopped a bad thing from getting into the state constitution, but there was no permanent organization, or a voter file, or an ongoing donor list. I also spent

---

* A statewide ballot measure which revoked the governor's order banning discrimination based on sexual orientation in state executive department employment and services.

** The measure's text would have added language comparing homosexuality to necrophilia and bestiality to the Oregon state constitution, and forced government institutions and schools to discourage such behavior.

two years building the LGBT rights group Basic Rights Oregon into a campaign-ready organization.

During that effort, someone said to me, "Would you like to come join our public relations firm?" I'm like, "What's public relations?" So I worked as a public affairs director, then an independent consultant.

There's been a thread in my life of being someone who listens and then helps to project ideas back out through various forms of media—creating ways for other people to engage with big questions.

In my last organizational job, I was working with parents and teachers to advocate for public schools. But as I was approaching my own middle age, I felt like I was really pretty far removed from the everyday stuff of people's lives. You go through these annual political cycles, and it can be really frustrating. I had gotten to the point of burnout.

Around that time, a friend read in *People* magazine about a burial ground in South Carolina called Ramsey Creek Preserve, started by a physician who believed that if people were buried in a natural wooded setting, it would give their friends and families a conservation ethic and also help to conserve land. My friend thought, *If this is in* People *magazine, and it's happening in South Carolina, why is it not happening in Oregon, the so-called green sustainability capital?*

We started our own personal self-study, wondering, "Gosh, would we want to open up a green burial ground? What would it take?" When we got in touch with the national Green Burial Council, they said, "You know, there's somebody else who's expressed interest in your town." It happened to be a woman who was a Life-Cycle Celebrant. I got together with her and asked, "What's a Life-Cycle Celebrant?" When she described it, I was like, whoa. It seemed to be a convergence of many of the things that I was interested in.

From the crisis intervention work that I did early on, I got a sense of what it was like to work in a social service setting. But I think I longed to work more culturally. I wanted to connect in other ways. Life-Cycle Celebrancy seemed like a way to work directly with people, to think about how we make meaning with each other, and to address the void that I experienced in my story with my own dad.

WELL, HAVE A NICE LIFE!

My dad was in fantastic health at age sixty-three, when, after a cross-country ski run, there was no longer denying that he had some sort of tremor. He went in to the doctor, and they discovered that he had a massive glioblastoma, which is a deadly form of brain cancer. They gave him six months to live. He was a surgeon, and he had gone into that field to have the power to fix things. He and my stepmom were extremely wary of living with any disabilities. They had an understanding: "If that ever happens to me, put a pillow over my head." They were quite clear with each other that they would not want to live in such a circumstance.

But my dad got there, both from the surgery and the tumor itself. He pretty quickly lost a lot of his speech capability, the ability to write, the ability to walk very sturdily and then to walk at all. But he wanted to live every day in that condition. My stepmother was, of course, very bereaved. They both knew that this was not a cancer that one survived. For her, it may have been more merciful if he had died shortly after his diagnosis. Instead, he lasted eighteen months.

My life had been formed around my dad's absence. My parents divorced when I was twelve, and my dad moved from Connecticut to Hawaii. My sister and went there for the summers, but, you know, that was a big separation at that age. The ability to be very present and engaged during his eighteen months of terminal illness was a huge gift. It was the best my relationship ever was with my dad. I think for my dad that time was a huge gift. You see this in people with diseases like Lou Gehrig's. People often investigate getting aid in dying through Death with Dignity, or maybe they even get the prescription because they think they want it, but then they don't use it. Because for some people, wow, once you get there, actually you want every day, alive.

After my dad reached the end of his eighteen-month illness, my stepmother was very clear: He hadn't wanted a funeral. It was also clear to me that she couldn't handle one more thing. But I'd gone through this amazingly intimate eighteen months, where I provided care for my dad and respite for my stepmother for a day a week. I lived with them for the last summer of his life.

Then when he died, the funeral home came in—it was just going to be direct cremation—they put him in a body bag, and they drove off. That's it. It's kind of like, "Well, have a nice life! Good luck figuring it out!"

My stepmother gave me a portion of his ashes in a yogurt container, and she thoughtfully curated some of his stuff that she thought I would want. Six months later, I put together a memorial for my dad in the backyard here at my house. I timed it such that my mom could attend. My sister didn't want to be here. She didn't need it. But for my mom, this had been her first love, and they'd been married for fifteen years. My mom had wanted to say good-bye to him, but he couldn't handle it. It was a very intense process.

Somewhere around that time I realized that the most common form of human memorial, among a lot of people I'd come across, was no memorial. Then I realized, as I was looking into the Celebrant Institute, that my partner Amber and I had done a commitment ceremony of our own design. Also, I had been asked to officiate the memorial when a friend's daughter died of suicide during her freshman year of college. At the time, I thought, *This is the toughest facilitation gig I've ever been asked to do.*

GOD IS LOVE

I slowly started to recognize that I was in a position to address some of this cultural vacuum. In some ways, it's the family business. I have a lot of clergy in my family, all women. My mom's sister was one of the very first women to be ordained as Presbyterian minister in the seventies. Her husband threatened to block her ordination if she divorced him, so she divorced him after the ordination. Her daughter, my first cousin, followed in her mom's footsteps. She met her partner—she's also gay—when they were in seminary. When the Presbyterian church cracked down with a "Don't ask, don't tell" sort of policy, she became an Episcopalian priest. I have another female cousin who's a Presbyterian minister.

I had some alienating experiences in the church early on, so that was never my thing, but I'd go see my aunt at her church in DC when I flew there for national meetings and marches. Sometimes I'd think, *Gosh, we're saying the same thing.* I'd be up at the podium at a Take Back the Night rally or another demonstration, and what she was saying was pretty much the same thing, except for the God part.

I saw the church as a patriarchal institution at that time. I asked her why she went that route. She said, "First of all, the power of the cloth." Then she said, "To spread the good word." I was like, "What is that?" She said, "God is love." And I was like, *He is? She is? It is? Really?* I hadn't gotten that.

Later, Amber and I had the opportunity to go back to our ancestral place in Italy with my mom and her sister. The cousins there would ask me, "What do you do?" My aunt would step in and say, "Same thing as me, but without God."

I'm not so sure it is without God, although definitely I don't use that language. When I explain to people what a Life-Cycle Celebrant is, I often say that it's like a secular clergy person. Because not only can I officiate weddings—and, technically, I do have clerical credentials to do that—but I am there for people in the process of figuring out what ceremonies they need in their life.

All of the needs that organized religion and social rituals used to serve are still with us. It's just that a lot of those forms have become archaic. Funerals are just a bad brand. A funeral director once said to me, "In the funeral chapel, you'll often see a man gripping his wife's arm, saying, 'Don't you dare waste our money on something like that for me.'" Because they see a retired clergy person mispronouncing the name of their best friend, and it's like, what's the point?

EVOKING A PRESENCE

I've always wanted to be a journalist. One of the things that I love most about what I'm doing now is feeling like I'm a curator of people's stories. It's fairly common—for celebrants who really take the time to uncover and tell the story of the person being honored—that after a memorial people will say, "How long have you known the person who died?" And I'll say, "Actually, I didn't."

I'm coming to see that one of the most powerful roles I serve is that I'm typically the first person to meet the deceased after they've died. I'm not a medium working metaphysically, but I am leading their loved ones through the memories and through the presence that is evoked through their stuff—a quilt they made, the letters they wrote, their emails, the impact that they had on others. Their legacy can be so much clearer to me, in a sense, because I'm coming to it fresh.

It's almost a midwife function, where the bereaved needs to make a transition from the relationship that they had with that person in the flesh to the relationship that they'll have with that person after their death. They need help navigating all the different ways that this person is going to manifest in their consciousness and their life. I'm there at that time of transition, helping to foster it. I hear things like, "I felt closer to my mother during the process of working with you than I did in the last months or years of her life." Perhaps she was suffering from dementia. They've gone through their mom being sick and dying, and it's still very raw, a very painful thing. Then they revisit, with me, the stories of their mom's early life and how she became who she really was, and how everyone else saw her. It's healing.

In one ceremony, the client generated a list of words, associations that reminded her of her mom. We printed them out on these really nice blank business cards. We put them in one of her mom's pocketbooks. She was a really sharp dresser and always known for having a pocketbook. During the memorial, a large family gathering, we passed the pocketbook around.

Each person pulled out a card, and that word—in connection to that physical object—evoked her presence.

For a service last Sunday, the family forwarded me every condolence note that they received. A lot of these people weren't going to be able to travel to the service, so I incorporated their voices into the service. Honestly, it was probably five or six hours of writing once I had all the source material. There's not really a recognized precedent in the marketplace for this sort of work because usually a funeral relies on a retired minister who interviews you for maybe an hour about the person who died. I'll often work twenty or thirty hours through the process. But it's super rewarding to see the benefits of that.

A woman came up to me after that ceremony, and I asked, "How did you know the deceased?" She said, "Oh, I just moved in across the street from her a few months ago. I just thought she was the neatest lady." Here she had gotten to hear this woman's whole backstory. She had only known her when she was sick, and she got to feel connected to the family and have the family hear from her. You know, "Here's how I saw your mom." In the absence of a public memorial, that wouldn't have happened.

Right now I'm working with another client to support healing from a painful event in her life. The first step is identifying ceremonial intent. What is it that you need to honor, witness, relieve, mourn, and express? Which of those verbs end up being most salient for you? In that regard, it's similar to the project management I've done for different organizations. I ask, "What's the goal? Let's use the things that are indigenous to your own value system, the artifacts that are most relevant."

In putting together a ceremony, I have a sense, from my training, about the importance of a beginning, middle, and end. How do ceremonies generally function? An incorporation ceremony that marks the change of status is about getting people to acknowledge this thing that has happened. Weddings and funerals are examples of that. Then there are support rituals, where there's a process that is still unfolding and it's about, "What are you putting in your backpack for this journey that you're on?"

It's not like, pick one option from column A and one from column B, which is how many weddings and funerals tend to operate. What I do is very personalized, but it's about the values and beliefs and stories of the particular client. More and more, I have a bigger picture in mind about the space between us as a people. While I appreciate the fact that individuals may be helped, I see my work as being about our capacity as humans. I want to see us collectively strengthen some muscles that are super atrophied. The opportunity to work with clients individually is a chance to do that, but the conversation side of my work is about trying to distribute that even more.

DEATH OVER PIZZA

I met a young woman in her thirties who was diagnosed with stage-four lung cancer. She hired me to help put together her death plan. She wanted to spare her husband as many decisions as possible. I created a lengthy questionnaire for her to use to clarify her wishes. Some things were clear—like, she wanted to be cremated—some things weren't. *Do you want to put together the playlist for the music at your memorial, or choose the food, or do you not want to? Are you planning a party or is it more like this or that person should speak?* I always say, with these planning questionnaires, just respond to those questions that really resonate with you. None of it is mandatory. She was like, "How can I possibly answer these questions on my own?" She brought together her ten closest friends from various parts of her life, told them there'd be pizza, and they talked about death. She actually did a post on the Death Over Dinner website about it. She selected a subset of my questions and invited me to observe.

What was phenomenal was that most of these friends hadn't met each other. They were from different parts of her life. Very easily, the first time that they could have met would have been at her memorial or at her deathbed. Of course, they are all very bereaved about her diagnosis and her living with this, but societally, what kind of permission is there to talk about that and for her to say, "Okay, I know I'm going to die, and I need you all to help me talk about that and to tell me what you think happens after we die?" It became, "I don't know what I think, what do you think?" It was like a mini-Death Cafe. It was like they were starting to do a workout together, you know? Because they're going to have to train to hold this grief together for her and to fully show up in a way that she's expecting, through her example and by giving them permission.

WE NEED MORE OPENING

Increasingly, people are saying to me that there may not have been any memorial or funeral for their parents because they didn't want a funeral, that sort of thing. But they start thinking of *their* kids. What are their kids growing up with? I'm working with one woman now whose parents died back on the East Coast, but she's going to do something here. One of her primary motivations is to give her son a place to have his grief for his grandmother acknowledged and to consolidate and incorporate stories about his grandmother into his life. Another goal is for him to see remembrance as a practice to incorporate in the family. She didn't want her son to grow up without knowing what to do for a person who dies.

The Celebrant Foundation director, Charlotte Eulette, often says about that word *closure*, which is so often used as a reason to have a memorial ritual, "Don't we need more opening?" While I do think these ceremonies mark the transition of a relationship with a living person, or the end of a period of sickness, it really does feel like a new beginning for people in that it helps them to think about what they might carry forward. Maybe there's a candle that gets lit, and then they light the candle on key anniversary dates or make a place in their house that's going to be a place of memory. Maybe there's some other kind of artifact or keepsake or memento, something that's viewed through the process of the ceremony that is an ongoing focal point—especially because there are now so few burials that provide a place of remembrance. Rather than "Check that box off, we're done," how can we create practices or have touchstones that will be about our ongoing relationship with this person, in a different way?

DEATH CAFE

My life has become heavily engaged in conversations about dying, death, and grief. In my personal life, I'm of an age where many people who I personally care about are sick or dying, or coming to me with their bereavement. Of course, I have a professional practice of assisting people in memorials and home funerals. At times, I think, *What have I done to my life?* Honestly, I think we never really know what we're embarking on. I did have this sense, after my dad died—which was a big part of my journey— "Okay, universe, you took my dad, but you can't take my mom or anybody else." Then I recognized that wasn't a very reasonable demand to be making. I thought at the time, maybe I could befriend the concept of death and just develop a greater capacity to handle it, be more prepared. The more I get into it, the less persuaded I am that it's possible to be prepared. But I thought Death Cafes would be a way to try.

Death Cafes are where people come together in a public setting, generally with those they don't know, to talk about whatever is on their minds about death. In Portland, they've tended to be fifty to one hundred people, but folks are always seated at a small group table of four to eight people. Generally, each table has a facilitator, although not always. They'll open with me or another leader providing just a little bit of background about what Death Cafe is, what its origins are, and how it came to the US. We mention that Portland—PDX Death Cafe—is actually the largest in the world, and people usually get a kick out of that.

I usually ask how many people have come for the first time, or have been before, and it's typically about half and half. I give props to people for being brave enough to check it out, and then I often open with some kind of gentle ritual just to get people settled in—a reading or a poem, oftentimes I will ring a bell—and basically welcome death into the room: the deaths of the past, the deaths of the present. We acknowledge that there may be people in the room who are living with concrete news of their own mortality, who are living with terminal illness, or caring for those who are dying, who may have someone who has died very recently in their lives. We try to name that right up front. Of course, the deaths in our future, that applies to every one of us.

We're very transparent about the role of the facilitator. What we say is, if you have a professional interest or professional standing, that's very welcome, and you don't need to hide the fact that you might have some expertise in a particular area—as an estate planner, or a funeral director, or a home funeral guide, whatever it might be. But we ask that you take off your professional hat and participate as yourself. The other thing that we are probably most rigorous about, after confidentiality, is that you don't promote your own business or service. We have a resource table so people, including myself, can have their fliers out, but it's totally optional. From the beginning we've been scrupulous about trying to keep it as a space that's not commercial.

There's not a particular path laid out. I'm generally explicit in saying, "We're not here to fix anything. We're not here to solve anything." I might even say, "You know, grief, and feelings, may come up." This may be an opportunity to practice holding space for that without having to manage it or handle it. That's what I've found around fresh grief. When it does come up, people actually find it an amazingly empowering and sometimes even exhilarating experience to go through being in the presence of that, and then getting to the other side of the moment. Generally, if someone's emoting, it's going to be very brief. It may feel excruciatingly long for them, but they know they're in a room with other people, and as they compose themselves, they can see the concern, the caring, on peoples' faces. Then the conversation moves on.

It's an experience of, *Wow, this is our shared humanity.* This stuff that can be really terrifying, really painful, we actually can hold it in a space between us. I'd say that's my personal passion. It's really about building our capacity as people to show up for and be connected through the big stuff that matters to us. It doesn't have be the exclusive purview of professionals or family members.

We encourage people to sit with those they don't know. We don't enforce it—sometimes people are very wedded, but we consistently get the feedback that people appreciate that. Sometimes they liken it to an airport layover where you might tell a stranger your whole life story because there aren't going to be any consequences. You're not going to have to worry about whether or not they're going to tell anybody else. It allows you to kind of step out and look at it together.

It's a very strongly held tenet of the Death Cafe originators in London that there be no agenda and no topics and no speakers. I still get probably an inquiry a month from someone: "Can I come speak at your Death Cafe? I have a story to tell. I have a product to sell." Death Cafe founder John Underwood's belief is that people have enough on their minds already about death, they don't need someone telling them what to think about.

WHERE IS THIS GOING TO TAKE US?

There is an art to bringing the conversation forward. Typically, we'll start with an opening question, and then there'll be other potential conversation starters. We used to ask, "What brought you to the Death Cafe?" Sometimes people would reveal tremendously vulnerable things, but a fair amount of people might say, "My friend told me to come," or they'd have a more esoteric or intellectual interest in death, which is fine, too. We crafted a new opening question: "Let's introduce ourselves by each sharing a death that was personally meaningful to us." Perhaps there hasn't been one in your life, in which case you can share that. People can pass if they want. We try to let people participate in their own style. But starting in that way gets right down to it.

During one of my early experiences going to a Death Cafe as a participant, the facilitator was very skilled. He asked, "Why did you all come?"

After people answered, he said, "Well, I noticed that everybody in some way used the word *fear*. I'm here because I want to not be so terrified." He said, "Do you want to talk more specifically about our fears?" One woman in my group had a very rigorous Buddhist meditative practice, where she had focused very specifically, as some Buddhist lineages do, on envisioning her death and investigating her fears around death. She spoke very eloquently about her fears, and I learned so much from that. I was going through my own mental checklist, some of which she named, but I was also like, *Wow, that actually isn't one of my fears. Huh.* With other fears, she really nailed something that for me had been an abstraction. I wouldn't have even been able to put those words on it, but they really struck a chord.

Just by hearing what's on other peoples' minds—whether or not you're taking away factual information—you can gain so much insight into yourself and the nature of the human condition. When there's fresh grief or, for example, somebody talking about being a suicide survivor, or someone who has experienced a violent death, it can be like, *Wow, where is this going to take us?*

I'm a Reed College graduate, and I did Death Cafes at several of Reed's class reunions. They were amazingly intergenerational, with current students mingling with eighty- and ninety-year-olds. I think because of the nature of reunions, you really notice who's not there. People were very honest, very raw, about their relationship with death. As we went around the room, I thought, *What have I gotten us into?* There was a little part of my brain, the limbic part, that wondered, *Is the roof going to blow off this room? Is the top of my head going to blow off? Are we going to be able to manage this?* It was all so real. It's not like anybody was inappropriately burdening the group—it was just, it was a testimony, you know. This other part of my brain was reassuring: *We can do it. This is life. This is real stuff.*

The last couple of Death Cafes were at the downtown library, an environment where there was a potential for drop-ins. In the foyer outside the room, Multnomah County sheriffs were intervening with someone who had passed out. A fellow walked in because of the refreshments, but also, I'm sure, his curiosity. The cafe was well underway, and my sense was that he needed personal attention, so I talked to him one-on-one. He disclosed to me his heroin addiction, which was long-term, and he was sleeping on the streets. He was a young guy. He had relapsed that morning, and of course, death was a huge topic for him. He told me about his friends who died, about how death sounds pretty good to him many days. I'm not sure every Death Cafe organizer or facilitator would be comfortable with this. I'm thinking about what's going on in the rest of the room, while also wanting to give him the best quality attention we could give him. That was a very, very powerful experience—it was not a bunch of people sitting around in a nice Irvington neighborhood home. It was testimony from the front lines. Someone who is manifesting basically everything that's going down for his generation and in this town—so is this the place for him to have his conversation?

Typically, people leave very uplifted, saying things like, "Who would have thought that a conversation about death could have had laughter, could feel so good?" The Death Cafe founders had suggested a closing question—a bucket-list question, like, "What do you want to do before you die?" Something they felt would help people get back to a focus on life. But I gravitated away from that because it reinforces this idea that death is the enemy, and it's life that we've got to embrace, when actually the two are really joined. There are other ways to wrap up and express that we've had a really powerful experience together. "What was it like for you?" That brings people a little bit back up out of the stories, without wrapping too nice of a bow on things. Not like, "Okay, bye, make sure you get into skydiving before you die!"

THE WOLF AND THE POODLE

I have two little visual aids—the wolf and the poodle. It's two ways of looking at and thinking about death. It comes from the fellow that I've been studying with, Stephen Jenkinson.

I first learned of his work after I'd organized the first Death Cafe in Portland. Over one hundred people had indicated interest in coming, and this was basically just by putting up a Facebook page and putting together a team of facilitators. It was just word of mouth. There was some national media coverage about Death Cafes that people were Googling, and they found us. I had the opportunity to interview the Death Cafe founder in London, and the woman who first brought Death Cafes to the US, who was a hospice social worker in Columbus, Ohio. People assume, "Oh, it's one of those esoteric California things." Actually, Columbus, Ohio, at a Panera cafe, was the first Death Cafe in the US.

One of the basic tenets of the Death Cafe founders was, "If you're in the white-hot experience of fresh grief, this is probably not a good place for you." We said, "We have designated support people if you feel overwhelmed and you need someone to talk to." But one woman said to me, "It's kind of like organizing an event about birth and saying, 'If you've recently given birth, please don't come. And if you do come, please don't tell anybody about how painful it is. And if you get upset, please go to your room because you might upset everybody else.'"

I found that pretty compelling, but I worried that someone might lose it. When she pushed back, I realized, someone can "lose it" in a Safeway checkout line. What she pointed out is that we live in such a grief-phobic culture that the chances of someone really letting go are pretty slim. I thought, *Where'd you learn to think like that?* She told me that she had been studying with this guy Stephen Jenkinson. He ran the largest in-home palliative care in Toronto for a number of years. He and his work were profiled in a National Film Board of Canada documentary called *Griefwalker.* He started a school, which he calls the Orphan Wisdom School, which looks at the roots of our death phobia, culturally.

Jenkinson's way of thinking, his whole method of inquiry, is, "What befell a people such that things would look like this?" You can tell from the name, Orphan Wisdom School, almost every people that came to North America, to form what passes as culture in North America, came as the result of some kind of traumatic circumstance. Typically, trauma cannot be sustained as trauma for more than one or two generations before it becomes something else—manifest destiny, that type of thing. You think of the women who came out west on the wagon train. Think of all the death that occurred on the wagon train and the circumstances of their lives, arriving here. So many children died. No wonder the women of that era were so often deemed "insane" and committed to institutions. There's all of this cultural amnesia around the trauma of these experiences. The parlor, which we now call the living room, was originally the place where the dead would be laid out. Today, most of us have never experienced actually seeing that kind of death as part of a family cycle.

Jenkinson was asked, "What do you think about all of this contemporary death talk? The Death Cafes?" When he keynoted at the Death:OK event that I produced last fall, he referenced "the rising fifth column of death hipness" and warned: Meet the new boss, same as the old boss. He says we have some deeply worn cultural ruts, and a lot of this new "Let's talk about death" stuff is in that same rut.

Like, when I talk to people about having "lost my father," well, where did I put him? I mean, he didn't lose himself, right? When you lose something, it's something I did—"I lost my keys. I lost my wallet." From Jenkinson's perspective, pretty much in every culture throughout time, people knew exactly where their dead where—they might venerate them on an altar in the house. They might believe they're in heaven or another kind of spirit world. It's a very contemporary, dominant Western cultural phenomenon that it's euphemistically comforting to say, "I lost someone." You experienced a loss. There's the grief, but your loved one being lost—it's a poignant underscoring of how disconnected we are from remembrance practices and knowing any kind of bigger story.

A lot of people are more comfortable talking about death as "end of life." Again, what does that say? When I die, life has not ended. Life goes on, and in fact my death is necessary for all life to go on. If we all take the longevity treatment, in a few generations we're screwed. Our entire lives are dependent on all of the deaths that have come previous to our lives. Yet when we see death as a failure, as the enemy, to be fought and conquered, what are we saying about our indebtedness to all of the death that has nourished me, you know, from the time that I got up today?

Given the lack of any kind of bigger picture conversation, what is our story about death? Some conversations that I'm involved with in the Death Cafe and other settings illustrate Jenkinson's observation that we have a great talent in North America for demythologizing—for turning a wolf into a poodle so that it can sit on our laps. Some of the Death Cafe tables that I've been at resemble a poodle-grooming session. It's like, look at that cute bow I've put on it. It's really well-behaved now. I'm going to have a good death. Look how pretty my poodle is. But then at other tables and other rooms, the wolf is absolutely circling. The hair on the back of everyone's necks is standing up.

A lot of people want to have a plan. They want to take care of death in advance. You've checked it off. You're cool with it. What Jenkinson says is that in his experience, all the people who are cool with death, once they're sitting across a desk from someone who says, "I'm sorry, there's nothing more I can do for you"—there's a wildness there. And a mystery and an engagement with something that's maybe outside the limits of our powerful individual control mechanisms.

RITES OF PASSAGE

The Celebrant Foundation and Institute that I attended was an online program that was eight months in duration. They based their program off of one developed in Australia. By contrast, many funeral homes now will tell you they have a celebrant on staff. That person may have been to a half-day or maybe a weeklong program. Some of those people at funeral parlors could be very gifted, and in other cases the funeral home just sends a front-office person and slaps the label on it so they can put it on their price list.

Some professional Celebrants are offended by the idea of DIY ceremonies, where family members or friends act as officiants. But I'm all about seeing that capacity being built and present in our communities. I'm also a Home Funeral Guide. In the home funeral movement, there's a very strong strand of practitioners who might call themselves home funeral guides, death midwives, death doulas, etcetera, who don't think that this work is about building up a category of professionals. It's about making sure these skills are resident in people's families and communities and keeping things totally paraprofessional. Even in these subculture movements, there are political differences around whether you should be able to make a living doing this or not. I'm kind of a pragmatist. I wonder how we get from here to there. You've got to have some people who help others to build those skills and reignite people's imaginations around them.

This interest in rekindling ceremony could be the start of something much bigger, or it could easily become another self-help program. You can buy kits online for your divorce party—so much ritual has already been commodified. Think about a baby shower: How do you mark a baby coming or a wedding? It's become all about the stuff that you buy, or these silly, giddy, frivolous activities. What about this threshold that these people are about to cross? What if you're becoming a parent for the first time? In a more intact culture, you might have access to rituals that really support you through that. Or maybe you're not a first-time parent, but what does this new child mean to your other children? Their role is changing in relationship to the newborn. In some ways, Celebrancy is about deconstructing what's out there now, as a commercial or frivolous thing, and saying, "What purpose is this serving, and is there actually something that would be more satisfying?"

One of the most fundamental rites of passage is what marks your transition from adolescent to adult. Do we have anything for that? Sex, drugs, and rock and roll are the default, and a lot of it is about you rather than the community. You get a taste of your death. Traditional initiation rites were children being forcibly removed from their parents by the elders. They're removed and often actually physically scarred or altered in such a way to make them unrecognizable to their parents because now they no longer belong to the parents. They belong to the village—they now have this purpose in society. From Jenkinson's perspective, all of us in mainstream North America are uninitiated, so we've got all these people dying who are basically still adolescents. Your job as a child, your world-view, is that the world is there for you. For your survival, for everything it can do for you. We can see the symptoms of this worldview all around. Most of us aren't living in a way that says, "I belong to the world, the world needs me." I think that's a big piece of our suicide epidemic: people not feeling needed by the world.

If we don't celebrate people's death, then they never really belonged to the bigger story. It's not that you need to know that you'll be reincarnated or that you'll live on in the afterlife, but if you've had this sense that you are part of something bigger than this tiny little thing that's your own lifespan, and if you knew what your death was going to enable and feed, maybe you could have a different relationship with the whole. What if we saw death not as our personal failure or enemy, but as our opportunity to step up in this next way, in the great bigger picture?

CONDUCTED FEBRUARY 2, 2016

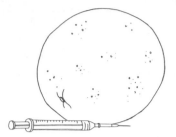

JOHN LAY

RACONTEUR, AUTHOR'S UNCLE

As far back as I can remember, my uncle John has offered me his unfiltered theory of everything. His opinions have always come via obsessively detailed stories that feel subversive and inappropriate in equal measure, be it because of their content (stories of masturbation, drug use, and perverse Catholic priests) or because of the lessons they contain (often about the destructive nature of capitalism). Even when I was a kid, Uncle John never bullshitted me. He spoiled me, he lavished attention on me, but he also treated me as a trusted equal even when the rest of the world seemed intent on telling me what to do. I presume that those impulses come from John's deep connection to the teachings of the lecturer and teacher J. Krishnamurti—who taught that self-knowledge was the only path to necessary social change—and from his own years of working with troubled kids at the Devereux school in Santa Barbara, California.

John ran away from home as a young man, despite (or because of) his family's considerable wealth. He married young, and had his only two children, Marcus and Doug, with his first wife, Edna.

John is a veteran, an animal lover, a pacifist, and a dedicated gardener who spends most of his free time sculpting the expansive, Japanese-influenced garden behind his house near the Oregon Coast. He is eighty-seven years old.

His late second wife, my aunt Shirley—my dad's half-sister, who died in 1989—is someone I never got to know as an adult. I remember her voice, her exquisite style, and her laugh from my childhood. I remember seeing her some weeks before she died, knowing that she had cancer. I rely on John to fill in all the blanks about who my aunt Shirley was and how they faced her cancer together, which he does here. While John's main contribution to this book is this love story, it's important to note that Shirley wasn't John's last love. He is happily remarried to a talented artist named Pat. They've been together for twenty-one years. "I think I'd be concerned if Shirley wasn't a large part of John's heart," Pat told me recently, when I asked if Shirley's legacy was ever a burden on her marriage. "Early in our relationship he would sometimes call me Shirley, and now, when telling me stories, he sometimes calls Shirley 'Pat.' Just requires a bit of translation. As you know, John doesn't love lightly, only forever."

REENLISTMENT

The story really starts with a clerk typist in Los Angeles, California. When I went into the service for a second time and had my own set of papers from being in before, I came to the recruiting office and said, "I saw the poster saying that I'd only lose one pay grade. So I'd still be a sergeant, but not as high a grade a sergeant?" They said "Yes, yes, by all means, you can come back in."

I thought for sure that I'd go back to a NATO headquarters somewhere because that was my classification and that's what I'd done before, in Germany with my family. They put the classification down, and I reported to Manhattan Beach Air Force Station in New York City for further assignment.

I get there in my civilian clothes. The sergeant at the desk, when I showed him my orders, says, "Yes, we got your orders a few days ago. There's one little thing that's out of order here. You're listed as 64152 instead of your real number. The 64152 is an RIF station outside of Oxford, England. Your actual number, 64151, is in French Morocco." He let me choose. I knew the French Moroccan would have been good in lots of ways, but it was nowhere near as tempting as going to a station right outside of Oxford. He says, "Good, so I'll just ignore that." I never would have gotten to England without that typing mistake.

I RAN AWAY FROM IT ALL

The point of me going in at all was that I couldn't support my wife and kids in Ojai, California. I couldn't get a job that was good enough to support a wife and two children. I had to drive somewhere else for work. I was a public weigh master at a cattle yard for a while, and then I worked for Sunkist, where I was a payroll clerk. But Edna said, "You're so smart. You have to do something better than statistics. You have to go back to college." She wanted to take over my life, you know? So I ran away from it all. I thought, *The only way I can do this is to go back in the service.* She'd automatically get the quarter balance of my pay, and I added more to that, and it left me enough that I could live on the base. It was free room and board, free laundry, free everything. Free movies every night. Well, twenty-five cents it cost, on base. You could buy a carton of cigarettes for a buck. I'd have drinking money and a nice private room in a male dormitory. And security. And I would know that Edna could stay in Ojai. I wanted my two sons to go to school in Ojai, and to know the Krishnamurti people that I knew there, and go to the Krishnamurti school. I wanted that for them. They were very important to my life, and I wanted them to experience all of that.

When I got to England, I'd go into London on Friday, Saturday, and come back on Sunday night. It was like a lark; it was vacation. But I worked my ass off at the base when I came back. At any rate, I usually went into town with this a guy who was stationed with me and had been there for three years.

In England, the pubs closed very early. You have to belong to a private club in order to drink, but this guy was a member of several clubs. He introduced me to the people there and sponsored me to get membership. So I had club membership in the Mazurka. At that time people really danced in bars. And young ladies who were attractive and very lady-like could always come in the bar and have a drink without being a member. There were always a couple of nice young ladies who you could talk to, and so on.

I met this young girl in the Mazurka Club, and I danced with her. She was very cute in a boyish, sweet kind of way, with short hair—just wonderful. Her mother and father lived in a large apartment right on the Thames River. But her father hated Yanks. Hated the Yanks. So I never met him or her mother. I started dating her, and she was getting really serious with me, you know? I thought, *Oh this poor thing.* I didn't go to bed with her. I think she was nineteen years old. That year I was twenty-seven: with two children, and married when I was twenty. I'd go to bed with anything that moved earlier in my life. But this whole burden of me breaking up with Edna and leaving the kids, I felt really guilty about the whole thing. I truly did.

There was a great deal of self-hatred in everything that I was doing. I tried to explain to her, "This just isn't right. I can't even meet your mother and father." I did want to meet someone I could make love to. I just thought this was the final straw that would break my back, if I lead her on, and then I hurt her.

One night I go to the Mazurka, and oh my god, she's at the bar, sitting there waiting for me. I walk in the door and I turn right around and walk out. I go down to the Star Club because she doesn't even know about that. I'm hiding out. And close to the bar is a round table with two young ladies and a bearded young man who I'd later find out was named Chev. Trouble, the three of them. It was apparent to me that the blonde lady was with the guy with the beard, and the other girl was by herself. She was tall and dark-haired and slim—quite elegant. I asked her to dance. She had great movements: very simple, sensual kind of movements. We touched bodies in a very nice way. Then they invited me over to the table, but the place was going to close soon. They invited me to dinner, and I came over. I remember the phone rang, and the blonde was talking on the phone to another man. By the way she was talking to him, I could tell just how in charge she was of everything she did. There was a self-confidence in her own beauty and her own attractiveness that put her in a class where she was always amused by men. I thought that was great. That was Shirley.

The next Saturday I went into town again. I was walking in Piccadilly, and I passed a restaurant called the Soup Kitchen. I heard this tapping on the window, and there was Chev. I went in, and he recommended a soup and I ordered it. We talked a little bit about the club that we'd gone to and so on. And he said, "What'd you think of Shirley?" I was very careful. "Well, she's just a, um, an English lady. There's no question about that. She's very attractive. You're a lucky man." He said, "Oh, I'm just her friend. I think she was interested in you." I said, "Really?" He said, "I'll give you her phone number. Give her a call. I think she would be happy to hear from you." So that's how we started.

"I AM JUST NOT WORTH IT"

We dated for months. She had a great job, she had a great flat to live in, and now here I was, the American. You know, coming and spending all my weekends, and then my time will be up, and I'll go home. This was a classic story. It's what happened all over Europe. The Second World War brought this all on, and now everyone wants to come live in America—all want to get married and come live in America. They think it's much nicer than it is anywhere else. And that was really true. It still was in the fifties. England was still recovering from the war at that time. But I just did not want anymore of that.

Now, we get that moment. Here I am, and Shirley wants to come and live with me in America.

I didn't want to stay in the Air Force, and I already had two kids. I didn't want to take advantage of this nice apartment, and this attractive girl, and then like a month before I went home, say, "Well, see you later." I wanted to break up before it became more entangled than it already was. So I came into town one weekend—it was about the middle of summer, maybe June of '57—and I go in with every determination. I sit her down in her living room living room, and I just say exactly what I am: "I am just not worth it. I have no idea how I'm going to earn a living, the fucking stripes are the only successful thing I've done in my life, and you don't want that life. And I just, I'm not going to wait until the last minute." And so on.

I thought she'd make some clever remark because she was so cool, you know, about everything. And she broke down. She didn't just cry, she sobbed and shook. I thought, *Oh god, what have I done?* I said, "This can't be this important." But it was. I had opened her up to Krishnamurti. I did open up her mind to a lot of things, and she really admired my way of thinking. She truly did. She was twenty-three, I was twenty-seven. She said, "We don't need money. Look what we're doing here. We can live this way." I knew that Edna and I were over, and I thought, *I just cannot do this to another person.* Edna wrote me a letter in the middle of all this, saying, "You know, the differences between us seem so silly when you're not here."

So I said to Shirley, "Okay, you've convinced me. For better or for worse, I promise you, I will never bring this up again. I will never dither about it again. So long as you want to go, we'll find a way to get you there, and keep you there as long as you want to stay. I will find some way not to harm you."

I came into that relationship feeling terrible about myself. I was very aware of the fact that I was a failure as a husband, and now I was a failure as a father, as well, because I was not living with my two sons, who I loved very much. I had a responsibility to them—I'd always be there. I wanted my sons to know that I was plugging away miserably in the military for their benefit. But it didn't turn out that way. It turned out that I had a wonderful time.

Shirley and I were totally honest with each other, and we didn't put any expectations on one another. She liked to go to bed with other men, for example. I didn't fight that. I didn't feel any proprietorship over her. I didn't feel that I owned her body. But we trusted each other. And it just gradually became this remarkable relationship. I grew within that relationship, and she became who she became. We spent thirty-three years together. We were made for each other. What else can I say?

THOSE WERE THE FACTS

I promised Shirley I'd be straight with her at the very beginning of her cancer. When we went to the oncologist, we knew he was going to offer us treatments, and we knew—because my son Marcus had talked to oncologists that he knew professionally—that if the cancer had metastasized into her liver, there'd be nowhere to go. Nothing was going to make that better. She'd live maybe ten months, maybe a year. The different oncology treatments that were available at that time could prolong her life for another year, maybe a year and a half. But that extra time would be miserable because they'd be injecting all this poison into her system to kill the cancer's poison, and in the process those injections would kill a lot of good things as well. She'd be sick, and she'd have headaches and throw up, all of that. Those were the facts.

So I told Shirley what Marcus said about the poison. I said, "The doctor is not going to offer us anything that's going to cure you or make you feel better." And she said, "Did Marcus say about how long he thinks I would live?" And I said, "Yes. Marcus told me that." She said, "Don't tell me. I want to try and live as long as I can in my own way, and I don't want to have it colored by that opinion." She didn't want that doom—that sentence of doom.

I said, "I agree. That's why I didn't say anything, but waited until you asked." And I'm glad she didn't know.

I WAS A MECHANIC

She wanted to try laetrile*, which is an extract from apricots or something. She found, through her sources, a nurse who had access to laetrile.

---

* A semisynthetic version of amygdalin, a fruit extract used to combat cancer as early as the 1840s in Russia. Laetrile and amygdalin came under intense scrutiny from the Food and Drug Administration in the 1970s, and that organization calls it a "highly toxic product that has not shown any effect on treating cancer." It was effectively a black market drug during Shirley's cancer treatment.

You would inject it in the same way you would inject heroin, once a day. Marcus sent me a whole bag of disposable hypodermic needles that I could use. It was sanitary that way. Doug came over and showed me how to do it. I practiced on an orange because the skin is tough like a human's. He told me the dangers of getting air in the needle. And I just shut my mind down about what I thought about laetrile, because what I thought about laetrile had nothing to do with what we were doing. I was a mechanic who was going to put some grease on something. She wanted me to do that. And Marcus thought I should do that. So I learned how.

I did it very well. I'm very proud of myself. And I have to tell you it really brought us together. It was something we did every day. It was much more profound than kissing or making love. It was much more. I did it for a period of time—I can't remember how long—and then she said, finally, "Oh, that's enough of that."

It was comfortable. She never had a time when she was physically in pain. She was in discomfort at the end because she had such trouble breathing—it was physically a difficult thing for her to do, even with the air that she was getting from the machine. She just used it at times, when she was short of breath and needed the help. When she was laying down in bed. But she never had discomfort, she never threw up, she never was sick to her stomach. None of those things happened. She just got weaker and weaker. And slower and slower in what she did.

I'M GOING TO BE WITH LITTLE EDNA

She still went to the acupuncturist, occasionally. He was a friend of hers, and she liked to go there. Our friend Pat* had come to see her, and when Pat realized that Shirley was really on her last legs, she said, "I'd rather be here with you, if you want me to stay." And I said, "Yes, yes." They were best friends. So Pat took her, a few days before she died, to see the acu-

---

* Not the same Pat who John would later marry.

puncturist. She took my car. I was going to take her, and Pat says, "No, no, you're doing too much. I'll take her." So she did.

When she got back, Pat came into the house and said, "You're going to help her in. She can't walk on her own." I carried her into the house. We went in through the backyard, then into the dining room. I got her as far as the living room, and she says, "I don't want to lay down in bed." I said, "Oh, good. Let's just sit here." We sat on the coffee table, next to each other, and I was holding her hand.

I said, "How was the acupuncture? Did it make you more comfortable?" And she said, "Oh, we didn't even do that. We just sat there and cried."

Then I said, "You know, I can cry. Are you ready for me to cry?" She said, "Oh, no, I'm not. I don't want you going around here crying." I said, "Okay. Sold."

She and I had very different beliefs, or disbeliefs, or whatever you want to call it, about reincarnation. She believed in it. She believed in it like she believed her name was Shirley. She believed that we had been together in previous lives.

A psychic had told her that we had been married, husband and wife, in Japan. We were Japanese. But Shirley was the husband, and I was the wife. Shirley said to the psychic, "Well, it's that way now, too. He's the one who takes care of the house and looks after me." Which was true. She had a more masculine approach to me, and I had a more feminine approach to her. It was part of our relationship.

I then turned to her, after we had settled the crying thing, and I said, "Well, you're right at the brink of eternity. How do you feel about that?" And she said, "Yes, it's true. And I'm going to be with little Edna now."

Little Edna was our French poodle. The first dog that we had. We never had a dog when we lived in Hollywood, or London, but I got two small little French poodles for her from our friends who had a litter: a male and a female. Shirley had wanted a French poodle when she was a little girl. It meant something to her. She really loved the poodle. We'd had cats when we were in apartments, in Arizona and Hollywood.

Those animals had taught us about unconditional love. They were able to give it to us, and we were able to give it to them. At some point I said to her, "Isn't it strange that we can love our animals in a way that we don't love each other? Why can't we give unconditional love to each other the way we do to little Edna and Smokey? We can see they're not doing the right thing sometimes, but that doesn't anger us." It really set up a whole different way of looking at things for us. We really realized that if you're in a house with animals that you really care for, that unconditional kind of love is possible. I'm not saying everyone who has animals gets it. People kick their dogs, you know, all kinds of things—but it's possible to have this, and it creates a harmony that is in the house.

Until the day she died, we talked about: "Oh, remember when little Edna did this? Or Little Edna did that?" She was always with us. Dead or alive. She was part of an unconditional love contract. And we knew that. For the English, the most important things in their lives they understate, or shorthand in a way. They don't ruin them with sentimentality. That's what I love about the English. I *reek* of sentimentality.

She told me she was going to be with little Edna. I knew her well, and I knew exactly what she meant. She meant that she would always be with me. She did that in the best way possible because it was something only she and I would understand.

NINE STORIES

She did the same thing when she died. The weekend before she died, Pat was there, our friend Mary came up from LA, and then Doug came over on a Saturday afternoon. And the doctor came to help Shirley die. He was a young man in his early forties who had great sympathy and empathy for people who had fatal illnesses and didn't want to go to the hospital. Shirley wanted to die.

The doctor came over on noon on Saturday, and she says, "I really don't want to go on with this. I'm so weak now." She really always told the truth, you know? She was unable to be deceptive about anything. By then she was so weak that she couldn't walk, and it was an effort to talk. The young doctor said, "I'll call the hospice people, and they'll send a morphine drip."

He felt good about it, I felt good about it, she felt good about it. As Saturday progressed, she got weaker and weaker. She wouldn't lay down because, if she laid down, she'd start choking. So I sat behind her on the bed, and the bed was up against the wall. I sat there with my legs spread as if I was in a toboggan with her, and she sat between my legs leaning back with her head resting on my chest. My chin was on top of her head. There was this group of people in the front bedroom in the sun. Beautiful, sunny afternoon. She had a number of books that we had got at the Santa Barbara library, and among those was a humorous book of Woody Allen's short stories, before Woody Allen became Woody Allen. Shirley asked me to get it. I used to read to her quite often. I have a nice voice, and I used to be an actor, you know? She says, "Why don't you read us a story? From the Woody Allen short stories?" I said okay. Everyone had tea except her and me. I read the stories, and it was just a very cozy and pleasant time.

It was about two weeks later, after she died, that it dawned on me that the very first weekend after I had met her in London, I brought Salinger's *Nine Stories*. I brought it to London that weekend. It was the first weekend that we had decided that, yes, we were a number, and that we were going to find a way for her to come back to the United States with me. I read a few of those stories to her, in her bedroom, laying in the bed.

And on her last weekend, in her English way, she had us do it again. But she didn't say, "This is what we did the first weekend we were together, and now this will be the last weekend we're doing it," or anything like that. You know, the way an American woman would.

"JUST MARVELOUS"

The doctor said, "I'll have the hospice bring over the morphine drip on Monday." But then he laughed and patted her on the knee and said, "I don't think you have to worry about that, anyway. I don't think you're going to live until Monday morning. You are so dehydrated right now that you could die at any moment."

It happened later that evening. I stayed in the bedroom all night, and Pat would sit with me in the bedroom while Shirley attempted to breathe for a few hours, and then she'd lay down and Mary would come and sit with me. It was around 3:30 in the morning. Pat and I were there, and Shirley was laboring for breath. Suddenly, there was this rattle, like a kid doing a machine gun noise, you know? Then there was silence. I said to Pat, "I think that's the death rattle." Pat says, "I'll get Mary." Mary brought her bag; she was a nurse practitioner. So she took out the stethoscope, and sure enough, she was gone.

The three of us went out in the kitchen and were just overjoyed, you know. She had died! She had died. We made tea and said, "Just marvelous." Then they went off to bed, and I was going off to my bed.

But you know me, I worry about things. I thought, *I'm just going to make sure.* When I walked into the bedroom, I didn't have to touch her. I could just see that it was, that her life wasn't there. I saw a dead body. Then I went back out in the kitchen, and I sat on the floor there and cried. Really bellowed.

It was just like the doctor had said: She lived for ten months. It was February 12. The day before her fifty-sixth birthday. A couple of days before Valentine's day.

I remembered what the young doctor said to her: "You're so dehydrated." And I thought, immediately, *The fucking hospitals. They get these people who are really dying and the first thing they put on them is that fucking drip solution to keep them alive, so they can run tests, so they can make money.* All you have to do is leave a person alone, and they'll live peacefully and honorably without pain.

THE ROSARY

A few days before she died, when Shirley was still functional in every way, I went over to the other side of the house where the bathtub was, and I opened the window and drew a hot bath. Really hot water. I was soaking in it. And I just, for some reason . . . Latin is a profound language. I started saying the rosary in Latin. "*Ave maria, gratia plena* . . ." There's a soothingness in that. The words in English are just nothing, you know? When I was in the seminary we did the rosary every night, and we would repeat that. "*Ave Maria* . . ." I can't remember where my trash can is, but I can remember "*Ave maria, gratia plena,*" make no mistake. I can recite the whole mass in Latin. There's something profound about it that was comforting to me. I recited the whole mass.

When I got up, out of the tub and dried off, I asked Shirley, "Could you hear me?" And she said, "No." I said, "I just said the rosary in Latin." She just smiled. Then when I read her journal after she died, she made a bigger deal out of that than any other thing I did throughout the whole year. But I understood it. I understood why that was so meaningful to her. I'm certainly glad I did it. We always seemed to do the right thing for each other. It was just a remarkable relationship.

\\

CONDUCTED FEBRUARY 10, 2016

JOSH SLOCUM
CONSUMER RIGHTS ADVOCATE

Josh Slocum is the national executive director of the Funeral Consumers Alliance (FCA)—a Vermont-based nonprofit organization which seeks "to ensure consumers are fully prepared and protected when planning a funeral" —and on the surface, he seems to genuinely loathe funeral directors. It's not a mean-spirited hatred; more like a giddy disdain. When I reached him by phone at the FCA's headquarters, I could almost hear his blood boiling as he described funeral directors who had passed themselves off as servants of the public good while fleecing consumers in the process.

Slocum may occasionally crack jokes at the expense of funeral directors, but his organization is serious about its fights for transparency and fairness within the funeral industry. This decades-long effort is not as high profile as consumer struggles with big tobacco or auto manufacturers, but Slocum might chalk that up to Americans' quiet reverence for the funeral industry.

The Funeral Consumers Alliance's blog, "The Daily Dirge," posts about the FCA's latest funeral cost studies and the battle for new alternatives to burial, but it also shares links to death-related sketch comedy skits, Yelp reviews of funeral homes, and red-baiting funeral industry brochures from the 1960s. After speaking with Slocum, one realizes that his personality—angry, thorough, and usually amused—guides the organization's tone. Slocum acknowledges that the pressures facing funeral directors are daunting, but his purest revulsion is reserved for those who play the virtuous mortician role with a little too much gusto. "That level of affectation just creeps me out," he says.

THE AMERICAN WAY OF DEATH

I fell into journalism. I have a liberal arts degree, and I'm all for liberal arts education, but it's not vocational school. It's not supposed to get you ready for a job with the corporation. I was good at it to the extent that I was a working journalist for three years, and I was pretty good at what I did.

I was a newspaper reporter in Lynchburg, Virginia, as my first job out of college. I was a cops-and-crime reporter, but I was looking for a feature story to run on the weekend that was completely off my beat and that I could really sink my teeth into. I was very interested in consumer protection and economic justice types of issues. That's just the sort of person I am. Somebody left a copy of Jessica Mitford's 1963 book *The American Way of Death* on my desk. I stayed up all night reading it, alternating between laughing so hard I thought I was going to piss myself and saying, "How the hell do these bastards get away with this? Why is nobody talking about it?"

I started investigating, or trying to investigate, what had happened to the prices and service at local funeral homes in Lynchburg after they had been bought by large, multinational corporations—this was SCI, or Service Corporation International, at that time. In the early days of the Internet, it was very hard to find out who owned which funeral home. There was nothing at all like Google searching, so I had to do things like send Freedom of Information Act requests to the state regulatory offices that dealt with funeral homes to see if I could get copies of price lists and other materials that the state collected as part of their routine inspections.

Basically, I was introduced to the idea of regulatory capture at this point. It became quickly clear to me that the state board of funeral directors was much more interested in protecting the profits and prestige of that industry than they were in actually functioning as a consumer protection organization, as the law requires them to. They denied me all sorts of requests for seemingly uncontroversial public documents. I simply could not get my hands on them. The attorney general's office denied my requests. I wasn't asking for anything that was personal information.

This wasn't a gray area. It wasn't something where a person should sit there and ask, "Can we really release this?" It was bullshit.

During the time that this was going on, the governor appointed the regional manager of SCI, who was the frontman for all these funeral homes, to the presidency of the state board. I was so disgusted by this that I started digging even further into the industry. I found the organization that I now work for, the Funeral Consumers Alliance, and that turned into a job offer. It was complete serendipity.

THINGS HAVE CHANGED, BUT THEY HAVEN'T CHANGED AN AWFUL LOT

We're a nonprofit charity. Our small office here in Burlington has two staff members. I'm one of them. We have seventy affiliated local organizations, things like Funeral Consumers Alliance of Eastern Massachusetts or Western Massachusetts, for example. Those are largely volunteer run, with the exception of one or two of our very largest affiliates that have enough traffic that they have paid staff. Mostly, these are volunteers who do funeral and end-of-life education at the local level. We watch legislation at the state and federal levels that affects funeral consumers—things like laws on how tightly regulated Grandma's prepaid funeral money is. We're mainly educational, but we're also a consumer lobbying voice.

This organization has been around since the early 1960s. Back then, the organization had a different name, and most of our local affiliate groups functioned as buyers clubs. They were known as memorial societies, and they were nonprofit groups. Back in those days, before we had any federal regulations that gave consumers the right to pick their funeral options à la carte and gave them the right to transparent pricing, the only way that you could really guarantee that people could get a decent price on a simple arrangement was by collectively bargaining. The consumer buying club would go to certain funeral homes and say, "Mr. Funeral Director, if you will agree to this price on a simple burial and this price on a simple cremation, we will put the buying power of our members behind you and give you our business."

The funeral directors who were willing to talk to those clubs in the late 1950s and 1960s took huge risks. Many of them were blackballed from their state trade associations. Some of them had their tires cut. Some of them were beaten up. Particularly in California, those who cooperated with the memorial societies often became embroiled in lawsuits or provoked legislation. California back in the 1960s had a law that made it illegal to advertise funeral prices. That was a reaction to consumer pushback. Things have changed, but they haven't changed an awful lot. If you're a funeral director, and you're willing to be seen quoting anything the Funeral Consumers Alliance says without immediately calling us "spawn of the devil," you're taking a risk.

In the 1980s, the FCA was the major consumer group behind the successful effort to actually get the Federal Trade Commission to regulate the funeral industry. So they had been doing an awful lot of this work for an awful long time before I came along, but I had never heard of the FCA. That's common for small nonprofits. But, especially with us, it's a bitter pill sometimes because what we do has to do with the universal human experience. Everybody is going to deal with having somebody close to them dying. Every single person is going to die. It couldn't be more universal, but it's seen as a strange, esoteric niche of consumer protection, when it's thought of at all.

PUTTING ON OUR GROWN-UP PANTS

I never got to publish those investigative stories. I couldn't even get my editor on board. I had a three-ring binder about an inch thick, full of documentation of the problems with the funeral industry—and particularly the well-known consumer exploitation by this company SCI—to back up all my claims. My editor called me into the office and said, directly to my face, "Okay, Josh, what is it? Did you get screwed by an undertaker or something?" No, I didn't get screwed by an undertaker, but this was a lesson to me in how very cloaked in secrecy the funeral transaction is and how very difficult it is—even for skeptical and reasonable people like newspaper editors—to wrap their minds around the idea that there might be something wrong with the way that funeral directors treat consumers. They simply couldn't conceive of it as a consumer-interest story.

One of our biggest problems as consumers is of our own making. We tend to treat funeral directors almost like clergy, instead of like business-men or -women.

First of all, we Americans have a really hard time putting on our grown-up pants when it comes to talking about death. We can talk about housing finance. We can talk about car shopping. We can talk about any-thing else, but nobody wants to talk about death. Because we refuse to talk about it, we also refuse to deal with it the way we deal with other significant life transactions—so we put it off. We don't comparison shop. We walk into a funeral home on the worst day of our lives, having no factual information about what our options really are. If we treated car buying the way we treat funeral buying, we would walk into the Honda dealer and hold our hands out and say to the first salesman on the floor, "Um, I need a car. What do I need, and how much will it cost?" But this is exactly how we buy funerals. We say, "Well, they're the professionals. They should know." Oh, they know exactly what kind of funeral you'll need, and it's usually one that costs a lot of money.

The only other profession that I think approaches this level of obfus-cation and difficulty in getting a sense of the value of what you're paying for is probably hospital billing. I find that very amusing because whenever my organization calls for funeral homes to be more transparent about pricing, or asks the Federal Trade Commission to beef up rules on price disclosures—which we're doing right now—some of the defenses we get from funeral directors include "hospitals don't do it." That's not really to their credit. That's not helping their brand.

NEVER PAY FOR A FUNERAL IN ADVANCE

We have a patchwork regulatory system where all fifty states regulate pr-eneed money differently. There's no consistency, no uniformity in regulation or safeguards, and very little guarantee of portability and transferability in many states for consumers. Some of the most stringent and best consumer protection laws exist in states like New York and New Jersey, where if you're a funeral director who accepts payment ahead of time, you're obligated by law to put that money into an FDIC-insured bank account. You can't skim the interest; you can't take a commission. You have to allow the interest to accrue on the consumer's behalf. If the consumer changes their mind and moves out of state before you provide the funeral, you have to give them all their money back. That's pretty good.

Then you get all the way down to places like Florida, where consumers stand to lose between 30 and 60 percent of what they have prepaid, should they ever change their mind, or move before the death occurs. Basically, states like Florida have legalized robbery.

That's just the regulatory side. You can see all sorts of stories online about hundreds of millions of dollars being stolen or misappropriated from prepaid funeral funds. That's a reality. But it is not the criminality in that portion of the industry that I think is the biggest problem. The biggest problem is that offering a prepaid funeral plays to unproductive, magical thinking on the part of consumer families. I'm constantly having to explain to people that prepayment is not magic. You'll hear the same phrases. People say, "I didn't want to leave it to my kids to take care of," or "I just wanted to make sure that everything was all taken care of." What does that mean? When you drill down and ask people, "What do you believe you have accomplished by prepaying?" they will say, "Well, the prices will never go up. The price is guaranteed, and the funeral home knows what I want. All my kids have to do is call the funeral home."

Okay, but what happens if you move to New York from Portland, Oregon? Who will they call then? Or what if you die on vacation? How do you know that whenever you die, be it fifteen or twenty from now years—how are you so certain that your funeral plans and what will be manageable for you and your family will be exactly the same, no matter what? It doesn't work that way. Prepayment is an expensive but easy way out because funeral homes make all sorts of promises that we desperately want to hear.

Some of the hardest people to help are the children of parents who have prepaid. This sounds absolutely counterintuitive, but those surviving children are even less prepared to deal with funeral decisions than children in families who made no plans at all. It's because Mom and Dad set up an expectation that "everything is taken care of, and one call does it all." Even in cases where the funeral director is clear, honest, and thorough, and sits down with Mom and Dad and says, "I'm going to price guarantee my services, but I can't guarantee the price you'll have to pay the cemetery. Some charges we can't know because we don't know how long you're going to live." Even when the funeral directors do it the right way like that, Mom and Dad go home and pat Susie on the head and say, "Susie, just go talk to the nice man at the mortuary. Mommy and Daddy got everything done for you."

That just sounds wonderful, doesn't it? But there's no such thing as "all taken care of." "All taken care of" is one of the ways that we adult consumers fool ourselves into thinking that we've done responsible planning. What we're actually doing—and this isn't a moral criticism—is we're telling ourselves fairy tales so we can sleep at night and not have to think about the fact that we're going to die.

DISTRESS PURCHASES

There's a lot of work to be done for consumer protection. There are auto loan scams, there are usury interest rate charges on credit cards, payday loans—all sorts of things. What makes it worse in the funeral industry is that funerals are what economists call distress purchases. It's never something you voluntarily buy. Nobody lines up in greedy anticipation to buy a funeral. Well, you know, maybe a few people—if it's somebody else's funeral and you totally hate them.

The fact is, you the consumer have more choice with a car dealer than you do with a funeral home. You can decide to walk out and go to another car dealer. You can make the choice to say, "I'm going to let my old car limp along a little longer because I want to check out some other dealerships. I'm not going to make this decision this week."

Even in the most strained of circumstances, you're not in the same position that you're in when your husband has died and you're standing in a funeral home.

A lot of people say, "Why do you pick on funeral directors? Look how much wedding planners charge." My answer to that is, frankly, if you're stupid enough to pay twenty thousand dollars to have somebody plan a party for you, I don't feel sorry for you. I don't feel badly for you because a wedding is a very anticipated purchase that you are voluntarily creating yourself. Right? It's not the same thing.

The history of the American funeral industry is peculiar, and it has resulted in a class of businesspeople who are way too big for their britches. There is an absurdly inflated sense of ego and entitlement on the part of funeral directors that is breathtaking. Even if they don't say this out loud and this candidly, the majority of the mainstream funeral industry comports itself as if they believe that they have a legal and moral right to the business and patronage of every family in their service area.

The history of the funeral industry has everything to do with American entrepreneurial capitalism, the Civil War, and industrialization in the last quarter of the nineteenth century. That industry has an almost complete stranglehold on the very way we experience death and commemoration, which have been completely absorbed by the logic of commodity purchasing. People can't even conceive of an alternative. "If we don't have a funeral at the funeral home, what do we do?" This is a psychological straightjacket that we Americans—and I don't mean Westerners; I mean Americans—have put ourselves in.

I had a lady on the phone about a month and a half ago who was calling to look for money to help pay for cremation that she couldn't afford. We get a lot of those calls. But this woman—when I got into her situation on the phone, it became clear that her husband had already died. He'd already been cremated. She had the urn at home. She was trying to find two thousand dollars so she could have what she called "the cheapest memorial service she could find."

Think about that for a second. It didn't occur to her to ask her pastor if the church would help pay for it. It didn't occur to her to rent a restaurant room at the Sheraton for half a day and bring photographs of her husband and some poems. The only thing she could conceive of was, *how much will it cost for the funeral director to give me a memorial service?* And when I said, "Hey, did you talk to your church first? Because if you're a member, they're probably not going to charge you anything. You might want to make a donation of a few hundred dollars." She goes, "Oh, I can talk to the church directly?" Now, that was a little bit extreme, but not that far out of the mainstream. It's astonishing.

I COULD NEVER DO THAT

I own a second house that has two apartments in it, one of which my parents live in, and the other I rent out to tenants. My downstairs tenant's thirty-year-old daughter died in her sleep the other day. She started apologizing to me that she hadn't gotten the rent check into the mail, and I'm feeling terrible for her. I said, "I want to remind you what I do for a living." My tenants downstairs are working-class poor folks. I know they don't have the money for a big funeral, so I ended up talking her through all the options. Then I said that, of course, she could take care of her daughter privately, interface with the crematory, and avoid the expense of the funeral home. The immediate reaction was, "Oh my god, no, I could never do that." Why? Why are you convinced of that? It's a reality that we create for ourselves by repeating that story to ourselves and to other people around us.

There's something weird about it. It's understandable, but this is not a universal part of the human condition. If you were to go back a hundred years, your family, my family, my tenant's family—all of them laid out their dead at home. This was how we did funerals. That doesn't mean that people loved death a hundred years ago. But they grew up in a different world, and necessity forces you to reconceive what you can and can't do.

Undertakers have been around for 135 years in their current form. Yet somehow humans have muddled through thousands of years without a professional class of undertakers. They see themselves as indispensable and pillars of society without whose presence the Earth would stop turning on its axis. They will make all sorts of claims about how they're essential guardians of the public health, but there are almost no public health implications with dead bodies.

"LAST GUY TO LET ME DOWN, RIGHT?"

There's a lot of cognitive dissonance in the mind of the average funeral director. They talk at length about how important engaging in death rituals is for people's mental health. The worst of them will make pop psychology claims that you'll have complicated grief for the rest of your life if you don't see your husband's body pickled and primped in a casket. But most discuss, almost rhapsodically, how important it is to commemorate the dead and to express something about that person who's now missing from our community—all of which are true sentiments. But then they get absolutely flustered or enraged when you suggest that the family follow that logic all the way through and care for someone at home. All of a sudden these funeral directors, who talk about how important the presence of the body is, go ballistic if you suggest that you dispense with them and do it yourself.

Having said that, it's just not the case that it's merely poor, innocent consumers and evil, duplicitous undertakers. I have a lot of unkind things to say about the mainstream funeral industry, but they are not full of crooks anymore than insurance sales is or medical device sales or retail books or anything else. It's the structure of the transaction that leads to the consumer abuse. Yes, it does encourage bad behavior that is particular to the way funeral directors sell funerals, but they are not, as a class, any more or less ethical than any other service sector. The problem is that they refuse to act like any other service sector, and we consumers have allowed them to elevate themselves to a status just below sacred. People treat funeral directors like they were clergy.

I do have some sympathy for the cultural place that they occupy in our society. It is a fact that undertakers are the butt of silly jokes because they represent our fears made real. I know how many funeral directors end up going to a cocktail party at somebody's house, and then Bill the dentist walks over and goes, "Oh, hey Sam, how you doin'? Last guy to let me down, right?" Ha ha ha. Oh, you're so funny. They do feel a certain pressure to always be in a suit and acting above reproach, but I think in many ways, as much as it's a trap for them, it's also a security blanket that they refuse to let go of.

I think a lot of things would get better if we dropped all the pretense and realized that they are in it to make money, and that's fine.

We consumers are also not honest about it. "I can't believe they charge this much." Well, I agree with you that XYZ Funeral Home's prices are absolutely outrageous. However, the tone of your voice says to me that you think there's something morally wrong with this. It leads me to believe that you're thinking of them not as capitalists, but somehow as almost demi-counselors or clergy. That's foolish. Funeral directors encourage that, of course! They even call their salespeople "family service counselors." But they are not counselors. They are salespeople. And it's okay that they're salespeople! They have to pay their mortgage, and they have to feed their kids, and their kids have to go to school just like yours do. If we dealt with this as the business transaction that it was, and not just as an emotional transaction, I think a lot of the difficulties would be ameliorated.

CALIFORNIA, FOR BETTER OR WORSE

The biggest thing that probably affects consumers the most is the rise in the cremation rate and the fact that, in many parts of the country, cremation prices are now actually competitive. All the way up and down the West Coast, you have to work to find an overpriced cremation. Back in '63, less than 3 percent of people who died every year were cremated. Almost everyone was embalmed and buried. Today it's 50 percent.

Even suggesting cremation in the sixties, in many parts of the country, was completely socially unacceptable. And of course that was heavily, heavily influenced by the funeral industry. They did a masterful job of co-opting religious terminology to justify their existence. Somehow over the past 130 years, a form of burial that includes chemical preservation, cosmetics, field-manufactured caskets—all sorts of things that have no history in any religious tradition or in the foundations of any society— have come to be regarded as a Christian burial. It's a complete triumph of the marriage of capitalism and religion. But most places, it's being changed and challenged.

I think we were responsible for some of that change. We certainly were agitating for the social acceptability of cremation. Also, in 1984 the Federal Trade Commission put rules in place that required funeral homes not only to transparently disclose their prices, no questions asked, but also barred them from requiring consumers to buy all-inclusive packages. This rule required that any funeral home that offered any kind of cremation had to offer a simple, no-frills cremation: That had something to do with it, too. A lot of it has to do, also, with the West Coast and California. California usually leads the way culturally and in terms of regulation. The population in California had a huge influx of immigrants and people immigrating from the East Coast, breaking family ties and moving away from the old homestead—when people do things like that, their attitudes about all sorts of things change. So a lot of consumer demand popped up on the West Coast, and that really helped propel cremation.

In the fifties and sixties, it was really popular to buy graves ahead of time. That's when so-called "preneed" really got started. It was the cemeteries, not the funeral homes, who started it. It used to be very common for young families in the fifties and sixties to buy up five or six contiguous graves at the local cemetery because, with four children, each of them will need their own grave, right? It seemed sensible in a world where you can't conceive of anything but whole-body burial. Fast forward to today, and the children of those parents are now in their seventies and eighties, and nine out of ten of them are asking how to get rid of these unwanted graves. We are in the middle of a big cultural change in how we conceive of the permanence of our death resting places, I think.

A NEW INTEREST AND A NEW ENERGY

I don't know when and why people suddenly become interested in talking about death. I could point you to someone like Caitlin Doughty, who is just a huge breath of fresh air, but that wouldn't tell you why the cultural landscape was ready for Caitlin Doughty.

There's definitely a new interest and a new energy among activists to really push back against efforts by the commercial funeral industry to shut our choices down—to shut down green burial, to shut down home- and family-directed funerals. When I first took this job in 2002, there were two women in the United States whom I knew of who would be considered experts on home funerals and were really out there educating the public about it. Now, in 2015, we have an organization called the National Home Funeral Alliance, whose entire existence is that advocacy, and they have almost a thousand members. When I started, there were two green cemeteries in the United States, and now there are about a hundred that are some shade of self-designated green. A lot of these folks are the same people who were advocating thirty years ago for the right to have birth at home.

The fact is that there's enough of that that they could actually form an organization and that there was enough of a network of volunteers and activists—both in Funeral Consumers Alliance and outside of it—that we got Senate bill 595 amended. That bill, as it was written and introduced, would have required all persons—even individual private families who are handling a dead body—to maintain that dead body in a mechanical refrigeration unit if it wasn't buried promptly. Or, in the absence of having a mechanical refrigeration unit, you would be required by law to contract with a funeral home that did. Honestly, I had very little to do with fixing it. And this is the first time I've had very little to do with it. [Laughs.] People really took off and did this on the grassroots level. That surprised me in a really positive way. That's hopeful.

\\

CONDUCTED MARCH 10, 2016

KIM STACEY
FREELANCE WRITER

Kim Stacey took a roundabout route to a copywriting career. She found free-lance writing jobs—mostly in funeral trade publications and websites—in midlife, after carving out a career as a copywriter for funeral home websites. I noticed Kim's byline in a trade magazine called Mortuary Management, *which has featured an idyllic landscape on each of its covers for the past twenty years. It's a funny juxtaposition, one that seems utterly out of step in 2016.*

Kim's columns, on the other hand, are shockingly of the moment. She has covered grief rituals across global cultures, "eternal reefs" made with human ash, and the history of funeral flowers. She writes about the funeral indus-try thoroughly and sometimes ferociously, using her insider status (she is a licensed, though not practicing, funeral home director) to go behind the scenes in a way that few other writers can. She has done this, for the most part, on her own dime. "None of the trade journals pay anymore," she tells me.

When contacted via telephone, Kim seems instantly familiar and en-couraging. I have discovered that, when it comes to people who are eager to talk about death and are fascinated by the industry built around it, it's a small world. Kim Stacey knows that world intimately, and her corner of it—writing about the funeral industry for print magazines—is itself a dying industry.

A THOUSAND DOLLARS A MONTH

We're supposed to get rain any minute. It's not raining now. So I'm going to go sit outside. I actually do it a little bit to annoy my landlords, since they booted me out on my ear. I got a notice to leave, a sixty-day notice, on Monday. It's a little converted garage, basically six hundred square feet. I pay a thousand dollars a month. A thousand dollars in this area is nothing. So, basically, I think they want to get someone else in here at a higher rate. But it has served my purposes. The seclusion was nice. Now it's time for someplace different, I guess.

A GOOD RITUAL WILL TRANSFORM YOU

I was twelve when my father took me to Iran. I was an only child. He worked for FMC Corporation. He was going there to build an irrigation pump foundry. He stayed there fourteen years, until he got thrown out during the revolution. I only stayed there six years. I came back to the states to go to college, but those were very formative years. You know, it was like Disneyland. I loved Iran, and I fully intended on going back.

Most of my life I've loved funerals. I think it had to do with my childhood. I was nine when Kennedy was assassinated, so that was the first big state funeral I saw. We had a lot of them in that decade; a lot of big people. Martin Luther King, Robert Kennedy. Funerals—I was steeped in them. My favorite book was on the Egyptian pharaoh Tutankhamun, and that was basically all about his tomb and his funeral and his embalming. So it's always been a part of my background—a little dark, maybe.

I think what I was really interested in was a spiritual connection. My parents were lapsed Catholics. I was an only child. If I even showed a glimmer of interest in going to church with a school friend—you know, how you'd go to somebody's church with them as a kid—they'd be horrified by that. But my best friend was a Catholic, and I loved the Catholic Church. It was so pretty.

Those were the old days. I would light candles, and my grandmother would send me little prayer cards. I'd set them up on my dresser. I got up at four-thirty in the morning, years ago, to watch Princess Diana's funeral. Ritual—I've always loved ritual. That's the hook.

A good ritual will transform you from where you were when you walked in the room to when you leave—you're supposed to be a little different. A good funeral can do that for you. Today's aren't quite as cathartic as they used to be because you don't get to grieve openly. You've gotta behave yourself. We've kind of hog-tied our grieving, and we're left to do it alone in the privacy of our homes. It's not very fair; it doesn't work that way. Grief is better when it's witnessed—where people can hold you, and it's a group thing.

At any rate, that was where I started as a child, looking for some comfort from ritual. Then when I went to Iran, I had all this opportunity to do amateur archaeology because there were archaeological sites everywhere. I got to work on three-thousand-year-old cemeteries. The first dig I ever went on was a cemetery, and I remember brushing off the skull of this deceased, and it had an arrowhead in the clavicle.

You talk about liminal spaces. Cemeteries are sacred because they're unique. They're not for the dead, and they're not for the living; they're not really for anybody. That was the focus of my master's degree—liminal spaces.

I did the fieldwork for my Master's degree on the grounds of Mountain View Cemetery, in Oakland, California—gorgeous place. Then I kind of put all that by the wayside and raised kids. I left my husband in 2003, and because I was homeschooling my kids, I wanted to do something from home. What do anthropologists do but write? I thought, *Well, I'll become a writer*. I took a direct-mail copywriting course. It's just a crappy little thing, but it got me understanding the concept of copywriting.

Anyway, then I put those two pieces together. I thought, *I could write website copy for funeral homes. They need me*. I was a little bit ahead of my time—most funeral homes weren't even on the Internet yet. I did some trade journal articles and just kind of cobbled together a life. I wanted to earn a living when I left my husband, and I thought that I would be clamored for by funeral directors. I wasn't, you know? They still don't clamor.

THE WOMEN'S PERSPECTIVE

At one time, *Mortuary Management* was the flagship magazine for the industry—but then you got all of your associations publishing their own trade magazines. Pretty soon *Mortuary Management* became—oh my god, it's down to about forty pages. It's next to nothing.

It's heartbreaking, really. I've enjoyed writing for them. Years ago I started the Association for Women Funeral Directors. I thought that would be a much-needed thing—that I could make money and do good work for women in the industry. I didn't know what the hell I was doing, so it fell flat on its face. Around that time, the National Funeral Director's Association got involved and started having women's conferences. So Women in that industry are getting some attention now. But that's how I got into *Mortuary Management*: I was the women's perspective, as a representative of my association.

It's a challenge every month to come up with something fresh. I used to write for *American Funeral Director*, and I'd get four hundred dollars an article. That day is long gone. There are so many people—so many consultants—who have something to say. There are almost too many people who can fill up cyberspace and print pages with content that no one's going to read.

Most of it is pure self-promotion. You run out of things to talk about. I write about books I've read, or my ex-husband's death and how it affected me.; I hope to get funeral home clients out of it, but for the ten years I've been writing for them I've never gotten a funeral home client from one of my magazine articles. Now I do it just because I like the editors, and I want to help. And I get to write about whatever I want!

SMALL POND, BIG FISH

You know, obituary piracy is a big deal. Third-party companies scrape obituaries off of funeral homes' websites and put them on their own obituary sites. The third-party sites have very high domain rankings, so when a person enters in "William Powell," looking through the obits, the stolen one is going to come up before the funeral home's own obituary does. The person's going to go leave the comments there, but the family will never be notified that anyone left any comments. The goal is to sell ancillary products, to accrue email contact details, and to send preneed planning information or push flower sales. If someone leaves a condolence on a third-party website, and wants to buy flowers, you can do it through them. Of course, there's a high markup.

When you're a funeral home, and you go to, let's say, FrontRunner,* for a website, they'll sell you a website full of content. Well, that's all mine, and it's all supposed to be customized. That never happens! So you've got this issue of duplicate content. Google hates dupe content. They'll knock you down. Websites all over the country and in Canada and Australia have my content, and that's doing them all a disservice. I go back and try and pitch custom content directly to them. Smart people will accept a bare-minimum package. I'll do the keyword research for your demo-graphic and plug in the right keywords. It's very basic. But most of the time they just limp along with the website as is, and that's too bad.

Of course, there's heavy grief content. I write about that. That's why I got my grief counseling certification.

When it comes to writing funeral home content, what they want me to do is promote funerals, promote rituals. Funerals aren't happening anymore, especially here in California, with the high cremation rate. So I have to pitch ritual: the importance of gathering together. I talk a lot

* A company that builds websites and software for funeral homes.

about pricing. I try and push every funeral home I work with to publish their general price list online. I think today's consumers want to see what they're going to pay. The unfortunate thing is that a general price list is such a confusing document that most funeral homes don't want to make it available because consumers don't know what they're looking at, and they just get more confused.

The law requires a certain set of information in a certain order, and disclaimers and stock rhetoric. It gets really complicated. Here in California, we have to post our pricing online. It's required by the state. Other states don't have that same mandate. In other states I often end up writing content about their pricing without actually disclosing the pricing. The call to action is always "pick up the phone and call us." We have to keep pushing that—"Get in touch, get in touch." They don't want their competitors to know their prices. That's another reason why they don't want to post online, but the bottom line is your competitor—they know everything about you. They can pick up a phone and call just like anyone else. They have their Aunt Martha do it.

Consumers are faced with a hell of a bind. They've gotta get grandma buried, and they've gotta do it quick. I had that with my ex-husband, Matt. He was adamant he wasn't going to die. He had stage-four colon cancer, so of course he was going to die. Nothing was done ahead of time, and that was tragic. My oldest son and I went down and set things up, and I got it just the way I wanted. Consumers don't know that they can have a witness at the cremation if they want one. They can push their loved one into the cremator. They can participate. But funeral homes don't really want you to participate, so they don't talk about it much. There are liability issues and such.

THE TEST

Funeral professionals are like wedding planners on a three-day schedule. It's a hard job, and it's an underpaid job. Unless you're a really savvy businessman and own a chain of funeral homes, most of the time it's a difficult business.

I became a funeral director myself. Not so that I could go into business, but because I wanted to prove it was too easy to become one in California. I was writing an article about licensing standards. You only need sixty units of credit, better known as an AA degree. You pass a multiple-choice test, and as long as you pay them two hundred dollars a year for the rest of your life, you have a funeral director's license. There's no continuing education required; there's nothing. I passed the test after a five-hour law-review course, which was basically about funeral law—the things you can and can't do. It didn't teach me to be a good funeral director.

I did it in a day. You only had to have a 60 percent to pass the class. I thought, *Jesus, you've gotta be kidding me. Lord, you could accidentally color in the right bubbles and get 60 percent.*

If you look into New York or even Florida, their standards are amazingly high. You have to be a college graduate, you have to go to mortuary school, you have to take continuing education courses, and you have to take the exam every third year. It's rigorous. California is just the opposite. My point was, if you want to be considered a real professional, you've got to have standardization. A doctor in California doesn't operate under vastly different standards than one in Tennessee.

There are other issues in the industry. There's a lot of attrition. Nobody stays in the business for very long. Mortuary college students on average stay three years. They can make more money doing other things, and it's very hard to have a social life as a funeral director. Especially the low man or woman on the totem pole.

Everybody's life is difficult, but when you serve families day after day who are grieving or angry—I was talking to a gentleman the other day whose son died at thirty-seven of stomach cancer. He was in the hospital and died within an hour of being given a morphine shot. The father is adamant that the hospital killed his son, and his anger was so strong that he couldn't focus on what needed to be done. Yes, he might want to sue, but that comes down the line. They've got to deal with the son's body. It's very taxing, people's anger and sorrow. It kind of pollutes your life sometimes. That said, in all these years, I have only met one funeral director who didn't love or at least like what he was doing. This man just didn't like life.

I love talking to funeral directors. Most of them are so committed. They are unlike anybody else, kind of a combination minister and counselor and bureaucrat. That's what funeral directors do. They're bureaucrats; they fill in paperwork and submit it to the right places and transport bodies. And it has to be done well. You've got to get that paperwork right. But it's the connection that matters. Every one of them loves the human connection.

They want to share their passion with me, as a writer, so I can share it with their audience. I did a website for one woman who specializes in Sikh and Muslim funeral in New Jersey, and this is what she loves to do. Writing for her was so easy because she could translate that passion into words. It's a little harder for men. Men don't emote well. They don't get down to the feelings of being a funeral director. But most of them are very caring individuals. They usually have a remarkable sense of humor, and I've never had a single one of them stiff me for my fees. Everything I write has to pass a plagiarism checker. I promise 100 percent brand-new content, and I don't know how much longer I can write brand-new content! I find that I'm plagiarizing myself. How much can you write about death and dying?

I WEAR MY HEART ON MY SLEEVE

Basically, I wear my heart on my sleeve. That was especially true when my ex was dying. I was taking care of him for two and a half years. My dog was dying at the same time; he had congestive heart failure. He was fourteen. I was surrounded by death, and I was just emoting all over the place. FrontRunner has a pet-loss website called *An Unforgettable Friend*, and I wrote all the content for that, including all the grief support resources—coloring books for kids and all kinds of things. I could do such a good job because I was grieving for my dog who was lying right at my feet, dying. It was because I could emote on the page that that content is so powerful. People write me about that, saying, "Oh my god, that's beautiful." I've touched people's lives with stuff I've written, and that means something. But the jobs are disappearing, and at sixty-two I think I'm running out of options.

I try not to tiptoe through anything. I like upfront language. When I write for Canadian firms, they usually don't want to have the word *death* anywhere on the page. They want to use silly-ass euphemisms like "passed on" or "passed away." You've "lost your loved one"—that just drives me crazy. You haven't lost them. They're not missing. They're dead. That's it; they're dead. They're right there, but they're dead. They don't want to be that blunt. They want me to pussyfoot, and I'm not really good at pussyfooting. I think the average consumer today doesn't want to be mollycoddled. I like to speak clearly because you are going to die whether you want to admit it or not.

Funeral directors are traditionally slow adopters. I've had them say, "What do I need a website for? Everybody in town knows where I am." Yeah, but the people in Chicago who are mourning the person who died in your town—they want a website. They don't understand. They don't understand search-engine optimization. Dear god, I barely do. It's exhausting.

They're overworked and underpaid, and a lot of times they don't get paid for the services they render. Many of them will bury children for free, infants especially. There's a lot of good work being done by funeral homes. They're very service oriented.

THE BAD DEATH

I had this horrible incident. One of my clients is a fairly well-known public speaker, and he asked me to help him develop a presentation. He was hired to speak to oncology nurses about how they can deal with the relative hopelessness of their job and maintain their sanity. It took me right back to Matt's death. I worked on it on Wednesday because it was due on Thursday. I was citing facts and figures about cancer—a million and a half people this year are going to be diagnosed with it, yadda yadda—and I was remembering the futility of Matt's care. I literally got physically ill. It brought up so much grief for me.

You know, I got that certificate in grief counseling. I like to think of myself as a grief facilitator. But mostly it comes from an academic point of view. Experientially, sure, I've lost dogs, and my parents are dead, but I was estranged from them. I've lost a few friends. Really, I was always talking like an academic. I never had the realization of how grief can slam you to your knees until Wednesday, when I was forced to confront all of it as a writer. To try and figure out how I felt about it—to try and talk about it. How can these nurses bring hope when there is none? I have no idea how well I did, but when I sent it to him at the end of the day, I was physically ill. I said, "Don't ask me to revisit the topic because I can't."

It was a very intense experience. I couldn't stop crying. My regrets came burbling up, the fact that he was essentially alone for two and a half years and dying. You know, I'd take him to chemo and take him grocery shopping and then take him home and leave him there, and he'd be sitting there alone. He used to tell me, "I'm just so lonely. I need a companion." I couldn't do it for him.

I took care of him for all the wrong reasons. Or not, I don't know. If it were me, I'd want someone to help me. And I did it for my boys. I needed to show them that family comes together. We were always family, in that I never stopped letting Matt see the boys. I felt I owed it to the three of them to do it. I'd have wanted him to do the same for me, but he wouldn't have. He wouldn't have touched me with a ten-foot pole if I were dying because I might be contagious. But as a Buddhist, this is what you do. It's not a religion; it's a way of living. You help people when they need help, and he needed help. Many times, he said, "Thank you. I don't know what I'd do without you."

Bottom line, I'm glad I did it. It was invaluable because all the hospice work I had done was with strangers, and when you meet them, you know they're dying, so you sit together in that space quite willingly. But when you've known a person for thirty years and they've been totally robust—Matt was a scuba diver and a dirt biker. He used to climb redwood trees and lop them down when he was a young guy. He had no fear about anything *except* dying, and watching him die was the hardest thing I ever did. It changed me. Watching other people die was part of the work, and it was expected. I thought he'd die at the bottom of the sea, that he'd get too deep or get the bends or something. To watch him shrivel up—it was a shocking experience.

His death was so bad, so ugly. I mean, he died screaming, basically, and I can still hear him. I was terrified of that kind of death. When you get to the heart of the matter, I'm not scared of dying; I'm scared of dying badly. Without grace and dignity and a sense of awareness and completion and calm. He had none of those things, and that's what scared me. He did not willingly let go of life. It exhausted everyone around him. His fighting exhausted us.

Now I know, were I today to get the same diagnosis he got, I'd do it entirely differently. It would just be acquiescence and an acceptance. There'd be a deep sadness because I do love watching the sun come between the clouds. There are precious moments. I'm also fairly hopeful and fairly resolved. Energy doesn't dissipate. My energy will combine with that of the universe, and there you go. I'll be a constant. I won't be in this consciousness, but I'll be a constant.

When I was your age, I was scared of not being part of the party; that everybody else would get to keep having fun, and I couldn't have any. That's not the way I feel now at sixty-two. It's different. I will miss—looking out right now, I have a maple tree with those flowers that hang, and they're actually blooming. They're gorgeous. There are drops of rainwater hanging on each of them, and the leaves are blowing and the flowers are moving. It's just gorgeous. I'll miss seeing things like that. Well, maybe I won't miss it—I wouldn't be around to miss it!

Death is going to be painful. One of the things I wept about on Wednesday—my youngest son and I lost his dog of fourteen years. Courage the Brave. And he just put a down payment on a new puppy, a Boston terrier puppy. He's going to pick up the puppy next week. My heart broke that he would open himself up to loss, because one day that dog is going to die and he's going to be heartbroken again, just like he was with Courage. He weeps about Courage—we both do—but you can't stop living. I admire him for being willing. See, I'm no longer willing. I'm too old; I've lost too many pets. I'm not going to do it again. Nope, can't do it. But he's willing. He's young enough. He's strong enough to go through that. I'm scared for him and proud of him.

WORK THAT NO ONE ELSE WANTS

Lifelong learning is my watchword; it should be my middle name. If I'm not learning something new I feel like my life is kind of wasted. That's what I want to bring these people, to educate them on the dilemma that they're stuck in—trying to bridge technology with what is essentially a rather archaic industry. We funeral directors are doing pretty much the same thing we've done for a long time. We're just disposing of the dead. And to do it with a consciousness of how other people do it, or how I as an anthropologist—this big, wonderfully holistic perspective that anthropologists have—to fit it in place, to remind them that they are doing sacred work, that's really important to me. That's the crux of it. Burying the dead is sacred work. We don't take the task on lightly. Most of us don't want to do it. We'd rather turn it over to someone else, and there was always the person in the village who did it or the family is responsible as a collective whole for washing and dressing and burying their relatives. You know, it is work that no one else wants, and it's not ordinary work—you're dwelling in this space between the living and the dead.

IT'S ALL VERY REGIONAL

One of my exercise classmates came to me—we're all kind of old. She's seventy-two. She had been to three funerals recently, and she asked me, "Is it normal for people to applaud at the end of a speaker presentation at a funeral?" She said at all three funerals people would clap after every speech or presentation, and she said, "I couldn't bring myself to do it. Was I wrong?" Well, I've never heard of clapping. But then I hit on it—in California, everything is entertainment. It's all like a big Hollywood. We're all doing this because you need to be entertained, so applauding kind of makes sense. But I'll bet you ten-to-one, if I go on Facebook and ask my morticians' group, people across the country have probably never heard of applauding. They still have that same rather sacred traditional view of the event. In California, we want it held at our favorite beach! It becomes more of a party.

It's all very regional. I was talking to one Georgia funeral home owner about his cremation rates. I was writing him some custom content, and in California everyone wants to talk about cremation. He said, "I don't think we really need any content on cremation." I asked him his cremation rate, and he said, "Six." I said, "Six percent?" He said, "No, I did six last year." Out of a case load of 450. It's very regional, our relationship with death.

INTIMACY

Around the time of the Civil War, we turned it over to the experts to care for our dead, and it distances us. I wrote a piece recently for *Mortuary Management* on desairology. A young woman who I know has started a company. She's a desairologist, which is a fancy word for someone who combines embalming with cosmetology. What she has fashioned is the "family dress experience." She goes into funeral homes and will work with families to help them care for their own dead—wash and dress them and cosmetize them, do their hair—the hands on. She doesn't just put them in a room and make them do it on their own. She guides them and helps them where they need to, and even if they just want to sit and watch somebody else do it, she'll do it for them. They can participate by watching and witnessing. That's what's missing. That one-on-one thing. Touching the dead, contacting the deceased body. We don't do that well. We don't do open caskets well.

In the back of my Ford Taurus wagon, I've got a pair of heavy-duty rubber gloves and plastic bags. One of the things I hate living in this valley is you always have roadkill. You have raccoons, skunks, cats—a lot of dead cats. I don't like it when people leave them in the road and just keep running over them. So, I pick them up. I stop my car and pick them up, and I put them in a bag.

I cannot stand to see the dead disrespected. That's another reason why I write what I do. The saddest thing I have is the thought that my kids would treat me the same way they treated their father. The reality is they and I both know what they're going to do. We've picked out the song—it's "Naive Melody" by the Talking Heads. That's my song. So that will be played, you can bet.

There was a lot of loathing, a lot of anger, between me and Matt, but the last thing we said to each other was "I love you." I think we both meant it. It was like two soldiers who had been in the trenches. There's a love there that can't really be defined. We had gone through this together. I remember holding his hand while he was in hospice at his house, and we're watching some horrible show. *Pawn Stars* or something. We're sitting there watching that, and I turn and look at him and he's just quietly crying. He knew he had hours to live. He leaned over to me, and he said, "So how long is this hospice thing?" And I said, "Honey, I just don't know." Then he got real quiet. He knew he had come home to die. That is intimacy, right there. To profess ignorance and to profess fear. This was a fearless man who used to climb redwoods, strapped in with ropes and leather, and hack them apart with chainsaws. But he was scared.

That's intimacy. That's what I think I was looking for in all the hospice work I did—that intimacy with another person. When you sit in that space in the doorway between life and death. There's nothing more intimate. Whether you're reading aloud from their favorite book or surrounding them with pictures of their deceased husband that they're going to join, there's intimacy there. It's very powerful, without a doubt.

CONDUCTED MARCH 11, 2016

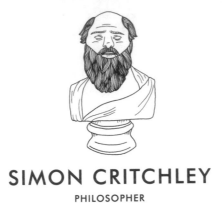

SIMON CRITCHLEY

PHILOSOPHER

Simon Critchley is a British-born philosopher and professor who has written or contributed to at least two dozen books since the early nineties. He also moderates a philosophy column called "The Stone" for the New York Times. *Death is a near-constant theme of his work, which runs the gamut from philosophical meditations to biography and fiction. His second book,* Very Little . . . Almost Nothing, *dealt extensively with the centrality of death to the human experience, and his more recent book* Notes on Suicide *delves nonjudgmentally into the ethics of taking one's own life. His most eccentric meditation on death, though, is* The Book of Dead Philosophers, *which provides thoughtful obituaries—some haunting, many hilarious—for nearly two hundred philosophers, along with their own thoughts on death.*

Despite his focus on mortality, Critchley's writing is playful and characterized by its sense of adventure and its willingness to cross-pollinate ideas from philosophy, literature, and pop culture. His experimental fiction book Memory Theatre, *about a slightly fictionalized Critchley stumbling on advance knowledge of the exact date and time of his death, reads more like a product of screenwriter Charlie Kaufman's twisted mind than what we might expect from one of the world's preeminent philosophers.*

I warned Critchley that I knew very little about philosophy—but that we at least shared a taste in bands. "The only reason to teach, apart from getting the money and the health benefits, is that you can get decent music tips from students," he told me on the phone. "I've constructed an elaborate kind of network over the years."

THE WORD *GRIEF*

If I tried to describe what I was feeling after my mother died last December in terms of the word *grief*, that wouldn't really capture it. I guess what I'm opposed to is the idea of grief being some kind of state of tears and upset, and then mourning as a process that one goes through with a series of stages. I think that for many people who experience the death of someone they're very close to, it's more a feeling of a kind of stasis. Things just seem to stop, and they won't budge. Time, in particular, doesn't seem to move. It just seems to be fixed. I cried after my mother died, but then that stopped, and then I felt a kind of deadness that was bound up with the feeling of time having lost its flow. I felt quite distant, as if I was feeling something that wasn't really in my head. It was a feeling that was being felt almost outside me and despite me. It was very odd.

It comes back, I'd say, every day for a period of time. It's not necessarily that I'm thinking about my mother, but I'm kind of gripped by a thought that's sort of thinking me—a thought that's having me. It's a very hard feeling to explain. There's almost a coldness to it. That sounds like what we're *not* meant to feel after somebody dies, but it is what a lot of people do feel.

The word *grief* just doesn't capture that. The idea of mourning, by which we mean the activities one engages in after someone has died—it's damaging because it means that after a period of time you're not meant to feel what you feel anymore.

You have about two months, you know? Maybe three months. That's the easy bit. When my mother died, I was doing a lot of stuff because I was responsible for the estate, such as it was. I had to register a certified death, arrange a funeral, all of those things. It's after three or four months that things really get difficult, by which time people have moved on. "Oh yeah, your mother's dead."

BOWIE

My mother's death definitely kind of paralyzed, suspended, me. And then David Bowie died in January. I had written a book about him, so on the morning of his death, I was asked to speak on various media, and then ended up writing something the Monday after he died. I spent the next ten days basically talking to people about Bowie.

What interested me about that was not so much what I had to say. It was what they had to say—and also how intimate the relationship to Bowie was, and then how intense the grief was because of the intimacy of the relationship one had with this completely abstract figure. Bowie could affect someone at this level of profound intimacy, in relation to something which is disorientating and bewildering, mainly life.

His death was profoundly troubling for people for that reason. A whole set of possibilities had closed down, but also, the flipside of it was that people thought more carefully than they had about the way his music, and music in general, was able to connect with them. There's something about the stupidity of a three-minute pop song that's able to hold a nugget of all of the stuff inside, which can be articulated in books and interpretations, but it's all there in some kind of form.

As human beings we kind of sediment, or at least we think we sediment, down into strata of routines and behavior and activity and careers and all the rest. But there's something about music which is able to reactivate all of that—to trouble all that sediment and get it spinning. Bowie reminded people of why that is important.

It was also an example of the way social media can, in certain circumstances, really work. Social media is a nightmare, we know that, but in circumstances like this it really is effective at offering a medium for forms of interchange, which I'd never experienced before. It's still going on. I'm in touch with a bundle of people who I wasn't in touch with before his death, with links being sent back and forth, and it's expanded into a whole range of other connections.

It's about being returned to that disorienting, bewildered space of adolescence, and the openness that one has at that point. That's what music speaks to. We forget that because we're all kind of hipster scholars of music, and we all know everything already.

I've been thinking a lot about process after Bowie's death. I'm reading everything I can find about him, watching everything I can find about him, talking with people about the way he writes songs. One thing that I've picked up, which I didn't really appreciate before, was how in a sense he didn't like what he was saying. At a certain point, he'd accepted that these were the sort of things he was going to say, and it wasn't an act of will on his part—it was some kind of invention which he was able to engage in for certain periods.

It produced the music that it produced, which indeed seems to circle around a set of themes, like isolation and schizophrenia. I think one has to accept that. As Beckett said, "Each man counts his rats." You've just gotta work out what your rats are, and know they're the ones that are going to eat your face.

"MAKE SENSE WHO MAY"

One's own death is always kind of unintelligible and incomprehensible because you don't experience it. There's that paradox of death, which has been the case ever since people have been thinking about it: It's not my death. It's the deaths of others. It's through the deaths of others that death comes into the world. And the deaths of others can be abstract, or they can be felt in relation to the people who you're closest to. When a young child asks their parent, or whoever is bringing them up, "Are you going to die?" The parent has to say, "Yes, I'm going to die." And then death enters the world for that child. Not through the actual death of their parents—although that can happen—but through the knowledge that their parents are going to die. That does change things.

One view of death is the old Epicurean wisdom: Death is nothing, so when death is, I am not. When I am, death is not. Therefore, why worry?

That line of thinking is very rational. We exist, you exist, I exist, other people around us exist, and we will exist until we don't exist anymore. And when we don't exist anymore, we won't exist anymore. That's something we can know nothing about, and it's a matter of idle speculation what, if anything, happens—so why worry?

Another rational response to death is to argue for the soul's immortality, which is the argument that Socrates makes in a number of dialogues, but particularly in *Phaedo*, which is where he's condemned to die. The philosophical content of the dialogue is a series of arguments for why the soul is deathless, the soul is immortal. You can say, "Well, yeah, life is mortal, that the body passes away," but there's a very strong sense that there is something about a self, some part of the self, which is not simply mortal. It's deathless. That's another rationality.

I'm sort of an existentialist. That's really where I came in, in terms of the writing that really spoke to me when I was young, and I'm still there. An existentialist feels like there are reasons we can give for what we do, and reasons why things are the way they are—but there's also a fundamental irrationality to human existence, which is bound up with our mortality and our relationship to our mortality. If philosophy is rational activity, then it comes down to the idea that we're these death-bound creatures who are possessed of another set of inclinations. It's not rational to fear death. There are a thousand ways to rationally quell the fear of death. The problem is that none of these seem to work. [Laughs.]

This happened to me the other night when I was trying to go to sleep. I just suddenly had an image of a friend of mine, a person I studied with called Will, who had a very serious head injury when we were together when he was twenty-five, in Italy. I suddenly had a memory of the evening of and the next day after his injury, and then I had the second thought of, *Maybe I won't wake up in the morning,* which is a thought I don't often have. *Maybe I'll drift to sleep and I'll never wake up.*

There's irrationality to such thoughts, and we all have them, and what we look for at that point are the capillaries that enable us to make sense of those thoughts: literature and music and anything else that works. I think death is irrational in that sense. We can use our words to try and make sense, but we know that making sense isn't really going to put an end to the worry.

I was reading Beckett the other week. I was reading the last dramatic piece that he wrote, which is called *What Where*, without question marks. The last line he wrote is, "Make sense who may." It's typical Beckett. He's constructed a bizarre little play with these characters called Bim and Bom, these old dumb names. It seems to me a description of some kind of scene of torture. It's not clear, it's not articulated, and then there's this final line, "Make sense who may." I think that's our situation. We may, if we wish, make sense. We can't but make sense, but what making sense is just an overlay that lays over something ultimately senseless, which is our own death.

SOME KIND OF FUTURE

After my mother died, I was reading a lot of things about bereavement. There's this poet, Denise Riley, who was talking about the death of her son—which is unimaginably more difficult than the death of a parent. She talks about the fact that she couldn't write because one can only write if one can imagine some kind of future. What bereavement does is it breaks that down. You think that you can't imagine a future for that period of time when you're in "profound grief"—in quotation marks—and you therefore stop writing.

The premise behind all of our activity as human beings is that there is some future into which our work is going to have a place. We hope that's the case, but we can't know.

Memory Theatre is about that. It's about the fantasy of me coinciding with myself and with everything I know, everything I want to know—coinciding with myself at the point of my death, which is controlled and mastered. In that fantasy, I go out like a lightning flash. But a more domestic version of that would be the fantasy that I want to die surrounded by my friends and loved ones, right? The good death.

In the case of *Memory Theatre*, it doesn't work out, and the Simon Critchley character is a little bit sad for a while. Then we find him engaged in an even more profound delusion, which involves this whole construction of an island which will, through the use of tidal motion, project an entire history of the world. We leave him outside of a local library in the Netherlands, waiting for it to open so he can consult tidal charts. That underlines the pathetic character of human existence, but I don't find it sad. I find the fantasy of everything meaning something catastrophic and sad. I find the vanity of human wishes a source of solace, actually. It's what makes us laugh. Humor is the capacity to sort of self-deprecate and to find everything ludicrous, ridiculous. And that's okay. Who do we think we are? Gods?

I'M A GREAT BELIEVER IN PHYSICAL INJURY

When my father was ill and then died in 1994, that broke through a kind of protective shell. It's almost like a membrane. You can think about death in all sorts of ways—and I certainly did—but the membrane of my narcissism was punctured by my father's death. At that time, for reasons that weren't planned, I was reading Beckett's trilogy as me, my mother, and my sister were taking turns nursing my father. Then I gave a talk—sometime after my father died—on Beckett. It was the first time I'd talked on Beckett. It was in Norway, which was kind of appropriate, and it was the first time I'd been to Scandinavia, and I hadn't given many talks publicly by this time. What I remember of it is a kind of electric quality I had about what I was trying to figure out, and I was using Beckett as a way of thinking about the immediacy of the impacts of my father's death. Death has always been something I've thought about. I think about it retrospectively now as a source of somewhat idle speculation, until something pierces through the membrane of the self and really addresses me. That can be an accident, as well.

I'm a great believer in physical injury. It's an absurd thing to say, but most of the time, a lot of people are asleep. Not all people. There's a tendency among young men to be particularly dead. Maybe they're not thinking about death, but in a sense they're inwardly, internally dead—and that's also a kind of self-protective thing. What can shake you up is the impact of bereavement, or indeed an accident where you suffer physical injury of some kind.

There have been a few nasty physical injuries which have woken me up. The big one was my hand being almost severed in an industrial accident when I was eighteen years old. I had classic effects of trauma; I forgot great chunks of the past, some of which came back, some of which was told to me—but then you're not really sure whether you believe it or not because you don't actually remember it yourself. But I was kind of erased as a self. It woke me up. It took years and years and years to work out that I'd woken up, but I had kind of woken up. I'm very interested in psychoanalysis, and Freud's very important. Infant development is crucial in all of those things. But I think things can happen later in life, what Sartre called "radical projects." I think there are moments in one's life when there can be external triggers or internal triggers where you wake up, and then you can invent something.

I think it's about—to sound really stupid—getting drunk and falling over sometimes. It's about situations of a loss of control or experiencing genuine danger when things like that can happen. This is obviously a risky thing to say because you don't want to encourage people to act recklessly, but there's something to that. If you could wake up to a ten-step process or by doing Ashtanga yoga really well, that would be nice, but in my experience, it requires more dramatic events than that. That could be anything from troubles in the place that one lives to living in times of change, times of war.

War is the mother of invention, but also it's philosophically, in a perverse way, productive. You could recount the history of philosophy as a history of war, in the sense in which very often the breakthrough moments—or the moments when there are a number of thinkers and things going on—are often situations of dramatic conflict. Or soon afterward, when there's been a cataclysmic event or series of events, and then people need to try and make sense of it. For example, in Germany, the last really interesting generation of thinkers was after the Second World War because they were trying to figure out that disaster. Peace, love, and happiness are lovely things, but they've not necessarily produced interesting cultures.

"MAN IS A USELESS PASSION"

If death becomes something that we have to make sense of ourselves, then the ancient schools of the Epicureans, the Stoics, the skeptics—they're all dressed up. That makes us all pagans. Now, what changed with Christianity, in particular, was that the question of mortality became a much more existential question. It was an existential question that was always raised in relation not to oneself, but in relation to God. If you think of people like St. Paul and St. Augustine, then all the way through to people like Luther and Kierkegaard, the question of "Who I am," which is a question of my mortality, is always a question that's addressed in relation to God. And so the question of mortality for us is difficult because we can't really believe in pagan answers to these questions, because we live in a post-Christian culture—and we can't believe in Christian answers to these questions. They don't really answer them, either. So we're in a kind of quandary. We have some existential doubts of saints and martyrs, people who gave themselves to God.

It's why Sartre says, "Man is a useless passion." We still live as if God existed, but we know that God doesn't exist, which kind of makes our entire activity futile. What I am compelled with in regards to religious traditions, when they meditate upon death—particularly Christianity, because they get particularly deep in Christianity—is the absence of comfort. You have to go through a real journey, a really arduous journey, and all that one has is faith. Faith is faith; it's not knowledge. It's an orientation that one can follow in life. Some people might want to add on to that "the afterlife, heaven, immorality of the soul," but much of Christianity is very skeptical about these things.

It would be great to be a real Christian, a real nineteenth-century, Kierkegaardian Christian. I can't do that.

STORAGE WARS

We're all hoarders, right? All the galleries and museums are hoarding—it's very well-funded by people with good connections, but they're still hoarding. That junk just gets to hang around, whereas most junk gets thrown away.

My wife and I watched this show the other day, *Storage Wars*. The pretext for the show is that there are these storage spaces, which have been abandoned because the people have left town or have died, and then they get auctioned off. These sort-of-real people, who are acting like reality TV people, are bidding for the imagined contents of the storage unit. Of course, what lies in these storage units are these kind of memory theaters—they are the contents of someone's life who's departed, either left town or dead. But their only value is the dollar value of their trash. There is that terrifying aspect to our lives: We go around collecting, shoring up fragments against our ruins, collecting things. To what end it's unclear. That's a very unpleasant thought to have about one's life.

WE'RE THE WEIRDOS

Ritual, particularly but not exclusively religious ritual around death, is so important because there's a temporal aspect to it. There are things that one does—how one dresses, what one says, whether one takes off one's hat—all those practices are kind of broken down for us.

Now we don't know what to say, and it's a source of huge disquiet, the whole topic of death. It's not that people had a clearer sense of death in previous ages. Maybe they had more of a sense of its presence because of infant mortality rates and all the rest being what they were, so people were more used to seeing corpses and being around death. If you look at every city, from the first time that cities were built, in present-day Iraq and Mesopotamia through to ancient Greece and China, what was at the center of those cities was a necropolis—which is a place where the dead were—and the life of the society was fundamentally bound up with the presence of death and the presence of the ancestors.

You could say that is the condition for living socially, the constant presence of death. One's aware of that all around you, and one knows how to act in relationship to it. But the main difference is that there were socially accepted rituals. One knew what the rites and rituals are. And that's all broken down with us. Rituals around death are really significant because at least they suspend the internal question. "You just have to do this. This is what you should do when someone dies."

People who work in hospices are in the presence of death, and I think that's how we should all be. I think we should live in that way. Not that we're all going to move into a hospice, but society *is* a hospice. People are dying. We just don't see it, and we've chosen to devalue it in the name of longevity and youth, and that is a terrible thing. It means that we don't cherish the connections that we have. We run after ones that we don't have, and that makes us even more miserable.

We're the weirdos. We've made this sort of social decision, and that's what fucks us up. Just think about the relationship to old age and longevity in China or Japan. It's just fundamentally different. You could experience that as being oppressive. But still, there's a sense in which you're surrounded by the presence of death—by people who are older than you that are going to die first—and one has to act in the right way, and one knows what the right way is. We don't. We're the exception.

Once you've lost rituals, as we have, can we just then invent new death rituals? That seems, in the United States, difficult to imagine. It's possible, but it's difficult to imagine—and probably unlikely.

One of my early memories is of a funeral in Liverpool and my great-grandmother, who we called our Ninny. It was an open-coffin funeral, and everybody in the family had to kiss the corpse. I was probably picked up so I could do that. I don't remember being picked up, but I must have been too small to get up there. I remember kissing the corpse. You don't forget that. Do you know what it means at the time? No. But retrospectively, you know what that means, and that's part of a kind of archive that you can draw on when you're thinking about questions of death. If you have those background practices and habits and rituals available, then in an unthinking way, they can be drawn on. A society who's decided to just eliminate all of that in the name of youth, vigor, and life—that's pretty screwed up. But can new rituals be brought back? Probably not likely.

Here in the US, we have the singing of the national anthem, display of the flag, pledge of allegiance. Those are not unimportant things, I think, but they're kind of national rituals that don't really touch on this fear that we're talking about, this fear of death. For most societies, there was a closely knit relationship between that public, national dimension and the private, familial dimension. That's what's broken down. The public and private have split apart, so we're left with fear of death. We're left with not knowing what to do and how to react when a death happens.

SUICIDE NOTES

The strange thing about a suicide note is that it's written for a future that you're not going to be a part of, as a last, desperate attempt at communication. That usually comes down to really quite strange details. "Please give my cat Tommy to Auntie Lisa, and my collection of toy soldiers should go to Timothy," or whatever it might be. It's sometimes like leaving a will. They're often extreme expressions of self-hatred, on the one hand—which is what leads to the kind of suicidal depression—and then extreme expressions of love on the other hand.

There is something narcissistic and optimistic about suicide because you believe that your death can affect something in the world, that your death really amounts to that much. Then there can be a kind of sober realization that it doesn't, and maybe you should stick around a bit and stop bloody complaining.

I read a lot of suicide notes when I was writing *Notes on Suicide* and then planning the day-long School of Death, where I held a workshop. The idea of a suicide note creative writing workshop was obviously ridiculous. It was meant to be offensive, which was part of the point, to poke fun at creative writing in particular. I talked for about forty-five minutes, about the history of the suicide note as I understood it, and then we handed out little cards and people just wrote what they wanted. Then, if they wanted, they could read them out loud. I think everybody did read them out loud.

What was striking about the class was how deeply people thought about the notes. They had twenty minutes or something to write them. It was a group of people in the very small room in a gallery in Chelsea, and they were incredibly thoughtful and moving. I was shocked. I thought they would be funny, ironic, or cutting little jokey expressions by people—but actually, people really thought about what they were going to miss and who they wanted to speak to.

The one that really sticks in my mind—I think this is in the book—is this Englishwoman who I never saw before and I've never seen since. She said, "When you find out those things about me that you don't know, the secrets I've been keeping, never let that diminish the love that I feel for you." God, that's powerful. She obviously was keeping some secrets. We all keep secrets, and she knew they were going to come out. I was shocked by the kind of things they wrote and the seriousness that descended when people tried to write suicide notes.

"CREATURES OF A DAY"

There's a very short poem by Yeats called "Death," and there's a line where he says, "Man has created death." I think what he means is that the human being has created the fear of death. This is an imponderable question. Certainly, we fear death. Is that something which is socially created? I think it is, but there's no way of checking otherwise because we're social beings. For as long as human beings have been the kind of beings that they are with each other, we seem to have had a fear of death. If it's a social construction, that doesn't mean it's any less real. The idea that then one will have to naturalize it and place it at the level of instinct strikes me as wrong. To be a human being is to inherit a fear of death. It's one of the things that we learn very young, that people die. It doesn't mean it's not real. It means it's absolutely real, but it's not instinctual.

People say, "I don't fear death, I fear dying." I fear the pain of dying, but not death itself. That could be true. Who wants to look forward to a future which will be designed by six or eight months or a year of terrible pain which will end in death? Death seems positively much more appealing. So there's that. There's also the fear of death in the kind of abstract thought—which can be deeply felt—that there will be a time quite soon when the world will continue without me, and I'll be switched off like a light. People, the city, life—everything will carry on, and I won't be there to see it. There's something painful about the idea that the world will go on despite you. We absolutely know it's true, and it makes perfect sense, but it can still be most painful if you think about it. I won't be here to see my great-grandchildren—something like that. We know that, but still the idea of a world continuing to exist without you is a source of melancholy.

The alternative would be to carry on existing. What would that be like? Well, that would be pretty terrible after a while. An example I always think of is in *Gulliver's Travels*. In book three, there were these characters called the Struldbrugs. The Struldbrugs have immortality in life. They don't die. They've found the secret to immortality, and they're depicted as these beings that are kind of slouched against the walls. They've lost any interest in life and don't understand anything that's happening, or have any interest in anything that's happening, because their world disappeared a long time ago. I think that's a good counter-example, that a possibly infinitely extended life would be a nightmare. The only thing that gives life shape and significance is mortality—the fact that we are "creatures of a day," as the Greeks used to say. It's hard to think of oneself as a creature of a day, but that's what we are. If we had all the days—if we had the life of gods—then it would very quickly become meaningless to us.

THE PARADOX

The paradox of life, if I may be so grandiloquent, is when one is young and there seems to be an ocean of time in the future, time can often be squandered and wasted in really quite silly plans and fruitless activities. Then when you become aware, whenever that happens—it happens to different people at different times—when you become aware that this will end, that really can focus your mind on the moment, on where one is, and then on trying to enjoy that moment and trying to live that moment and not be such an arsehole.

I think that's something: that the prospect of death can have a kind of sobering power, but can also make you a nicer person. There's a great story about this. There was a guy, Freddie Ayer, who was a very famous British philosopher and introduced logical positivism into Britain. He was a kind of public intellectual from the fifties into the eighties. A complete atheist. He had a near-death experience, or rather, he died for a few minutes on a table. He choked or something and lost consciousness and was technically dead for a couple of minutes. Then he had a vision of what came next, and he was aware of looking at himself walking up and down somewhere. It was dark. He was walking up and down swinging a watch because he knew that something about the fabric of space and time was out of order, and he had to contact the god of time and put it right. At that point he was revived and lived for a good few years after that.

Some time after he'd died and come back, there was a party. His wife, Dee, was there at the party. Someone at the party said to Dee, "Freddie seems to be in really good form." And she said, "Yeah, he's so much better since he died." There's something to that in the sense that death can perhaps begin to make you a slightly nicer person. That's something.

YOU WORK IN A GRAVEYARD,
YOU'RE SURROUNDED BY GRAVES

In Plato's *Phaedo*, which is an account of the death of Socrates, Socrates has been condemned to death. We see him on his last evening, and he's going to take the hemlock. He's discussing this with his friends, his followers. He appears calm, he appears in control of his faculties, and he discusses the nature of the immortality of the soul.

It's really unclear how we're meant to think about those arguments, but the point of the story is that here we have the philosopher Socrates, who knows he's going to die. He's able to take the means of death into his own hands, namely the hemlock. He's sanguine about it, although death by hemlock was apparently extremely painful. Socrates describes what's going on in his body. He describes the poison making parts of his body cold. It's an extraordinary description of his hands and feet and legs becoming cold, and his last words to someone who is there called Crito. He says to Crito, "We owe a cock to Asclepius," meaning we must sacrifice a chicken to Asclepius, who was the god of healing. So the last thought he has is one of healing and one of the observance of ritual. What one did as one was dying was to make a sacrifice to the god of healing.

To philosophize is to learn how to die, so that's the activity that I'm meant to do for a living. Philosophy is an art of dying. That's how it's been since Socrates, and arguably how it is in different forms throughout the history of philosophy. It gives you an extraordinary vocabulary for thinking about death, and that's good. The worst thing is the dumbfounded response to something that befalls you, and you don't have ways of thinking it through. My job gives me countless ways for thinking it through, which are consoling in a funny way. It's the opposite of morbidity. Death is what we do, and the more of a presence that has in our lives, the more we'll kind of cheer up.

To think through the nature of things, as philosophy's meant to do, is to obviously focus on our mortality in a way that enables us to talk about it. So that's what "to philosophize is to learn how to die" means. The wisdom that Socrates teaches us is the wisdom that he exemplifies in his personal life, the manner in which he goes to his death. That became the ideal for the philosopher. That's how you're meant to die. Of course, it can be ridiculed and complicated and made funny, but that's the exemplar.

This is a spectacularly privileged way of passing one's time. I think it's like working in a graveyard. You work in a graveyard, you're surrounded by graves. It doesn't mean you're morbid. Like the gravedigger in act five, scene one of *Hamlet*, who's playing with the skulls and making jokes about them. It's like that. To do what I do is to always be working in a kind of cemetery, and I think that's great. I'd rather have that than work somewhere where you don't believe a cemetery exists. Everything that we stand on is a field of skulls. Everything is Golgotha, and we know that. We just choose to hygienically hide it away. So much the worse for us.

\

CONDUCTED APRIL 15, 2016

ANDRE COBERLY

HOSPICE VOLUNTEER

Andre is a sometime coworker of mine from a small record store in Portland. He's warm, a little loud, and has a tendency toward sarcasm. I have worked a lot of shifts with Andre over the years, but they were so full of blue jokes and music talk that I never really got to know what made him tick.

When Andre told me recently that he'd been working in hospice for years, I needed to know what made someone want to spend time with dying strangers. We met at a sleepy bar in North Portland, not far from our shared workplace, and drank a few beers while delving into our off-hours lives. Turns out, the guy contains multitudes.

Andre has been present for dozens of deaths. I thought somehow those experiences might have given him a theory of what happens next. No such luck. "The not-knowing actually makes me feel better about it," he said. Then, perhaps sensing my frustration, he offered this book a potential epilogue. "As far as a tale to be told with an ending? It's never gonna happen until you go through it."

WORM FOOD

When I was a kid, somebody told me that when we die, we all become worm food. I thought, Ah, that's great! But for some reason, I took it to mean that we all become worms. I don't know why I calculated it that way.

That was fine with me, though, if I died and just became a worm. The world needs worms, you know?

"ARE YOU A GOOD LISTENER?
DO YOU HAVE A CAR?"

In 2004, I moved to Portland from Seattle, just for a change of pace. I started working at the record store part-time. I didn't want anything full-time at that point because I was looking for another line of work. But I was bored. I was really bored. So I decided I'd start volunteering.

I looked online for a couple things. I said, "Oh my god, I would have so much fun volunteering at the Humane Society." Always liked animals. I told my sister about it, and she started laughing at me. She said, "You realize your twelve-year-old niece volunteers at the Humane Society, right? Only twelve-year-old girls volunteer at the Humane Society." I thought, *Okay, well, fuck that. I can't do that, I guess.*

I started looking again. I literally Googled "volunteer opportunities in Portland." There was a lot of Meals on Wheels–type stuff. There was a lot of working with at-risk youth. A lot of rehab kind of stuff, adults who need help getting back on their feet. Then hospice popped up, and it was all about, "Are you a good listener? Do you have free time? Do you have a car?" It sounded perfect. I never knew anybody in hospice. I never had a grandparent die in hospice. They just *died.* I don't think I even had friends who I knew of who had anybody in hospice. I just thought hospice was some place that you went, and that was it. That there's no other avenue after that. I assumed that they took care of you, and they made you comfortable. That's what I thought hospice was.

So I found out about this program. The volunteer coordinator said they were looking for people to go and visit their home patients, people who need somebody in their lives who they can talk to and hang out with, because the family can't be there all the time. That was part of the deal— the family needs their time away, so if you're there, at least they can take a couple hours to go grocery shopping or something. So I said, "Okay, this sounds great."

The company's headquarters was in an office park. It was nondescript. They could've been selling life insurance. It could've been a lawyer's office. They could've been book editors. There was nothing in the office that said anything, except for a few "Death Isn't the End" kind of corny posters on the wall. "Live Every Day Like it's Your Last," that kind of shit. Other than that, it didn't say anything. It didn't scream "hospice." It was an office building.

I went through the training, which was just a day's worth of, like, "Don't steal from them, don't beat them, don't let them beat you"—that kind of stuff. But I still didn't know what I was getting into.

The first day, I went and visited my lady. I'll call her Diane. She was in bed. She was weak. I was a little leery: The place had a smell to it. Diane was dying of emphysema and lung cancer, but she was still smoking. She was on oxygen and smoking the first day that I went in there, and I didn't really put it together in that first moment. I finally realized how dangerous that was, and I said, "You can't do that! You can't smoke and have oxygen in your face." You know? And she's like, "Oh sweetie, I do it all the time. You guys are such babies about this stuff." She was so curt that I instantly liked her. I instantly knew that we were going to have a good time. I said, "Well, smoke all you want, but you gotta take the oxygen off. Or don't smoke while I'm here. You wanna blow yourself up when I go, you can do that if you want." She laughed and said, "Oh, that sounds great."

I got to know this lady over the next couple days. I found out she was a big Elvis fan, she was from the Midwest, she loved playing cards. That's what her family did. They had a farm, and they played cards and listened to Elvis. I love playing cards. Elvis I'm fine with as well, you know? She liked young Elvis, whereas I like fat Elvis. But she actually *met* young Elvis, and so I think that's why, you know, she was such a fan. It was one of the stories about her life that she shared with me, and it was kind of amazing—this lady who I never knew before this, and who never knew me, we got to know each other really well over the next couple weeks. It kind of blew my mind.

I really relished our Thursdays together. I would just go over there, and we would play cards and listen to Elvis. Some days she would be so tired, so we would just watch a movie. Or she would sleep and I would just sit and read and be next to her for two or three hours. I was there while the family was gone and her caretaker was coming in—so it was a good little window of opportunity for having somebody around. Some days she didn't want anybody there, which was also fine, and I would leave.

Then she decided that she was going to die. But she also decided that she liked how chemotherapy made her feel. That doesn't happen a lot. But in her mind, it made her feel better. So she decided to go back on chemotherapy. Even her doctors told her it was worthless. Her hospice was revoked because of that, and that kind of struck me. I wasn't allowed to go see her anymore. Even in my off-time I wasn't supposed to see her because, even though I was a volunteer, I was still part of this company. This was my first rodeo, and I decided I didn't think that was fair. I didn't think that it was very prudent to not allow me to go and see this lady just because she wanted chemotherapy. She was still going to die. Some people need blankets for things, and chemo was her blanket. So, she died, and I never got to see her again. That pissed me off. That made me upset. I said, "Fuck hospice. This is ridiculous. If it's all going to be run by some sort of Medicare protocol, and it's not run by person-to-person experience and formula, then I don't want to be a part of it." So I left.

A PRESENCE

A few years went by. I matured a little bit. I'd read about it more, and I'd realized, you know what? It's not really in their hands. The bureaucracy doesn't make people's need any less. But I felt like I'd burned my bridge with the first company, so I went to another one. It was closer to town, anyway. I went back to it with different eyes, and right away I loved it.

This time, my first patient was somebody who was awake but not alert. Wasn't going to talk to me. So many strokes that it just wasn't going to happen. Alzheimer's, as well. So, I started to hang out with him, and I kind of had a little bit more of a challenge this time because he couldn't tell me what he liked. I used the room, and I used cues that way to see what he'd like. I saw a lot of fishing stuff. I saw a lot of things about mysteries. I figured this guy liked mysteries, and he liked fishing. So I just started to read *Moby Dick* to him.

He couldn't respond to me at all. He was sort of locked-in. But I would walk him outside. I would talk to him. I kind of felt like there was a presence there, like he knew that I was around.

I FEEL HONORED, AND I'M SAD, AND I'M TERRIFIED

I was getting very interested in hospice, but I wanted something more. I looked one place up that had an actual live-in facility. All these other things had been private companies where you could go to somebody's house or an assisted residence. You could go to any sort of place. But you weren't guaranteed to go to the same place twice. This place was an eleven-bed, in-house care facility run by a local hospital. It was essentially a twenty-four-hour ICU for hospice patients. So, somebody's at home, and they can no longer be on home hospice. Their nurse or family says, "Dad's symptoms are out of control. We cannot do anything about this. Please take him." Around 50 percent of the people that go in there die there. Some, by the time they get to the facility, they're pretty far gone. At that point there's nothing you can do. It's just a comfort measure. Other patients, though, there's a lot of simple things just to get them back home. Even though they're going back home to hospice—you know, the goal is to send them back home. Nobody really wants to die away from home.

I started to train there and instantly liked it because for the first time I could do hands-on work. At the private companies, as a visit volunteer, you can't do any of that. Even if they fall on the ground, you'd have to call somebody else. This was the first time that I got to really do hands-on care, and in fact you are expected to as a volunteer. This is the first time that I figured out, "Oh my god, I get to help turn patients. I get to help wash patients. I get to help patients eat and brush their teeth."

My sister is a nurse. I have several good friends who are nurses, and I felt like if they could do it, I could do it. I got trained, and my first day on the floor, it got *real* very fast. People were soiling themselves. People were needing turns. And it hit me how real this was. Actually getting to do the hands-on stuff made me see that, shit, this wasn't just reading books to somebody or playing cards with somebody. This was actually taking care of somebody.

I didn't know how I was going to feel the first time I had to clean someone. I thought to myself, *There's no way I can do this.* The first woman I helped had C. diff, which can really attack the senses—it essentially produces liquid that is coming from the deep, deep gut, and the smell of it can blow you away—and I was in the room with this young certified nursing assistant. We had to clean her up, obviously, and he saw that I was a little gray, a little unsteady. He said, "Are you cool? Can you do this? We can get somebody else." It was at that moment that I saw her. I saw the whole circumstance and realized that this was a human being. She's not doing this on purpose just to gross me out, you know? At some point I'm going to need this as well. So, I dove in and did it. And it was very—it's hard to say the right word—it was very satisfying to at least make somebody comfortable. It struck me instantly that it was pretty important, taking care of the physical needs people have at the end of their lives when they can't take care of themselves anymore.

Their families aren't always around. Really, families shouldn't have to do that. I always feel like the family should be there to be the family—they shouldn't have to be the caregivers. It's great if they want to be, but it would also be nice if they had the opportunity to just be present.

It was always interesting to me to see how people who worked in the healthcare profession acted when they were there as patients' family members. A lot of times they would just let us do whatever because they realized, "I'm a family member. I'm not at work." They wouldn't be hawks and sit over us and watch us. Whereas people who weren't in the field were often very uneasy with people touching and handling Grandma.

Eventually I got my CNA license so I could work there full-time. I worked the night shift, which was 11 pm to 7:30 am. Before, I was a volunteer. I could leave after four hours, once a week. But once I was there full-time, the things that I saw just started piling up, and they were incredible. The human things: what can happen to your body when you're dying, what can happen to your psyche when you're dying—I mean, it's fascinating and very scary all at the same time. But I was really, really enjoying it at that point. The hands-on stuff was just feeling better and better. I was talking to family members. I was talking to patients. We were getting into questions that were very existential— that were unanswerable. Just to be a part of those bedside conversations was amazing. I felt honored, and I was sad, and I was terrified all at the same time. I picked up extra shifts when I could, because you don't make a lot of money as a CNA and because I really did enjoy the work. It's back-breaking work. It's brutal work, medical care. You're lifting people. Just because they're dying doesn't mean they're all scrawny. Some of these people are very large. And a lot of them, their level of consciousness is like a minus-one. So even if they wanted to help you, they couldn't. Aside from that, though, I was seeing more and more things. I was having a really good time. I was moving up pretty fast, too—working my ass off and just—I felt like I was making a difference.

THE FIRST GUY

There were people who I walked in on who had already died. There were people where I came in on a shift, and I was asked to care for the body. We wash them, clean them. We have a ritual there. We send them out with a passage quilt that these very nice people sew for us every year, and we send them out with flowers. The whole staff walks out with the patient who dies. So, I'd done all that. I'd been a part of that, and I helped clean the bodies and get the bodies dressed and ready—even though they were going to a funeral home, and they would redo it all there anyway. It was good for us. It made us feel like we had done our service to that person. It was more important to us than probably anybody else, but a lot of the family members shared their appreciation for the ceremony part of it.

Anyway, the first guy: I walked in, and it was probably about three in the morning, which is the weirdest time of the night shift. It's that 3 to 4 am switch that's just the most bizarre. I mean, a lot of things happen. A lot of people die in the night, too. So I walked in there and called the nurse in, and I said, "I don't know, there's something different now." He had been doing agonal breathing the whole time, anyway. It was . . . [imitates gasping]. Then there was a lot of apnea, and the eyes were rolled back, very glassy. I couldn't feel a pulse. There *was* a pulse, but it was very, very tiny and weak. I just remember thinking, this is odd. I feel like this isn't right.

The nurse came in—and she's a very, very gifted nurse, and very observant. She said, "I think he's getting ready to go." I remember saying, "Oh, I haven't seen one yet." I didn't mean it like that. It's just how it came out of my mouth. Thinking, *I don't know if I'm ready.* Part of me was like, *I don't know if I'm ready to see this.* But it was happening. I was holding this guy's hand. I was scared and confused, but at the same time I knew I wasn't letting go of that hand. I could feel the warmth still in the hand, and I was not going to let go. There was nobody else in the room. He didn't have family. I figured it was the only decent thing to do, to hold onto that hand. I watched it, and it took probably two or three minutes, and the nurse stayed in there with me, and she was stroking his head and stroking his arm and saying. "It's okay, it's okay." Very sweet and tender. He just took a couple sharp breaths, and that was it. It was nothing else. That was it. It was all done.

We sat and looked at his face for probably another minute or two. She got a stethoscope and checked his heart, and there was nothing, and that was it. She said, "I'll notify the family. If you want to start cleaning up the room a little bit, that would be very helpful." I just realized, *Shit, that just happened.* You know? He was just here, and he's still here, but he's not doing what we do anymore. That was it.

I will always remember him. I'll always remember what he looked like because he was the first. He went so serenely. He went so *textbook*, as they say, that it would be hard to be like, "Oh, that poor guy." I mean, he was at level of consciousness minus three.* Then he just had some apnea, and he died. I'm not discrediting the pain that I'm sure he was in before I saw him, but that was the base that I knew him as. He came to me at LOC negative three. He died two days later at LOC negative three.

YOU'RE NOT THERE TO CRY

I've probably been there for about two dozen deaths since that one, people actually dying in their rooms. I've seen some real violent ones, and I've seen others that are just real soft and quiet and sweet and in their sleep. They're all different. I've seen a guy that looked just like me. He was thirty-eight years old, never smoked a cigarette in his life, and died of lung cancer. He held my hand, saying that he didn't want to die because he had babies. He died four days later.

The amount of raw emotion that goes into it is amazing, and as somebody who works there, you kind of have to keep your cool, keep it together. You don't want to react too much. There have only been a few times that I have, and I tried my hardest to get out of that room as fast as I could. Sometimes it gets built up. You don't want it to be about you, and you want to be professional. You also want to be the coolest person in the room. You want to keep your head together because they're going to be coming at you with questions. They're going to say, "What's going on? Why is this happening? What's going on with him?" You need to be upfront. You need to be blunt. You need to say, "This is her moment, and I'll leave you alone if you want, or if you need anything you just let me know."

---

* There are various scales for measuring consciousness, but on the LOC scale that Andre refers to, one is alert and negative four is totally unconscious.

If you're crying—if you're as emotionally attached as they are—you're not going to be there for them in the way you should be. They need to be there to cry. They need to be there to hold each other and scream and everything else. Not me. I'm there to do my job. There were a couple times that it was very hard. I'd be lying if I didn't say that there were some people that I got really attached to, even after a short amount of time. Not to say that the other people weren't lovely as well, but you just have different attachments to different people. It could have been something they said to me on the first day that drew me to them. It doesn't matter. But it's your position that you're just there to give comfort. You're not there to cry. A priest doesn't go in there and cry. A priest does what the priest is supposed to do. Doctors don't cry. They go in there and do what doctors are supposed to do.

Nobody ever asked me to not show that level of emotion. It's something that they don't tell you. You just have to learn how to do it. Like a soldier at war, you can't show too much. You have to suck it down. At the same time, another very important thing that I would say to anybody who was interested in going into this is leave it at the door. I know that's a really hard thing, and it took me a long time to learn. There's a chef at the facility. He's a big baseball fan, and we became good friends. When I worked the night shift, on my way out after work, I would make it a point to go in there and talk to him about baseball. Just to get my mind off of things. Or I would tell jokes to the nurses on the way out. Or the nurses coming on shift next, I would tell jokes to them to get my mind off it, to leave it at the door. It wouldn't do anybody any good if we took all that baggage home.

THE FAMILY DOG

A man throwing up to death is something that I'll always remember, but then there are emotional things that I'll always remember.

There was one in particular—it was this lovely, lovely couple. She was such a sweet lady. She was there for her husband. He was dying. They had this little dog. This made me go home and squeeze my dog after work, and of course I cried. The man died, and the wife was in there with this little dog that she had in her lap. I remember being in there and saying, "I'm going to clean him up now. If you guys want to be in here, that's up to you. If you want to step out, that's totally fine, too. I'll be done very quickly." The rest of the family stepped out, but the wife said, "I want to stay," which is very rare. They usually don't stay in there. But I said, "Okay, that's fine."

She had the dog on her lap, and I remember the dog was just watching me the whole time. It was just this weird thing. The dog was just watching me, wondering what I was doing to its second owner. I cleaned him up, got everything going. Everything was fine. The dog was still very leery of us. When I got him all cleaned up and we had gone out of the room, the funeral home came. And the funeral home guy, rightfully so—it's kind of one of our things—closes the door when he goes in so other patient families don't see him. This was at three in the morning, so it wasn't likely to happen, but at the same time, it's just decency.

He goes in and closes the door, and the dog notices and he runs up and sits just outside the door. The dog sat right by the door, and would not move at all. Even with family calling him, trying to pick him up, he just would not move from the door. When the funeral home guy came out and opened the door, the dog jumped up on the gurney.

It was just one of these emotional things that was at the same time kind of funny. The family was laughing, but everybody was sobbing, too, including myself and the nurse. That this dog didn't realize what the hell had happened: that he was no longer going to see him ever again. Didn't make any sense to him whatsoever.

I've seen that with children, too. They don't get it. They're just like, "But he's here. Why can't he just still always be here?" The reality that an adult understands—we're losing a father or a mother—we get it. God forbid a parent loses a child, but it happens. You lose a loved one. You're going to lose your brother or your sister. That makes sense in the world. It's shitty, but it makes sense in the world. To a child—or even a dog—it doesn't make any sense at all.

"HOW LONG IS IT GOING TO BE?"

There's a process to death. Not everybody's the same. Actually, everyone is really different. A lot of the hospice job comes down to talking with families. They might say, "I notice his breathing kind of changed from yesterday." And I say, "Well, the breathing does change. That doesn't mean that this is the end. That means that his breathing has changed, and he's at another step right now." They might say, "She seems hot." When you're dying, your internal thermostat—that's the way I would put it—flips up and down. Your top half could be sweltering; your bottom half gets frigid. That could flip a couple hours later.

Keeping the patient comfortable is what I do as a volunteer, it's what I do as a CNA, and it's what nurses do. It's what doctors do. Everybody who's in that room is there for the comfort of that patient. If a patient says, "I'm too hot," we open a window, take the blankets off. And that's the thing that you need to talk about with the family because they don't get it. They think, *Oh, Granddad's dying, he doesn't know any better. He needs to be covered in blankets.* Everyone wants to cover everyone in blankets! He's boiling. He needs to be uncovered. You go through these things very diplomatically. You talk to them. You rationalize with them and say, "Well, think about when you get sick. Do you want all these blankets on you? Sometimes you want the blankets off."

What I like to do is delegate tasks. I like to say, "I tell you what, you let me know if this changes in the next hour or two." Then they're a part of it—they're aware. They have something to do other than be freaked out by what's happening in front of them. I say, "Why don't you touch his feet every half an hour or so. Let me know. Do you feel like they're changing a lot?" You give them things to do, and it takes their mind off things really quickly.

Everybody who works in hospice kind of has different ways to do that kind of stuff. I work with one lady, she's so amazing, and she has what we call "morphine voice." She just walks into a room and starts talking to people. She's just like, "I'm just going to make everyone feel great." She just does it. Everyone has their own approach. There's other people who talk very literally about what's going on in their bodies and what's happening. That's also a good approach.

There's all sorts of different things you can do with the family. Mostly the family wants to know, "How long is it going to be?" That's what they want to know. That's what they keep asking. And that's the question you can't answer.

There's a few that you can say, "Next few hours," but the next few hours could be twenty-four of them. There are some where you're like, "It could be a couple days." The reality is you don't fucking know. It's up to that person. That's what I say to the family all the time. With hospice, it really is up to that person. This person could be stubborn, this person could be a fighter, this person could have no fat on their body at all, so their body is just willing to fight naturally, even if their brain tells them they want to die. People who are younger, their body's going to be stronger.

The family can get pretty tired of the emotional prison that is somebody dying in front of them. You don't sleep, you don't eat—you barely even leave the room. So they want to know, when is this going to end? And there's no answer. They could go on agonal breathing for days. They could have apnea, they could do everything. Their heart rate could slow down to such-and-such. It's just impossible to say when that person is going to go because it is up to them. It's not just "they've done all these steps; it should be anytime now." Sometimes you do say, "It could be anytime now," but still don't know what that means.

It's so hard to see that done to the family. The dying person usually doesn't know what the hell is going on at that point. They are already at the stage where they're just waiting for the exit. They're waiting for someone to show them the door. But for the family—the family that's come in from out of town; the family that's been there for days, weeks, months on end, sleeping in the same room; the family with members who are close to losing their jobs—they don't know what's going on. That's horrible. It's horrible to see, and it's horrible to deal with, but you just talk to them. You just say, "This is not fair. This is the shittiest circumstance you could be in, and I want you to know that anything you need, I'm here for you." That's how you deal with it.

NOW I CAN DIE

It's not a rule or anything, but one thing I've noticed is that when the really inseparable families finally leave for a while—to go out to dinner, to go home to shower—the person often dies. I think deep down, we all kind of want to do that. We don't want to burden the people around us.

All that shit is real. I never thought it was real before I started doing this. I thought it was all hokey, like, "just because your spouse dies doesn't mean you'll die within a year." It's not concrete, but all these things that people talk about—they really do happen.

All these things about your grandpa talking to his mother in a dark room, and his mother has been dead for seven years or however long. And then he's dead a few days later. All this weird shit happens. All this stuff really takes place, and often there are telltale signs that somebody's going to die soon. Not just the physical signs, but the mental signs. Like people looking off and pointing at things that aren't in the room and laughing. Or they'll be very scared the wall is on fire inside the room. That's a popular one. I've never understood that one.

I do think that people who are dying, people who are comatose, people who are even, like, asleep—they know when someone is in the room. And if you're in the room and watching them like a hawk, they feel that. When you leave, they feel that. A lot of time it's a pressure that's lifted off of them, and they feel like now they can die.

I WAS NEVER FULLY ASLEEP

For me, something happened with the night shift where I just couldn't physically do it anymore. It started out pretty easy, minus figuring out how to sleep. I was cool with it because it was exciting and it was new. The winter time it's fine. You find time to sleep. But the summer time is shitty because you realize there's so much going on. I like to hike, I like to go out camping, I like to do all that stuff. But I was spending my days off sleeping because I couldn't figure it out. There were a couple nurses who had been night nurses for a long time, and they switched their whole lives around for it. Even on their days off, they were still night people. I just wasn't ready for that. A lot of people aren't ready for that. The burnout on night schedule is pretty quick. It's usually around a year or two years. You figure it out real fast that, *holy shit, I can't do this*. And you physically just can't. I mean, I got fat. My sleeping was so crazy. My metabolism was all off. My dog was ready to divorce me because I wasn't walking her. It was all crazy.

The problem was not that I was never fully awake. It's that I was never fully asleep. Even when I would sleep during the day, I was never fully asleep. I would do these things where I would nap for three hours, wake up, and go to work. On my days off it was even worse. Some people are good at it. I just couldn't do it. Also at this point I realized that the money as a CNA—it was not gonna cut it, and I was having real doubts about nursing. I love nurses. Again, some of my best friends are nurses. My sister's a nurse, my sister-in-law is a nurse, my cousin is a nurse. I have nursing around me all the time, so this is not a knock on nursing at all. It's just a knock on *me* being a nurse. I didn't like the hierarchy system that nursing has, and I didn't like the fact that the nurses, even though they wanted to they're in the room for five minutes, and they're charting for ten. To me, that was just something that I didn't like, and I didn't want that to be my hospice experience. I wanted my hospice experience to be something a little bit more fluid, something that I could really be in there with them for.

So I quit. It was very sad. It was the first job that I've ever quit where I really, really was torn. It took me a long time to realize that it was the right thing, and even when I had realized that it was the right thing, it still took me a long time to actually say, "I quit." I quit with the caveat that I would come back as a volunteer, which I did, and I do, every Sunday night.

I realized that I'm best serving people when I'm using my words and my focus and my humor and my listening. I'm better at that than at giving somebody comfort medication and then charting symptoms. For me, I want that one-on-one interaction. The physical body to me is fascinating, but it's not as fascinating as what the mind has to offer. I'm going to get my psychology degree, and I want to be a therapist. You know, be a grief counselor. For patients if they need it, but family mostly. That's how I'm going to maintain my hospice longevity because that's what I want to do. I've realized—since 2004, when I first visited that lady and we played cards and listened to Elvis—that this was my calling. Not knowing anybody ever on hospice in my life, it just fucking happened to fall into my lap. But it's my calling.

NOT TO BE MORBID, BUT

I've always thought that I would die violently—but then it'd be *over*. Car crash, explosion, something weird like that, where I don't sit suffering. I think that's probably how a lot of people imagine their death will work. They think they'll maybe die in their sleep or have a heart attack. Keel over, fall down the stairs, and break their neck.

I never thought, *I'm going to get cancer, and it's going to be a very long and brutal death*, or *I'm going to have a bowel obstruction, and it's going to be the worst thing I've ever encountered in my life. I'm going to get emphysema, and I'll pray for death. I'll get ALS, and I'll be trapped in my mind, and my body will be useless.* I never thought about things like that, starting out in hospice, but now that I've done it, I realize, you know what, there is a possibility that's going to happen to any of us regardless of what you do with your body. You could be straight *livin'* and get ALS. I've seen it. You could be an eighty-year-old man who smoked cigarettes and drank whiskey your whole life, and you're there visiting your dying wife. It's just bizarre stuff. I never thought about it until I went there. Now I can tell you, quite honestly, I don't want it to happen like that to me.

I think anybody would say the same thing. Anyone who worked there would say the same thing. It looks brutal. If I had the option for compassionate care [Death with Dignity], I would take it. The guidelines are very strict for compassionate care. If you're maimed in such a way that you can't actually drink the cocktail or verbalize that this is something that you want to do, you don't get to do it. I think about that. I actually think about it in a planning way. Not to be morbid, but I think about it like, *Shit, if there's something happening to me and if it's confirmed by medical science that, yes, I have Alzheimer's coming, I'll stop it.*

I wouldn't want to do that to anybody. I wouldn't want to kill myself and then somebody else has to deal with finding me. Probably some poor guy that like, that's his job. But compassionate care? Absolutely glorious. I believe in it 100 percent, and I think that it's the only right thing to do. We do it with animals; why can't you do it with yourself?

At the same time, I commend the people who say, "Fuck it, I'm doing every single day until it's my last." I commend it, whether it be religious or whether it be just sheer stubbornness. I love it. I love that those people are out there, and I will take care of them until I'm old and gray and almost in the bed next to them. But I couldn't do it. I feel like I've lived enough to where I'm okay.

IT'S PROBABLY JUST GOING TO GET WORSE

I didn't really think about death when I started volunteering. I just thought about volunteering as something to do. At the same time, I was coming out of my twenties, when you're immortal and you're a moron. I didn't think about it like that. I still don't really think about it. I think it's because I'm comfortable with death. I'm comfortable with the notion of it. I certainly don't wanna die. I don't have a death wish, but I'm more or less okay with the fact that it's gonna happen. That could also be the fact that I'm going on forty and starting to really feel my body. Hell, ask me when I'm seventy. It's probably going to get worse and worse and worse. I'll just be like, "Shit, take me." I've had patients say that: "Take me!"

It doesn't make a lot of sense to question your mortality. Just try to be the best thing you can be, and you know, help anyone that you can.

We're all going to go through it, and what you want is to be comfortable at the end of your life. I feel like if you take that approach to it, what you'll find is that you'll give comfort a lot easier, knowing that it's going to come back to you at some point. Not to sound selfish, but it's a "this tree keeps growing" kind of thing. It goes back to that first time I had to change that lady. I remember the way I amped myself up—I thought, *Someone's going to have to do this for me at some point.* That was it. It's going to happen to me at some point, too, and I want to give before that happens, so I can really feel that people are going out comfortably.

I WANTED TO CUT DOWN THE CURTAIN

I think that, for me, there was a mystique to death. There was a curiosity around death. There probably was a fear of death inside me, but really I had just never seen it before, you know? When I first started out, I wanted to know what I could do to see what this process was like. I wanted to cut down the curtain, to see the Wizard of Oz. It wasn't a morbid curiosity, but . . . okay, maybe it was a morbid curiosity. [Laughs.] But a lot of it came down to the fact that I didn't know anything about it. For me, hospice was mostly like, "What is this thing?" And I stumbled across it.

So I feel blessed, more than anything, that I stumbled across this thing that happens. "Life and death are the two constants," that's what they always say. "You should see two things: a birth and a death." Well, I was there when my sister gave birth, and it was disgusting. Death, there's something kind of beautiful to it. There's something very rewarding in exhaling when it's finally over.

\\

CONDUCTED APRIL 18, 2016

TERESSA RAIFORD

COMMUNITY ORGANIZER

In the three hours I sat with Teressa Raiford, she had one visitor, two missed phone calls, and dozens of text and instant messages. Raiford is an activist and community organizer from Portland, Oregon, who is generally associated with the local Black Lives Matter movement. She's a regular at city hall meetings and rallies held at the state capital in Salem (many of which she organizes). She has been criticized and even jailed for her activism, most recently in 2015 for disorderly conduct (a charge she fought and won). Despite a reputation as an antiestablishment agitator, Raiford has friends and allies across Portland's political landscape. Upon meeting with her, I understood easily where the goodwill comes from. Before I could tell her that I don't usually drink coffee, she set one in front of me and began to answer my questions about her tumultuous life story, without melodrama or pulled punches.

It quickly became clear to me that Raiford's near-constant activism—she's the cofounder and lead organizer behind Don't Shoot PDX, an organization that protests police violence, among other issues—serves in part to keep her own grief at bay. Her work is a tribute to dead family members and friends, and it's also a coping mechanism. She is relentless in confronting what she sees as institutional failures and the people who enable them—but the resulting battles can take a heavy emotional toll.

BEING KIDS, WHERE YOU
GONNA GO, ANYWAY?

I grew up in Portland. I just recently got my transcript from Portland Public Schools. I wanted to know exactly where I grew up in Portland because I grew up in foster care. That's a trip because you're moving around so much. I know that I went to a whole lot of different schools, but now, going through all the stuff that we've been working on, I wanted to kind of take myself back and figure out like—what schools did I go to, where did I live? Kind of put together memories of growing up so that I can create some kind of chronological order of things that happened in my life. You know, growing up in the seventies and eighties, it was pretty crazy out here for children like myself.

My mom didn't want to marry my dad because she thought he was a bad guy. She was like, "He go to the penitentiary too much." [Laughs.] That's because he thought he was a Black Panther or whatever. So she picked the square dude, and he went into the marines. He had the family home. His family was in the church and everything. It was a great opportunity. He had good property and manners. Don't hang out with the guy with the afro when you can hang out with the nice guy.

But he was a monster. When he came back from Vietnam, he was, like, all the way transformed. My mom went through domestic violence. I was a little kid, so I don't know exactly what was going on, but I know there was a lot of abuse happening. He used to beat my mom in front of us, and he would abuse us. He would physically abuse us, mentally abuse us. We were his weed team, for distribution. He would have us manufacturing the bud. I remember the matchboxes, and I remember taking seeds out. I remember even sealing the bags with a machine. And this was in seventies, maybe '78, because my brother was about four years old at the time. Can you imagine?

My mom ended up leaving, but she left us with him. At one point, me and my sister started to save change that we were getting, and we buried it outside the window of our old house in Northeast Portland. We told my brother one night that he needed to get the money, and he needed to run away to the Fred Meyer grocery store and find my grandma and tell her what was happening, and then come and get us. He tried to do that, but, you know, he was a kid. He put the money in the gum machine, and while he was doing that, my grandma's sister came into the store and was like, "Mondo, what you doin' here?" And he was like, "Oh, I'm getting some gum, but I gotta get my sisters. We looking for grandma so we can save them." I guess he kind of tried to tell her what was going on, but she didn't understand, and so she brought him back to the house.

Of course, we all got in trouble because the boy ran away, and whatever he was trying to say probably didn't make sense to all the adults. We ended up getting ferociously beaten, like beat bad. After that, he put plastic around the windows and kept us locked up in the house. He would take us where we needed to go and bring us back in. Then when he wasn't there, we would be locked in. There wasn't a way for us to get out. But being kids, where you gonna go, anyway?

My auntie and my grandma knew that something wasn't right. I remember my auntie coming back and talking to us through the mailbox. We told her what was going on, and a little while after that we got out of the house and were living with my uncle Joe. That was still foster care, even though family was able to take care of us. Because of the family dynamics, we changed hands so many times. My grandma got sick, my uncle died— all kinds of things happened. We ended up going back and forth into the system. Being in the system with your siblings, if you guys don't all behave in a certain way, then you have the issue of being removed from each other, separated. Just all kinds of crazy shit. I know a lot about all of these social service systems, and as an adult—as somebody who has raised children myself now, and lived through that system, and seen the dirty and painful parts of it—I want to tackle it and to dismantle it. I know how it can be, and I understand what these children are saying. It's not falling on deaf ears, you know?

MY HEROES WERE MOSTLY TEACHERS

In my world, I didn't know that anything was wrong. If somebody would've said, "Are you okay?" or "Is something wrong?"—well, if you grow up in a fucked-up-ass world, you don't know what's wrong or right, so you're not going to be like, "Aw yeah, everything's terrible." I don't remember no great days, so it's like, what's the expectation of better or worse?

My heroes were mostly teachers because, when you'd go to school, everything that's happening—like chores, manners, abuse, whatever's happening in your home—when you go to school that stuff is a little more decent. Or at least they used to have some order in school. Schools now seem to be just as terrifying as foster homes, but back then it was like a refuge. I remember teachers like Mrs. Anderson, Mr. Johnson, Mrs. Kendricks, Mrs. Rittenauer, and Mr. Wilhelm. All of my heroes were frickin' teachers.

The social service person was obligated to pick us up and take us to different places. They were not really listening to us when we were saying that we were getting abused because they didn't want us to have to be separated. Now, as an adult, I can understand why maybe they didn't listen to us—because they didn't have an outlet for that, and it would've caused us to be separated. I understand those dynamics now. It couldn't all just be malicious, right? I'm still thinking that after all these years: *It couldn't just be maliciousness.* [Laughs.]

I really question that, because we have an opportunity to dismantle and to influence policy, and to see that this is not a rocket science situation. It just takes courage and sometimes just a little integrity and a willingness to say, "Okay, this is my job, but this part of my job is inadequate for my client. To serve them better I need to bring it up so that it can be addressed."

THE EIGHTIES CAME, AND ALL
OF OUR FRIENDS STARTED DYING

I remember somebody died at our house. I think it was on Shaver Avenue. It might be apartments or a parking lot or something now, but we used to live in a fourplex over there. This lady had a heroin overdose in our bathroom. I saw her.

We ended up going to foster care because of that—because of course, if there's a dead body in the house and everybody's doing drugs, then you gotta figure out what should happen. If there are kids there, they're going to foster care. It was probably a good time for us to leave because we were going through a lot of abuse over there. I don't even know how old I was. I really don't. Maybe seven or eight?

The stuff that we used to see as kids was horrible. I remember somebody dying when we lived in another spot, too, and there was blood all over the place. It's crazy. When you think about society and how we look at people who have had death and poverty and pain and violence in their lives, and you're wondering what's wrong with them. It's like, "No one's encouraged them to have any kind of counseling or do anything about that trauma. What do you think is wrong with them? What's wrong with us for allowing it to fester?"

When the eighties came, and all of our friends started dying, at first everybody was taken aback, like, "Woah, what's going on?" Then at some point it set in to where it was, like, customary. "Let's just get T-shirts." [Laughs.] "Let's go to the funeral dressed a certain way. You know, let's pour out a little liquor." All that time, I kept thinking to myself, *These are people we went to preschool with. These are our best friends. How do we just go and buy a T-shirt that has somebody's name on the back of it to celebrate their death?* That's a loss for our community. Who's going to pick up the slack for what they were going to provide, as far as being a member of our community? I'm thinking everybody has a value—it's so necessary for all of us to work together. We have to have a desire to take care of one another. When death takes us out of that, most of the desire can't be just to celebrate the death. It has to be, how do we make up for that person? What else is gonna be adequate to build in the space of what we just lost? Funerals became a trend. Dying became a cultural thing. Where we would celebrate life and birthdays and holidays and do festivity type things, you were going to houses and you would see pictures of obituaries. You would have everybody throwing an anniversary party for so-and-so's death. You couldn't get anybody to come to a birthday party, but if you have a funeral, then everybody's going to pop up to come to the funeral. If you're celebrating that death every year, then everybody's gonna remember that death every year. We got RIP pages on Facebook, and everybody's celebrating the damn day that seventeen-year-olds and nineteen-year-olds and twenty-year-olds died. Those guys didn't even turn twenty-one, and there are forty-seven-year-old men honoring seventeen-year-old dead boys as the OGs. You know what I'm saying? That's weird.

I didn't ever think that that was supposed to be anything normal, and that's why I really started doing the activism when my nephew died—I didn't want his death to just be like, "Oh, he the dead homie." I was like, "Oh no, he's gonna be *great*." If he didn't get an opportunity to put into this world his desires and the needs that we have, then I'm gonna do something to make up for that space.

BLACK PEOPLE DON'T GO TO SCHOOL TO GET KILLED

School was super violent. There was a lot of gang violence. A lot of our friends were dying. My friend Bobo was a victim of the first gang violence that I remember, and we didn't even know it was gang violence. This was maybe '85. I was going to Jefferson, and Bobo was in alternative school with my cousin Clarence. The day that he got killed, he skipped a field trip. He was going to go out to Grant High to get Clarence's Fila hat from this guy that took Clarence's hat, right? My cousin used to breakdance and think he was a hip-hop artist, and somebody saw his little hat and snatched it up. Bobo was like, "I'm going to go get Clarence's hat back." He went up to the school to get it, and the guy who took the hat was like the new kid at the school from California. He had access to a gun somebody gave him at the school—at Grant High School.

Everybody told the guy that Bobo was up there to get the hat. They gave him the gun, and outside in front of all the students he shot Bobo in his leg. And Bobo was like, "Woah, why you shootin' me?" He fell to his knees, and the guy walked up on him and continued shooting him and executed him in front of all the students out there. It was a trip because, that same day, I'm walking home from school with Bobo's brother Rabbit and my friend Karen, and we stopped by my grandma's house. She was like, "Come in here. There was a shooting at the school." And I was like, "What? What do you mean?" Me and Karen went in, and she was showing us that there was a shooting up at the school on the news. It's this little broadcast, and I was like, "Them white people are crazy." And my grandma said, "Why do you think it's white people?" I was like, "Black people aren't gonna kill each other. Plus, where would they get the gun, anyway?"

I never could think that somebody in our city who was black could go to school and get shot at all. Black people don't go to school to get killed. That's the crazy white people shooting up the school. Everybody knows that. But that's what happened, and that blew my mind. I had pictures of him on my camera because I was in photo class. I had pictures of him from the day before. We were at the park when he was talking about going up there, and I kept tripping because I was like, "Dang, all the pictures of Bobo have my thumbprint in the way." There weren't any clear pictures. I wasn't a good photographer.

That was the first one that we knew about. After that it was my friend Miles. Miles got beat up, and—well, he went to go beat somebody up who had beat somebody else up, and he got shot. It just kept on going— like all these people from Portland who were like the big brother or the person who'll stick up for somebody. It was like all these bullies came in and started bullying people, and when somebody would come to help, they would get killed. And then the next thing you know, within two years, our parents—everybody was calling the police and telling them that there were problems because people were getting jumped into gangs and everything.

After a while, when my brother said he didn't have a choice but to join a gang, I didn't have any choice but to understand why he made that choice. People tell you they gonna kill you, and you saying, "Okay, I'm down with the movement." That's literally how it is because you've seen everybody around you getting killed, and nobody's going to jail for it. What do you do if they come to you and they keep beating you up? They beat my brother up so much. He got knocked out at the swap meet one time, and people brought him to my house in the back of their car, knocked out. After that I couldn't make him wear his African medallion no more. He put on flannels and a T-shirt and hung with whoever wasn't going to let people come and hurt him.

If you're in the neighborhood, you need to tell them that you got a relationship with them. It's like the tax man back in the colonialism days. "Oh, who are you? Let me see your papers. What are you doing here? Where's the property that you live on? Who do you work for?" Because if they ain't gettin' paid for you being here, then you really shouldn't be here. That's what was happening to the kids. It was a trip because Portland's not that huge, you know? Portland's small. And the majority of kids dying from gang violence are wards of the state.

If that was happening within their parents' houses, you would have a lot of parents in jail for neglect and for all different types of crimes against their children. They call those kids "at risk of harm." But our children are dying within your system, with your oversight and accountability intact. That's crazy.

Even a lot of the people who came up to sell drugs were wards of the state of California. They grew up in foster care together. When they graduated out of that system, and they had nowhere to go, they went to whatever homie would pick them up. They adopted whatever opportunity they had available. The foster care system doesn't tell their guardians that they need to make sure that these children continue their education, or avoid getting pregnant, or learn how to fill out housing applications. All the bad stuff happens to you while you're in foster care, so you're kind of fucked up when you turn eighteen and all you got is a plastic bag. If you don't kill yourself then, society's gonna help you.

SO THAT'S HOW MY
LIFE GOT ALL FUCKED UP

One day I was walking my friend Karen home, and I had recently had stomach surgery, so I was bent over. And these two guys rolled up in a red car with California license plates on it. This is still kind of before we realized that gangs was all the way in the community. Nobody was saying, "Hey, these are gang members." But one guy asked me if I needed a ride home and was like, "Are you okay?" I was like, "Oh yeah, my stomach hurts." So they were driving me home to my house. These guys are in their twenties, and I'm not even seventeen years old yet. I'm talking to them, and we build a relationship. I'm thinking, *They're gonna come over and hang out, and Karen's really gonna like them because they got bud.* They're like, "Do you got other friends?" I'm like, "Yeah, I got friends." It wasn't anything serious. We were just hanging out with them. They would buy us coolers, do all kinds of little shit.

One day, dude kidnapped me, and he didn't bring me back to my house. At that point he raped me and all kinds of shit, but he would not bring me back. For probably almost seven months, I had to stay with this dude, even though I had had the stomach surgery. After he raped me, he was like, "Woah, I can't take you back to your grandma because, if you tell anybody what happened, I'm gonna have to kill you and your family." I didn't think he was serious, but then I really didn't know what to think.

I done seen guns, I done seen drugs, I done seen these guys talk about hurting people. Now he has me with him, and I'm seeing him actually hurt people.

I'm not cool. This is not a cool situation for me. But there's no way for me to get out because when I keep trying to run away and get home, my grandma's like, "No, don't come back over here." He had gone over there and told her that if I didn't stay with him, he was going to kill her and my whole family and all this other stuff. So she was like, "Naw, you wanted to choose hanging out and doing all that other stuff, so you go and do that." So that's how my life got all fucked up.

I had my son right before my eighteenth birthday. The guy kept me with him because he was scared I was going to go tell the police on him. I wouldn't have because I didn't even really realize that what he had done was abusive. My life was already so fucked up. For me, it became, as long as I survived and he didn't kill me, then we're cool. There's not a problem. We can still even be cool. But you're really not gonna take me back home?

One time he took me to my aunt's house to pick up my cousin, and instead of just waiting for my cousin to come out, I was like, "Let me go in and see what's taking her so long. I'll be right back." I walked into my auntie's house—and this was probably about two or three months before I was going to have my son—and walked out the back door. Then I went to my other grandma's house and stayed there until I had my baby and everything. I never had to deal with him again.

TWO DEAD POSSUMS

I remember the police officers dropping off the dead possums when I was eleven, to basically threaten the lives of my uncles and let my grandmother and my grandfather know that, you know: *y'all niggas.*

The Burger Barn was a business that my grandma owned. Before she owned it, she used to work for this tavern, the King's Tavern. When the guy died, he left her most of his property and money and everything because she used to run the business for him. She bought the property next door to where my grandpa had his gambling shack. She wanted it because she wanted to keep an eye on him. She opened up a twenty-four-hour soul food restaurant so that she could see what was happening in the community and what her husband was up to over there, playing poker or whatever.

The Burger Barn made a lot of money because she was from Mississippi, and she really knew how to cook. This was twenty-four-hour soul food, available in Portland at a time when there were a lot of jobs here. People were coming in and out, and there was a busy gambling shack next door, too, where you could get you some hooch. [Laughs.] At the same time, the police had a relationship with the business owners. The police commissioner, Commissioner Jordan, was my grandfather's friend. Charles Jordan. The guy with the afro.

My grandmother was making so much money with the Burger Barn. She didn't do nothing wrong up in there. She served people, she gave people jobs, she spent the money that she was making there on sending people's kids to school.

In Mississippi and in the South—my grandma is from Natchez, Mississippi—when there's a threat on your life, usually you'll get some dead rodents or something thrown around your house. They came and dropped the possums off on the steps, right there in front of the door. You couldn't open the door without hitting the possums, so there wasn't a way for people to come out. My grandpa had to move them.

We had already had threats from the Ku Klux Klan, where they would throw dead chickens on the steps. That's why we had the cameras up when the police did it because my uncle was like, "Well, next time they come, we gonna see them."

My dad called Commissioner Jordan, and he said, "Some of your officers just got through dropping their possums over here." In the time that it took my grandpa to move the dead possums off the steps and for the officers to make it down to the police precinct, Commissioner Jordan and his staff came outside and inspected the officers' cars. They saw that the floor mats had blood on them. So he didn't even have to ask them too much more.

They ended up putting it on two officers who didn't have anything previously on their record. Commissioner Jordan fired them, then the union challenged it, and they were reinstated. Basically, he would've been probably our first black mayor because everybody loved him. After that, people were like, "Lynch him! How dare he fire these fine, upstanding white officers because of this black garbage over here? They're over there gambling."

My grandma was horrified. She was an introvert, too, so after that she turned into a total recluse. She wouldn't come outside. If she wanted to go get food, she would have one of us go. I don't think people know how much they devastate families and people's lives when they do stuff like that.

My whole view of police was always that they were everyday people that could be good or bad. It wasn't about what they had on as a badge. That wasn't representative of the people. Don't tell me about their authority and professionalism. That's not gonna work. I gotta see who they are as far as the character of the individual. That's how you know who people are.

THIS DREAM

When I was in my twenties, my grandmother died, and I had just gone through some severe domestic violence. My mom was throwing barbecue grills through my window because she was on crack. People in our community were dying left and right.

Then this boy got killed across the street from our house. My son had been talking about this dream he had about this black boy with this short afro and curly hair coming in to our house through the window. He said, "We were in the room making art, Mom, and this boy came in through my window and sat down and ripped up our paper and laughed at us and then kept on running out the back." I was like, "What? That's goofy." But my sister was like, "No, Teressa, we have to listen to him." I'm like, "We're not gonna entertain the baby. We're not gonna go back to all the stuff from when we were kids." She thinks she has ESP, and I'm always thinking logically, like, "Oh, those are coping mechanisms, and she's been watching too much *In Search of* . . . with Leonard Nimoy." She wanted my son to describe what the little boy looked like. My son described every-thing, and my sister was tripping because she was like, "Yeah, that sounds like Michael."

Next thing you know, not even twenty minutes later, one of my other cousins came in: "Y'all know so-and-so got killed last night? Somebody came into the house across the street. They was in there playing domi-noes. Somebody opened the door, and they started shooting. When he heard the shooting, he jumped up and ran out the back door." His back door would have been coming toward our house. It was this boy Michael. They said that he was running out the back door to get away from the shooting, and he got killed on the back step.

I was like, "I'm getting the fuck outta here because y'all think this stuff is normal, and I don't think it's normal, and I want my kids to have a better life." Within six months, I was gone. I used my tax return and I took my kids. I wasn't going to get beat up no more. We were not go-ing through anymore of this. We were not going to think that gangs and drugs and all this stuff is normal. We were gonna go have a normal life away from all the weird stuff. When we got to Texas, it was like, it couldn't have been anymore normal.

MY RESUME WAS ON SOME BEAUTIFUL PAPER

Black people don't move out of one black community and go to another black community unless they know people in that neighborhood. They go to a community and live. So I moved to Texas, and the communities we lived in were beautiful. My kids went to Anne Frank School, and then when we moved up a little bit more, they were going to Barbara Bush. [Laughs.] And Tom Landry and Valley Ranch. It was a totally different world, like, "If you want to work, then you can have a job, and if you're good at that job, then we'll move you up." It didn't matter if you had college degrees and a good family and all that stuff. It wasn't political. It was based on your abilities.

I bought a house within a few years. We bought land and built a house. I didn't have Section 8, food stamps, welfare, nothing from the time we got there. I started out as a stock person for Nordstrom. Then I ended up working and doing purchase orders for the buyer. Then I went straight to Bank of America in a sales support position. Someone recommended the job, and I said, "Shoot, what they gonna have me do? I'm cleaning the toilets?" I'm an introvert. I'm scared of people. But they were like, "Just go for it."

I go into the interview—no college education, nothing—just a mom of two. I'm twenty-six years old. I'm in the interview at this big old oak table in Dallas, Texas. I don't understand how I'm sitting here with these people who are like, "I got a master's in finance!" I'm like, *Who told me to come here?* But my resume was on some beautiful paper, and it had all the stuff that I had actually done on it. I had been a file clerk in Portland, then a client services manager. They knew, and they hired six of us out of the twelve who interviewed. I was in that department for five months, and a job came up for the manager over a bigger department. I was managing twenty-four people, and I hadn't even been at Bank of America for six months.

NO SUN EVEN CAME UP

My uncle Denny was getting out of jail. I think he did twenty-seven years or something. Everybody was like, "You know, you gotta be home because Uncle Denny's coming home. His parents are dead. He went in when he was nineteen. The whole city is different. We need people here who he can recognize, who know him, who can help reintroduce him and just be home." I was coming home for what I thought would be a couple of weeks, nothing longer than that.

When I came back, immediately it was death again—death, death, death. It threw me for a loop. Not only was I not around poverty at all in Texas, but when you're not around poverty, and you're not around people who you love, you're not usually around the pain and hurt of violence and death. That goes for anybody of any color. The violence still happens when we're not around, but you know more about it when you're around it.

At the same time my daughter was like, "I want to check out some art schools out there." When we came in on the plane to Portland to visit, they were talking about some bomb threats at the airport. Then everybody was talking about how it was summertime and how violence was up, and I was like, "What? Violence in Portland?" I'm like, look at all this pretty shit. Are you kidding me? Being gone for fifteen years, you're not seeing what everybody was talking about with the gang violence and all that. I'm looking at brand-new buildings, beautiful streets, nice houses. Everything looks good to me.

Not long after I got back, the Methodist church—along with all these other community members—was being called to come to Multnomah County to talk about community violence and what could be done. "We're gonna get everybody together, and let's have a rally and talk about it." They had this group that I guess was in line to get a sixty-thousand-dollar grant from Multnomah County.

At the public hearing, I was like, "I'm from this community, and if you guys really have a community violence issue, and you're talking about buying diapers for gang members and doing a talent show and some of the goofy shit that I just heard here—none of that's actually going to work." If they're actually in a gang, that has to mean that there's some racketeering involved, which means that there has to be money involved, which means that they probably don't need your money for diapers. If they're not making money and you just think that poor kids are gangs, let's go ahead and dismantle that, and let's do it with some job opportunities. These kids don't know that lawyers work for Nike. They don't know that architects, graphic designers, and good writers work for Nike. They don't know that there are all these industries within that industry because no one has introduced it to them. Let's do that with your power. Give them an out.

They were like, "Yay, let's do that. Let's create a steering committee. If we create a steering committee, would you be willing to be a part of it?" I was like, "Uh, yeah!"

I stayed for so many damn meetings that I was getting frustrated. I'm sitting here arguing with these broads over, you know, "What are you guys gonna do to apply an effort toward resolving these problems right now rather than giving it to another system and forgetting about it and feeling like you did something?" They started saying that I was vindictive because I was in foster care, that I didn't want things to work. I couldn't take it. I walked out of that meeting that afternoon. I told them to do what they were going to do. I needed to take my ass and spend time with my family. I walked away, and it was a beautiful day.

Then the next day, no sun even came up. My nephew was dead. Before my uncle even got out on his date, my nephew was dead. He got out the same day as my nephew's funeral. That's what's so jacked up. I'm like, *damn.* I came home to see my uncle who went to jail when he was nineteen, and I came home and my nephew who's the same age as my uncle died. It's like, you don't get a life no matter what happens. You could die or go to jail, and you still end up nowhere.

I remember that night when we were at the hospital. My brother had called us up, saying, "Come up here, something happened with Andre." I was like, *No, this is crazy, no way.* That was just my second time seeing my brother the whole time I had been in Portland. My brother just looked at me and said, "Teressa, what are you *doing* here?" I was like, "Mondo, I don't know. How in the hell would I just happen to be at home during some stuff like this?" I said, "Last time I came home, grandma died. I don't know if it's just the universe allowing me to be here with you, but I'm not going nowhere." And I haven't.

"WE'RE NOT GOING TO SAVE ALL OF THEM"

I don't think that I knew what activism was. We had always done food drives, different kinds of volunteering, and I never knew that that was activism. When I was in Dallas, I sat on a lot of different boards and committees for different organizations, like Habitat for Humanity. But I didn't know it was activism.

When my nephew died, people were like, "We're not going to save all of them." And I was thinking, *Woah I'm not leaving. I'm gonna throw myself into this, and we really need to do something.*

Every time someone would say something to me about how messed up the system was, I would say, "Well, how can you continue to work for it?" They'd say, "Well, because I gotta retire next year, and I'm working on this, and you can only do what you're doing." I was researching, investigating, and working as a business development manager. Every single day since my nephew died, that's what I've been working on. I'm doing business development for the community of Portland. [Laughs.] That's why we call our activism a community action plan. It's like, if the community starts having this discussion, regardless of what level of community they are at—if there's people who are willing to work, then there's stuff that can actually be done.

Anybody who calls me, I'm there for them. I've had victims call me. I've had police hit me up, giving me their cards and asking me to get them subpoenaed. Everybody calls me for all kinds of shit, and I just do the work. I'm just like, "Okay, environmentalism. I don't know anything about that, but send me over some information, and I'll call my people that do that, and we'll go ahead and build a campaign that gets people involved. I'll find out if we can advocate." To me it's just advocacy.

THE PAIN OF LIVING SEEMS
TO BE WORSE THAN DEATH

I'm just now dealing with the trauma and death. I'm not dealing with it in a good way. The activism and the protesting, I think that's helping me. That's like therapy or something, right? I've gone through all this shit, and I've never talked to a psychiatrist or a counselor or a therapist or anybody about nothing. I just kept going because I was like, *I'm the oldest and I got my kids.* I always had an excuse for not dealing with taking care of myself. Everybody's like, "Teressa, you gotta take care of yourself," and "Why don't you take care of yourself?"

This is the first time I've ever lived by myself in my life. I had my son, and then I had my daughter, and we always had our community. Me and my friends always lived with each other. This is the first time that I've ever had in my life to be by myself. I wouldn't keep moving, but the people who support me, the community—I have a GoFundMe account, that's how I pay my rent. If the kids call me and I gotta make a hundred dollars off of speaking at a college, I'll do that. I haven't been able to stop. I need to stop. They want me to stop. They're like, "Teressa, just stop and deal with your pain. Deal with your hurt, just live, just breathe and be a person because you deserve it now. You done did it." But I feel guilty about everything, so I don't stop. I won't take a break, and I won't take care of myself. That's shameful. It's like, dang, I do think that I'm a person worth saving. You know what I'm saying?

At some point you gotta think that people who are in a lot of pain, especially people in hospice, they get to a point where they're like, "Okay, I gave you guys enough of my time, now I'm tired and I'm gonna go." I'm there now, but I'm still alive, so I don't know how to get past being there and not wanting to continue. You don't know what else is going to happen. The pain of living seems to be worse than death. Resting in peace sounds all right.

I don't cope with it. This is why you got people who go crazy or have emotional issues, and I'm having them, but I don't know how to deal with them. I drink coffee, I stay in the house, I look outside. I'm scared to go take walks. Because now with police investigating you and assaulting you, and your lawyer saying, "Hey, you're not paranoid. They really are investigating you, you might not be safe"—that shit don't make none of this easier. I'm like, *How'd I go from trying to be active for my nephew to wondering if my safety is an issue?*

You got racist people who want to kill you because you're saying "black lives matter," and then you got people who think that you're bad because you have an issue with police brutality. I've got police officers who are friends. I got police officers who have had to stand off with me who are also telling people in the community how much they love me. They help install security systems at my church so that the ninety-year-olds in our congregation can be safe. I got the mayor of Portland, every time he sees me, he tries to hug me. I'm like, "Don't you be hugging me in front of people, Charlie. They gonna think we get along."

I'm a normal human being. I'm just somebody who wants to help make things better for us, but I don't even know how to make things better for myself. You do what you can, right?

PEOPLE DON'T KNOW HOW
MUCH OUR KIDS ARE WORTH

The thing that got me about Michael Brown's death in Ferguson* was when his mom said that he didn't think he was going to live, anyway. She said she was always trying to get on him about going to school and doing his homework and graduating and all that. And he didn't really think he was gonna have a life. He kept saying things like, "It don't make no sense

---

* Unarmed black teenager Michael Brown was shot and killed in 2014 by white Ferguson police officer Darren Wilson, setting off protests locally and nationally that helped to kickstart the Black Lives Matter movement.

because they gonna kill me, anyway." I hear kids say that all the time, like, "I ain't never gonna make it, anyway. I ain't gonna never be nobody."

I was like, damn. People don't know how much our kids are worth, and they don't care. But his friends knew. When you would see those images on the news about what was happening in Ferguson, those were kids. On Twitter and Facebook, they were like, "Meet me at my grandma's house." You would see kids talking about getting batteries and keeping their cameras going and getting water. What I remember about Ferguson is that when the police put a curfew in place, the kids went on boycott. They stayed outside, and they were building tents and camps. This was for days. They were streaming what they were doing outside, and they were organizing. They were ordering food and connecting online and communicating with people. They's kids! Everybody's connecting communities to give them resources to stay outside. It lasted months. Every time something happened, they had the communication line. It was going through the buzz. Kansas City might've just sent water one time, but now Kansas City is a buzzline. If somebody tweets in Ferguson, it's gonna tweet in St. Louis and tweet in Chicago. Beautiful. That's what made it go: The kids were pushing it and everybody else couldn't ignore it because they were calling for help.

RUNNING FOR OFFICE

I had already been doing Trayvon Martin rallies, and I had been doing community town halls at Portland Community Media. I had been doing a lot of community outreach that didn't nobody want me to do. My family didn't want me to do it, the community didn't want me to do it, the people that I call the gatekeepers didn't want me to do it. I ran for office. To me, running for office was radical because I had to Google, "What is a city commissioner?"

I only ran for office so I could do community advocacy. I thought, *If people know that I'm a community leader, then they'll call me if they need stuff.*

That's what I would use the platform for. The whole time, everything that I said I would do if I was elected was the stuff I was actually doing while I was not elected.

You don't get paid for activism. You lose your teeth, you lose your hair, you lose your home. You can't have friends because everybody has something to lose if they're around you, and they have to defend you. It ain't cool. I could probably have a great, beautiful life, but I don't even know what that is. When I lived in Dallas and I was building my house, I bought the marble for my floor and I paid for whatever the kids wanted. Everything was beautiful. We were making it, but we still wasn't happy.

The shit that I'm doing every day now, that kinda works. Being with students and helping them figure out what they want to do with their life, that makes it better. I tell them that when our friends die, it's like, "How do we seed that back into where we need it?" I feel like I'm seeding. Like, okay, let me go ahead and give some things because I know a lot of dead people that didn't get an opportunity. I loved them a whole lot. When you have that capacity, you can give more. So you try.

THOSE ARE BULLET HOLES, RIGHT?

I'm not the leader, but I'm the lead organizer of Don't Shoot Portland. I made the event page, and I kind of tell everybody what to do. I do safety patrol. But everybody else is doing the work. If you look at the Don't Shoot Portland banner, it's red and black and it looks like it has all these dots on it. Those are bullet holes, right? We call our plan a "community action plan"; that's CAP. We were like, "We're gonna bust a CAP in the problems that are happening in our community!" [Laughs.] The community action plan is dismantling those issues as a community. It's how we come together. We create our plans, and then we go into action, so the nonviolent direct action, testimonies, the workshops, the trainings, all of that is part of busting the cap in the system's ass.

I was calling myself a first responder before Mike Brown died because, again, if people had issues with the police, if they had issues with the school, if they had issues with foster care, if they had issues with the health care—I was there. I sat with people for months in hospice, cleaning up their houses and trying to get their family and their insurance and stuff together because nobody else would take the time to do it. Everybody keeps dying, so there's less people to take care of each other. These are my friends' grandmas, and just everybody. Them getting older don't make the pain disappear. It just makes less opportunities for people to be there for them. So, I keep myself busy.

EVERYBODY GOT WOKEN UP BY THESE KIDS

There's a segment of my generation—people who are in their forties, thirty-somethings—that grew up in poverty around the crime and the violence of crack. That generation, the systemic issues of the society that was around them, the culture that was created from that, it loves death. Death is a superior value to life because it's better for you. You *rest in peace*, you got your dead homies, and everybody is glorified. Movies like *Boyz n the Hood* and *Friday*, everything was about chasing bullets and dying. Having something to live for and die for rather than staying here and being treated like a dog. It's like they created a suicidal culture that makes it seem to be acceptable to be taken out. Everything glorifies death over life.

It's all violent death. A lot of people are killing each other and killing themselves, and nobody's even talking about all the suicides from the pain of having so much loss. It's ridiculous. My godson killed himself two years ago.

Nobody wants to believe that these are suicides—they wanna call them accidents. No matter how traumatized a person's life is, nobody in our community is saying, "Oh wow, you're a talented artist and that's great that you went to school and you finished even though you didn't really believe that you could, and that's good that you made records while you were doing it so that you could channel your pain and make that part of the power of going through this." They are like, "Aw, your hair look cute." You know? That's because that feels better than the pain of struggle. When you're struggling every day, you don't wanna talk about struggling every day. You wanna get light and deal with something different. Especially when death is on the table every day, all the time.

I'm thankful now that these children have shown us, through what happened after Mike Brown was killed, that they are not feeling that. When those kids did that, it was a surprise to the world, because our generation had glorified violence so much. We were so cool with black death that when our babies was like, "No, we can't have that," my generation was like, "What? What's going on, y'all think this is a problem?" And now everybody's waking up.

Everybody got woken up by these kids who told us, "Yeah, Mike might've been a big kid or he might've done bad stuff, but was it worth him getting killed? Who would accept that?" Then it was on us as adults to say, "What is acceptable when it comes to children being killed in our country? Is it okay because they lived in poverty? Are children who live in poverty less valuable to society than those that don't?" That's a big, serious wake-up call, and everybody has to question their values when they have to answer that. You can't say that because he lived in poverty and was thug and might've stole some cigars or some other shit, that he didn't deserve to keep breathing.

How absurd is it when you go to the bank and you see an armed guard outside, and you go into the bank, and on the counter it says, "Protected FDIC insured." Why, if the money is protected and insured, why do you have a gun? If somebody comes in and says, "I want the money," just give them the money so that they don't take your life or the life of any of the people there, and let them go. You gonna kill the person for stealing money? That's just money!

That's the fog. We stopped listening. Remember in the eighties, when that song came out, "Video Killed the Radio Star"? The radio star could have you seeing and thinking and feeling everything that they were talking about because you were *listening*. Video just looks good for a second.

Yesterday was the anniversary of Kent State. American law enforcement was going to college campuses and shooting students because they had taught society that these kids were low-life scum. Hippies. The media basically said they were nonhuman scum, fighting the system. Well, the system must be great if these kids that are fighting this system are scum. They taught society—this is the generation that is over us right now, that is still running shit—that if they weren't part of the good, elite society, that they were part of the hippie scum society. To keep that society in order, they had to stand up to the opportunity to lead society into a better day.

If you were killing kids on campuses back then, a better day is killing them while they're little kids, so that they don't go to campus. Let's kill them while they're in preschool, let's kill them while they're in high school. Let's not let them go to the campus. Let's create jail systems that keep these impoverished people, who are eventually going to be mad about capitalism, locked up. Let's lock 'em up. Let's medicate them. Let's create a society of mental health that keeps them sick, so that they don't use their minds to go anywhere. Let's call it ADD. Let's tell the kids that they have learning disabilities, and minimize what they might do in society that could take away our advantage of power.

THE FUNDAMENTAL STRATEGY
FOR DISMANTLING BULLSHIT

If you start listening to the children, they know everything that's happening, and they know the answers. The children have been telling everybody to wake up. They don't stop. But nobody listens to them. We wanna put them in a picture and be like, "Aw, look how precious they are." Why don't you take the picture down and listen to what that child is saying? In two minutes of listening to them, you'll understand so much more than what that little picture told you. Some of our most active activists are nine. We get lectures by twelve-year-olds. It's crazy, but they know what's happening.

If we adults woke up and realized that instead of judging the kids we should be making sure they have a safer, better world to live in, we'd be so much more productive. We have power. We have a lot of power. Can you imagine if a whole bunch of people just said, "Let's give a fuck about the kids and really do something"? We live in a society where you have to get paid to play with kids. You have to get paid to do something that helps somebody. Even if you have an organization that you work for nine to five, if there's something special that people need, you will not move until that funding comes in. Like, really?

That's the fundamental strategy for dismantling bullshit. If the system doesn't exist because of a relationship that it has with the people—and a knowledge and understanding of the people—it's not gonna work. It's a bullshit system. It's a scam. It's built to keep people unable. It's built as a disabling system. It's built to adequately box in people so that it can accommodate numbers, so it can look at data. "How many did we have born this year, how many died, how many died of this type of death, how many died of that type of death? Ooh, is there another kind of data process that we can implement so that we can get more of this data, and how much money can we make because we accommodated a connection with these numbers?"

The bureaucracy—that's a dope-ass machine. It works. The propaganda machine works. It'll have you thinking that you're doing something useful. It'll have you participating, it'll have you putting money in, it'll have you coming out and making it look good, and it'll be fucking all of us. So people need to know how to do things on their own.

WHAT "BLACK LIVES MATTER" MEANS

Being black in America, you hear "rest in peace," and that sounds fucking spectacular to somebody who has not had peace in their life. When I say "black lives matter," that basically changes that paradigm. If kids and adults are saying they don't matter, and they're not going to try because it's not going to work—and everything in your society, including cartoons and commercials and movies, shows that you're a second-class citizen—that makes you feel like your life ain't worth shit. Saying "black lives matter" and doing the work, it's believing what you don't believe. It's taking the opportunity to think for yourself, "Does my life matter? Do black lives matter? Do we matter at all? What does that actually mean?"

All the exhibits of black life and culture are propagated on our deaths. When Dartmouth rolled out a ten-week curriculum based on Ferguson, which I learned about in February, I was so excited. I'm thinking it's going to be on economics and poverty and anthropology. But the ten-week course was on artwork and music—the sermons and the songs sung at the funerals, the pictures of the faces and the expressions and the signs people held. I'm like, wow, for ten weeks, a course of curriculum about Ferguson to an Ivy League school is about death.

You're going to give these people the dignity of death and the songs of sorrow as the value from Ferguson? It's the building! It's the understanding of policy! It's the value of civics. It's reading about the civil rights that many were hung and murdered for. It's bringing that reality back to this society that was told that none of that shit worked, that they shouldn't be connected to it. That's what the fucking curriculum is supposed to be.

That's what "black lives matter" means. It doesn't mean that the death of Martin Luther King is what we honor. It's the life. It's what he worked for. We learned after they gave us the damn holiday that his death was the value of his work. Everybody honors his death every year on his birthday. Dr. King died for our sins like Jesus, and now the world is better. [Laughs.] We should be thankful that Dr. King did all that work. Now what are *you* doing? Well, nobody says we're supposed to do shit.

"Black lives matter," to me, means that the life is better than the death. We have to fight for that as a society because it would be better for all of us. Our kids, none of them should have to grow up with the guilt of racism. Because they didn't do it! Who would give their children that inheritance and have them bear the burden of holding it and thinking that it's honorable to have it? That's sickening, you know? But that's what it means to me. The life is better than the death. Even if that's a hard lesson, we can make it better for the next generation if we try. We got to.

If you want to do something, just do it, because the world needs it. There's not enough of us. Just be proud that you're able because it's not an ability that everybody has. I think it's something that's spiritual.

CONDUCTED MAY 12, 2016

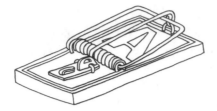

ART SPIEGELMAN
CARTOONIST

"Death is on my mind daily," Art Spiegelman said when I reached him by email. "I'm sure we can find something to talk about." There was just one thing I wanted to avoid. I was pretty determined not to obsess about Maus. The cartoonist's seminal graphic novel (first serialized in Raw magazine from 1980 to 1991, and collected in two volumes, the first in 1986 and the second in 1991) is a hybrid of journalism and memoir that humanized the Holocaust for a whole generation of readers—and did so through the unlikely lens of mice, cats, and pigs. But Maus is only one piece of Spiegelman's career in comics, which have frequently addressed complex topics—including death. For example, in the 1972 comic, "Prisoner on the Hell Planet," Spiegelman addressed his anguish over his mother's suicide. In the career-spanning collection Co-Mix (2013), he shared a series of grim-reaper-laden drawings that he made while awaiting surgery for a brain tumor. And in his willfully disjointed response to 9/11, In the Shadow of No Towers (2004), he relied on smoke, falling bodies, and vintage cartoon characters to capture the nation's temporary insanity. (His wife, Françoise Mouly, is the art editor at the New Yorker, and their initial joint response to the attack was a New Yorker cover: a black-on-black silhouette of the towers against a starless sky.)

Yet when I finally got him on the phone—while Spiegelman was on a late-night, three-hour train ride after a lecture in Boston on "Forbidden Images"—that little mouse seemed to show up in spite of us. Even when our conversation covered well-worn territory, though, Spiegelman was the perfect combination

of graceful and irreverent. At sixty-eight, he still bristles with th
dignation of a much younger man. It's a trait that most of the great comes ...
teurs seem to share. But he's at peace with the whole Maus thing. "Whatever I
do, I know that the first line of my obit is 'author of the Pulitzer Prize-winning
Maus.' That's just the way it is," he told me. I asked him how he'd like the
second line to read. "Huh, that's interesting," he said. After a moment, he con-
tinued, "I don't know. I never thought I'd get a two-line obit."

BIG ART

I wasn't interested in religion at all until I read the *Tibetan Book of the
Dead* when I was in my psychedelic phase. If I had any religious notion of
death, it came with my first LSD trip. I was in a house with some college
friends. We were on holiday, and their parents were out on a cruise, so we
stayed there on our own trips.

I believe we'd gotten some terrible LSD. It was my first trip, and I felt
like I was dying at some point. I was lying on a very plush carpet in a parent's house, and a realization came over me that "This is it! This is going to
kill me, this drug that I took!" Eventually, I remember hearing a voice that
I'd never heard before in my head, which after that moment I determined
was Big Art. There was Big Art and Little Art. Little Art was dying, Big
Art was the one who was going to explain it to him. I didn't have a good
vocabulary for it, but I thought, *Okay, now you're going to die. This is not
a problem. It's just what's happening.* I might have used more psychedelic
phrases at the time, but in retrospect, I was just explaining the nitrogen
cycle to myself. Everything recycles, and dying just means going into the
ground and feeding worms. You can call it being reincarnated as a worm,
but it's just you providing food.

It was a cosmic change where there wasn't any of this birth and death
stuff. It was just this ongoing recycling project going on. And there's
no reason to fret about it. It actually gave me great comfort and sort of

stopped the anxiety about dying, because one day, Little Art was going to die—he didn't have any special franchise on being alive, so what the hell?

I read the Timothy Leary translation of the *Tibetan Book of the Dead* after that first trip, trying to figure out what I had experienced. It gave me a vocabulary, some words to understand exactly what had happened. A cartoonist pal of mine said when he first took LSD, he had visions in his head of Walt Disney-like characters. Then he found out he was supposed to see paisleys, so he changed his trips after that. For me, it just gave me a slightly more mystical way of understanding what happened rather than my banal, "yeah, that's the nitrogen cycle we're all part of."

I guess it all stuck with me somehow. Although, Little Art, the person you're talking to now, is a mess. Big Art is often a cosmic buzz somewhere. It's funny because when I went to talk to my kids about death, I had to tell them about my LSD trips. When they got older, they told me I was weird. Not everyone explains religion and life in terms of psychedelics and cosmic visions.

I took things from Hawaiian woodrose seeds to opium to any other drug that I hadn't sampled to try it at least once. It was available, and people seemed to be having interesting times on these things. I know people who took lots more LSD than I ever did, but I must have had, altogether, like fifteen or twenty trips. Some of them were terrible; some of them were great. But those were all value judgments that I could only put on them when it was over.

I didn't stop doing any of it because it was a "bad trip." It was just, "Okay, I get it." I thought it was a serious experience. On the other hand, I always found marijuana much more disturbing than LSD. It made me more uncomfortable and paranoid, and not cosmically paranoid, which was more interesting.

I definitely don't believe in any religion, and if there's a god, it's someplace in the nitrogen cycle. There's a universal logic of some kind that isn't human, but it isn't what most people talk about when they talk about god, either.

ROSEBUD

I can't remember my "Rosebud" of death, but I know that pretty early on I was made aware of what my parents went through, without them telling me. I did find out fairly young that most people had grandparents, and I didn't. I guess the earliest thought of it was seeing a framed photo of my dead brother on the wall, which was when I was quite young. I knew that there was such a thing as being a kid and dying, as opposed to getting old and flabby and wrinkled before you died.

I can't remember thinking, *Oh my god, really? This doesn't last forever?* I'm sure that it had something to do with the traumas that my parents were leaking out to each other in Polish every day.

They lit candles and stuff, but to me it was just part of the weird mystery of the grown-up world, the same way that my parents had weird candles for cupping, that Eastern European quack medicine that involved putting glass suction cups on people's backs. This was just something else, where you mumbled nonsense words and lit candles and put them up in the window somewhere. It was really lost on me.

"CMON, BUDDY BOY"

Death is always an awareness for me. Either from the side of "I'm thankful to be alive and I think it might end soon," or "Oh man, it's time to get off the merry-go-round now." Somewhere between those two states is my reality.

When I'm slacking off, I say, "C'mon, buddy boy, you've only got so much time." I slack off and then feel terrible about it and wish I was dead. I've had suicidal periods, thinking about wanting to rush the process, but at this point, I'm just aware of it. A number of friends have started dying on me. I'm sixty-eight. For me it's just sort of like, "Wow, I got old someplace when I wasn't looking." I'm pretty old for a young fella, but nevertheless, I notice that people say "sir" to me now, unless I stop them.

I've thought about death, always. Now I can say, "It's because I'm getting old, and I have friends who've died," but I thought about death when I was in my twenties and thirties almost as much. Maybe I was more suicidal then, I don't know.

LONG-TERM SOLUTIONS
TO SHORT-TERM PROBLEMS

I was kicked out of college for being crazy. I don't know that I was thinking about death in the nuthouse, but it changed my outlook. It changed what people could expect of me. It allowed me to be more myself in that way, and it took my parents' expectations off of me. It also kept me out of the draft. The draft made me think about death a lot more than my own psychotic episodes did. By being crazy, I didn't have to worry about the draft anymore.

I was only recently released from the mental hospital when my mother killed herself. One of the conditions of my release was that I move home with my parents. I was twenty. That's not exactly an adult, from what I'm reading now about how brains develop.

My mother was very depressed. When I went off to college, her mission was in some ways accomplished. I was a big part of that mission. She wasn't happy with the choices I made. We kind of drifted apart around that time, when I'd always been in some ways her closest companion. She'd sit around the house and smoke cigarettes and not do anything for long stretches of time.

Living with her again, I didn't feel loved. More like that umbilical cord being tightened around my neck. Affection and understanding were the last things I was feeling.

One day I told her I'd be back from Central Park, where I'd gone with my girlfriend, who she didn't approve of. She asked when, and I said, "In the middle of the afternoon." Instead I came home in the evening. Before I came back, my father got home from work and found her body in the bathtub. So I missed this thing that was arranged for my benefit, somehow. Maybe she'd timed it in a way that, if I'd gotten home when I was supposed to, I could have saved her. I don't think so, but it's possible.

In the immediate aftermath, it was a combination of numb shock and an awareness that I was supposed to find her body. She'd planned it that way, and I didn't come through for her, so there was this awful guilt that came with the whole thing.

It was a heavy load, and I think that's why I cauterized the event and shut it off from being something I remembered. Now, after all these years, talk about long-term solutions to short-term problems. She would have been so overjoyed to know her grandkids. That's something that is just...impossible.

At this point, I don't think about her all that much. It's not like every day I think about my mother. But I do think about how something was stopped that didn't have to be, how she could have just waited it out. It would have all turned out differently. Even *Maus*, when I was cut off from the mandates she had given me in life, would be a different book without a missing mother. A kind of continuity would feel like it existed in my life that feels like it doesn't. I was very close with her until a little after puberty, and then we began having issues of one kind or another. But in some ways I'm not in touch with those memories. I don't sit around going, "Oh yes, I remember when we were both reading the same book and then talking about it after." We would do that, and I do remember that. But it's not the kind of continuity with my past that I would have felt if there wouldn't have been this giant chasm of her suicide.

There have been times when it's been difficult to exist, but I don't want to do that to anybody who I love. Her suicide short-circuits my following through. It protects me from caving in to the impulse. But it also keeps the idea of suicide very present for me. As Nietzsche put it, "Thoughts of suicide have gotten me through many a bad night."

When I'm able to, I try to give other people my reasons for not killing myself, and I hope that it'll take with them. I think one of the things that was very special about Françoise for me when I first met her was that she was fucking crazy and suicidal. Being able to, in quotes, "rescue her," was very satisfying. Early on in our relationship she was talking about killing herself, and I said, "I can't live with somebody who's going to blackmail me with that. I can't be with you. It's too fraught." She actually took it to heart. I mean, *I've* brought up suicide since then, but she's gotten furious with me when I've had my episodes. She'd say, "How can you do that to me when you've made me promise not to?" And I get it, it's kind of a double standard.

"PRISONER ON THE HELL PLANET"

"Prisoner on the Hell Planet" really came in a flood of memory triggered by an argument I had with an old girlfriend. At some point I realized I wasn't mad at her, but I was really furious with my mother. At that point, I wasn't thinking about doing a strip. I just wrote it all down so I could remember it. I wrote down everything I could remember from those years—it was only about five years behind me, I guess. This was about 1972. Before that I'd managed to really not think about it.

At that time, what I was working on had no real reason to exist. I was doing a real dopey story that I didn't even realize was based on the old Chuck Jones cartoon, *One Froggy Evening*—except that it was about a talking turd.

I was literally working on a piece of shit. I think it was even called "Just a Piece of Shit." It was not well-drawn. I looked back at it and winced, and right at that time I thought, *Well, the heck with it. I'm much more interested in this.* So I polished that one off, or quit, I don't remember which, and immediately started what became "Prisoner on the Hell Planet" without knowing whether I'd publish it or not. For me, that was really strange. Publishing is how I know a strip is finished. A comic is something that one can reproduce, and that reproduction is the ultimate original. I didn't even know if I could publish it; I just knew I had to make it. I thought of it as more like art, you know? I had only recently begun to take art that wasn't comics seriously. Expressionism was the art movement that I had the easiest connection to. First of all, it had a lot of black outlines and lines in it, and it was all kinds of overwrought and anxiety-ridden, and because a lot of those guys seemed to me like they were cartoonists, basically, even though they considered themselves painters. It seemed like the right approach to drawing what I had to draw.

I am not, like, a champion ice skater. Getting the line right the first time is not obvious to me. Some cartoonists just have these beautiful, snappy lines, and they come down singing. I usually have to scrape away, white-out, patch, do whatever it takes to get a page functional. With "Prisoner on the Hell Planet," as soon as I decided that I was going to allow myself to echo the styles of expressionist woodcuts, I was using scratchboard, and scratchboard has the great advantage that you can scrape away, put a line down, scrape away again. You have more than one lick at finding what you're looking for. The medium had that very congenial aspect of being able to use it as a system for discovering the visual as I was working.

Only when I finished it did I realize, *Oh, I need to print this.* It was four pages. It had no more weight than the "Piece of Shit" story that I had been working on.

SUCCESS BUILT ON SO MANY DEAD

Sometimes I'm just grateful for anything that will keep me busy, and sometimes there's something that I really want to see and understand and make. *Maus* is what I'm best known for, but it's the most anomalous thing I ever did—it's a long narrative piece. I'm actually built for shorter-distance runs. It's a lot to choose a style and stay focused on it for thirteen years.

The little button we used to wear was "Don't Trust Anyone Over Thirty." I assumed I'd be dead in a motorcycle accident by thirty, but I hadn't even learned to ride a motorcycle. So when I turned thirty, I thought, *I should at least try to do something ambitious.* That ambition was to make a very long comic book that would need a bookmark and would beg to be read and didn't meet the ambitions for dopeyness that comics seemed to demand back in the day.

I had a couple of ideas. One of them was called "A Life in Ink." I wanted to do a book about someone from birth to death, a cartoonist who lived a hundred years. He was going to be a successful cartoonist modeled after an amalgam of people I've read and daydreamed about. It was all going to be done on Françoise's printing press. It would consist of a journal of his, an anthology of his comic strips, the magazine he did when he was living in France and trying to be a painter and failing. The magazine considered cartoons and comics an art form back in the 1910s and had Picasso and Gertrude Stein writing strips for him. Just various things. That would have been fun in terms of using the press.

This was after I moved back to New York and was in proximity to my father. I could only for so long pretend that I was talking to him long-distance from California. That added pressure to doing the *Maus* project instead of this other thing. The only way I could talk to my father was about [his past and the Holocaust]. It was in the zone of possible conversation without me flipping out and getting angry at him.

Then, ultimately, we started a magazine called *Raw* like two years after I'd been doing the research and figuring out what this book *Maus* might be. It was ideal because *Raw* was self-published by Françoise and I. We decided to call it a biannual because we didn't know whether that was twice a year or every two years. Those seemed like deadline parameters I could meet. I put some of *Maus* into each issue of *Raw*. After I finished each chapter, there was a feeling of satisfaction in seeing it get published, moving ahead a bit, but also being able to take a holiday from it and do things that were more graphically experimental or whatever. That was the rhythm of it.

Then, after I finished the first half of the project and it came out in paperback and achieved what seemed to me to be astoundingly large success, I got completely depressed and had to stop everything and just deal with my depression.

Success confused me. Basically, the world I had to reenter after experiencing all this acclaim was walking through the gates of Auschwitz, and that's no fun. Much more fun to just be out on the literary circuit. Altogether, it was just very difficult to climb back in past, with all of the success built on so many dead. That's included in that chapter with the image of me working on a pile of dead bodies. But I did eventually get back on board and make the second half of *Maus* happen. Somehow that all took thirteen years.

ALIENATED, COSMOPOLITAN ATHEISTS

I really don't think about god very much. I really don't. I mean, thinking about life, thinking about death, doesn't involve or conjure up the word god. It's not a problem, it's not an issue. It's not something I have to get straight with. A lot of the Bible is getting people scared enough that they'll act well in terms of its morality, and I don't need these old men with beards. I don't want to be stuck somewhere with harps and milk and honey. That corny traditional notion just seems stupid.

I've never been able to take comfort in the religious rituals that are there, presumably, to give comfort. The Jews who I admire are alienated, cosmopolitan atheists. It's a tradition of sorts. It includes Kafka and maybe Freud. I think Einstein had some vague remnants of belief in him.

I know a lot of people, when they get old, they have some kind of deathbed conversions. This last year I've spent a lot of time with this ninety-eight-year-old artist named Si Lewen. I just finished a book about him. His father was a pretty thorough atheist, and his mother seemed to go along for the ride but had these residual magical notions that came from her ethnogenetic connections to her grandfather, who was the Rabbi of Lublin—they called him "the seer." Si was always a thoroughgoing atheist his whole life, but he's the most god-fearing atheist I've ever met. As he gets closer to death, he talks about wondering what's on the other side. I'll say, "I thought we talked about this once, Si, it's nothing. There is no other side."

He'll say, "Maybe, but who knows?" He was hedging his bets as he was turning ninety-eight—and rather sheepishly, just saying, "Well, you can't know anything for sure, so I don't know this for sure, either."

Of course, the odds against whatever happens after we die being what living people have reported seem pretty long. Nobody's quite come back. The most they can come back is a stroke-like experience, and they say, "I saw a tunnel," or something, you know?

Last week, Si told me he was going to start painting again. He retired for about a year at ninety-seven because he was still working fifteen hours a day. About a year or two ago he had something that made him unable to use his right hand, and now he's retired. He says, "Art, I know I've said this before, but I have to come out of retirement. An artist who doesn't make art is not an artist." He's about to pick up his brushes yet again. For most of the past year, I thought he was dying—but not of any ailment, just boredom.

IF I HAVE A CHURCH, IT'S
THE CHURCH OF THE ABSURD

A few years ago I had a pituitary anomaly, they called it—a growth in my brain. I was going to have brain surgery. This was actually the second time. I had it successfully scraped away once, and then it grew back. It wasn't cancerous, but it was dangerous. It could burst, it could make me go blind, and if the doctor did something wrong, it could kill me. I had this weird notion of what a brain operation was, based on seeing Don Martin cartoons of a blade going over the top of your head, and someone cranking your ear to pop the top of your head off so they could get the brain out and do whatever they do to it, toss the brain back in and crank your head down, then slop some paste on the crevice, and it's over.

It was really a lot more like a very intensive version of something like a root canal. They go through the nose and mouth, use micro-imagery to do whatever they're doing. Before this surgery, I did feel my mortality especially keenly. The second time the tumor was bigger than the first time, so I couldn't get too used to it. I had to get surgery relatively quickly. But in the days leading up to it, I thought: *Okay, I may die on the table. What am I going to do about this? Should I switch to being Catholic and get last rites or something? No, that's idiotic, I can't do that. Should I become an orthodox Jew and figure out what Jews are even supposed to think about this sort of thing? Nah, that's boring.*

What I ended up doing was, I decided I would read as much Beckett as I could before I died. I got through most of the plays, but not all of the novels and prose writing. As I was going through these plays, I realized, *Yeah, this sounds about right.* If I have a church, it's the church of the absurd. Beckett was a cold comfort that came complete with irony and humor, much better than most religions. You're stuck, you can't win, enjoy the ride. Try again, fail again, fail better. The fact that there's no one right thing to do just seems to be a given to me.

Then, when the operation went even better than expected and I was out of the hospital within twenty-four hours and perfectly fine, I was kind of annoyed that I hadn't had time to read the rest of the Beckett stuff. I haven't made time for it since. I guess I'll save the prose until the next time the tumor comes back.

Reading about Beckett, though, made me believe something that a wise shrink, who has a bit part in a couple chapters of *Maus* and survived the camps, had said that struck me as really profound. I was going out with him around midnight, after a session had gone on for two hours or more where he dozed off and I kept talking. If I thought there was anything he really should hear, I nudged him awake. So we were walking down to feed the stray cats in Central Park, which was a ritual for him, and he said he was a nihilist, and that he couldn't think of anything more sick than behaving ethically. So maybe he didn't read Beckett, but he got it.

DRAWING MOHAMMAD

I don't think of myself as a political cartoonist in any standard sense of the title, but I know that when I did a piece for *Harper's* after the Danish cartoon thing happened*—that was about five months after—it felt somewhat but not terribly dangerous. I just felt that, well, this is worth doing. I didn't feel like I was really jumping off a cliff by doing it. I was aware that there was some risk. But the magazine was publishing them for the right reasons, and we were willing to take the risk together. I was proud of them for being willing to do that.

I don't feel like, *Oh good, there's a suicidal cartooning mission I can go on. I'll go grab it.* Although, I was trying to figure out what I could do after the cartoonists were killed last January. I knew a couple of those people. I couldn't let it go unmarked, and I had to at least, in solidarity to these brave and strange people, find some way of thinking that through. I made a page called "Notes from a First Amendment Fundamentalist," and I did a page where I drew a stick figure with an arrow pointing to it with the word "Mohammad" as a way of crossing the line. It was only because I was dared to, not because I wanted to. It was just out of some kind of solidarity with the *Charlie Hebdo* artists. I didn't think what I was doing was especially dangerous, but you never can tell.

I just felt that it was genuinely brave of them, and my position was to only respect what they had done even though it seemed more and more foolhardy to do it. I would never have the monomaniacal desire to draw Mohammad, ever! It just isn't part of the vocabulary that I'm interested in expressing. But I can imagine myself in some situation getting into hot water by having a misplaced conviction.

---

* Al-Qaeda terrorists killed twelve people, mostly staff members, at the offices of the the Paris-based satirical newspaper *Charlie Hebdo* in January 2015.

SHOOTING AN ARROW INTO SOME FUTURE

I always thought I'd be famous posthumously, which is an insane thought. I now realize it was just hubris. I was not decades and decades before my time, but like, twenty minutes.

If anything, success gave me more self-doubt. It has obviously made my life more comfortable in some ways and more difficult in others. It's a mixed bag. The economic wolf has stopped breathing down my back, thanks to the success that came in the wake of *Maus*. But I don't remember striving for wealth or anything. I just wanted to do the best I could as a cartoonist.

I wanted to be posthumously famous because then nobody could get in my way. I was trying to build what I was working on so it would last, let's say. That came from not wanting to accept the fact that everything is as ephemeral as it is. One of the theories of art-making is that you're shooting an arrow into some future, but it's just such an abstraction. You can never tell what's going to be appreciated in the future. As my friend Ken Jacobs, the filmmaker, said, "If I really worked for posterity, I'd be making my films for cockroaches."

Now I think posthumous fame is absurd. I subscribe to that Woody Allen line. I'm not interested in posthumous fame unless I'm here to enjoy it.

PAPER LASTS LONGER THAN PERFORMANCE ART

That mouse mask has been grafted onto me in ways that are not exactly removable. It's a pipe dream to think I can remove it. It's my skull underneath it. Very often, when I'm signing a letter or something, I'll sign it with a mouse head because it's organically part of me now.

I just don't want to be limited to only drawing mice for the rest of my life, and I've found ways around it. I can compete with myself or not. I can do whatever I do. I don't mind having had it come through me. I'm proud of it on a certain level—but it sometimes does grate me to be living in that shadow. I've done as many strips, metaphorically, about that as I could do. Now I'm just left with whatever comes to mind, without having to specifically allude to it. I know that *Maus*, historically, has had an impact on my medium.

I've seen, even now, people who are genuinely affected by *Maus* and are making art that's a response to it—some of which I cringe over, but every once in awhile I see something that's really terrific that was made because something I did catalyzed it. I don't know if that's exactly posterity, but it feels like it's the intellectual version of the nitrogen cycle.

On some level I care, but it's insane. And on some level I don't. There's this illusion of knowing that people will still be reading *Maus*, perhaps, after I stop being here. I don't know why that should make me happy, but I'm happy that certain works from artists I admire are here to be appreciated. They made me at least think more of being a pen-and-ink artist, because paper lasts longer than performance art does. Performance art takes maybe more of a genuine existential commitment than I could make. But paper doesn't really last all that long, either.

I'm sure that the root art that inspired me—that goes back many generations farther than EC Comics or Krazy Kat, whatever inspired them and inspired the people that inspired them—is a long legacy, most of the members of which are anonymous, especially when you're taking the long perspective. That's all a part of the process that allows some kind of creative work to happen that, to me, is one of the few justifications for humans being on the planet.

It's one of those things I've never thought through to its logical consequence, but there's a feeling of comfort in the idea that something I made might be read by people long after I'm no longer around to promote it.

\\

CONDUCTED MAY 26, 2016

ZACH WILSON

VIDEO GAME DESIGNER

I play video games, and not infrequently, but I still hesitate to describe myself as a "gamer." Some fraction of the hours I've spent playing games has been regret-free: building virtual cities, gaining a richer appreciation for sports, fighting neon aliens with distant friends over the internet. But a lot of it has felt like addiction. Many times I have found myself still awake at four in the morning, playing some violent first-person shooter, thinking, This is it—this is the last round.

As a level designer on major games like Homefront, Battlefield 3, *and* Battlefield Hardline, *Zach Wilson is one of the people I should curse for some of those lost hours. Designers like him build experiences that feel immersive and cohesive enough to sustain continued and/or repeated engagement. But increasingly, I find myself asking whether addictiveness is enough. It's a question that Zach Wilson has been asking, too.*

Days before I called Wilson, he had accepted a job offer from Bethesda Softworks, perhaps the most critically respected major game studio in America. For Wilson, working for Bethesda represents a chance to step away from the intense, military-style first-person shooters he has helped build for the past decade, as well as to leave the increasingly expensive San Francisco Bay Area, where he was then living. But he's also hopeful that he'll get to contribute to the next step in the evolution of the medium: one that is less focused on killing and more focused on player freedom and powerful storytelling.

While some game designers loathe critics who focus on story and content, Wilson is inspired by that. "The critical conversation afterward, divorced from the reality of the development, is the thing that's really interesting to me," he says. "It can be a propulsive and powerful means to effect change in games."

VERBS

When game creators think about actions that the player takes, we call those verbs. The verb "to kill" is very different from the verb "to sneak" or "to jump," and those are the actions that we give to the player. And there's this huge gradation of possibilities of how you represent "to kill."

You've got *Mortal Kombat*—where it's these horrifying, just unbelievably gruesome torturous deaths—versus *Minecraft*, where you shoot a blocky zombie and it disappears into smoke. *Dead Space* is another example of that, where you're killing the undead by cutting of their limbs. That's pretty gruesome. It's definitely a spectrum in terms of how you actually represent death to the player and what that actually means.

When you're playing a game like *Mortal Kombat* or *Killer Instinct*, you're playing that to witness interesting ways of people dying. *Mortal Kombat* goes into X-ray mode, and you can see the bones breaking, and that's kind of what *Mortal Kombat* is about for people. That's the expectation players have. If you added that to *Super Mario Bros.*, it would totally clash with what the fans expect of that game. You're still *killing* goombas, but in a way that's not gruesome.

I'll tell you the reason that in so many games the verb "to kill" is the primary means of expression—it's uncomplicated. The feedback in most cases is immediately satisfying. You pull the trigger, the gun fires, the dude dies, you get points. Some games are really, really good at this feedback loop. There's any number of proven models that you can use as a starting point, or basically rip off, and create a functional base game. The weapon and gadget model in *Call of Duty* or *Halo*, for instance: You would be surprised at how many games start by trying to duplicate an existing system and extend or reskin it. It just takes the time and meticulous effort of very skilled professionals.

And they sell like a motherfucker. Sixty percent of the top-selling games of 2015 focused on the verb "to kill" as their primary means of interaction. I'm including *Mortal Kombat* in this because it literally means "combat ending in or causing death," despite the lack of guns.

"WHY DO I HAVE TO DO THIS?"

Minecraft is going to be very disruptive. There's a whole generation of kids being raised on it. One of my friends told me a story about his thirteen-year-old. He thought, *Oh, he likes open-world games like* Minecraft, *he'll love* Fallout. But the first thing that happens when you play *Fallout* is that you get an objective, and you have to complete the objective. His kid was like, "Why do I have to do this? This is stupid." I think that is going to have a huge effect on games.

If you're playing *Minecraft* in survival mode, the best thing to do is not to and kill hunt zombies, but it's to build a house and to stay safe. I think that's also going to positively affect the way gamers approach games.

Hopefully we'll see more games like *Dishonored*, where it's a completely viable option to play the game without killing people, still within an objective-based situation or scenario. I think that's what kids growing up on *Minecraft* are going to crave: "Why do I have to do that? Why do I have to go and kill?" These are elements that we're used to just accepting in games. I think we're going to see players and developers questioning that.

EVERYBODY WANTS MY JOB

I've been making military first-person shooters for the past ten years. If I could have one effect on games, it would be to push them in a direction that doesn't involve *just* killing. I would love to see more games where it's possible to achieve goals completely through persuasion, or completely through some other means. I think that's really important.

I'm extremely fortunate to have the job that I have. Everybody wants my job. There are an infinite number of twenty-two-year-old kids who are just getting out of school who would work on *Call of Duty* for free, and they're probably not focused on "What does this mean for the grand scheme of things?" or "How does this fit into the culture?" And more power to them. Maybe one day, they'll start to think about it, maybe not. But I'm at a point in my career where I really want to see more of the kind of stuff that they do in *Dishonored* and in *Minecraft* and games like that, where it's all about you being the kind of player you want to be—being able to express yourself.

Being able to put those philosophies into practice, it's hopefully something I'll have the opportunity to do. I think players crave that. I think by taking away death as the central verb that the player has to work with, it opens the doors to more people because there are a lot of potential gamers out there who don't want to kill people. The more opportunities for players to sneak around or talk to people to achieve an objective—the more they can naturally be themselves in this world—the more you're going to have people who wouldn't normally find themselves playing games playing your games. Games like *Dishonored* and *The Elder Scrolls* are perfect examples of opportunities to allow that nondeath method of expression.

DEATH AS A FAILURE STATE

I was thinking about the legacy of death in video games. If you think all the way back to where games started, in arcades, you had a quarter and you would put a quarter in a game and your guy—Pac-Man—had three lives.

Pac-Man was very obviously not human, and the ghosts were not human. It was all very representational. It just kind of became this understandable currency, like, "One quarter equals three lives, and if I'm really good, I can make a quarter go a long way." Life is not really tied to death, in that sense. It's tied to success or failure, and it seems to me like the idea of life and death as a failure state just echoed out from that. It is something that we never broke out of, really. Death is a state in video games—you're alive or dead, and it's represented by a Boolean value, true or false.

There are games that have been really successful in using death and emotional attachment. The Firaxis version of *XCOM* is a great representation of that. You create these characters, custom soldiers, that you bring into battle. The first time I ever played, I named everybody after my family members and made them try to look like my family members, which is what you naturally do.

You play with these characters, and if you play in a particular mode, then once a character dies, they're dead. They were soldiers, and they died, and their names get written up on the wall, and you have to move on with new soldiers. People who play that game develop a profound attachment to their characters. Part of it is you're putting resources into these characters, and then you're going into the field of battle with them, where they act in a very realistic, soldierly fashion. When they die, it's a loss to your team. I think they handled that in a really interesting way. It's not grizzly: They die on the field of battle, like, down in the mud, killed by an alien in service of humanity. We equate that as a noble death. And players feel it. You feel that loss. Especially when it's a character that has been with you for a long time.

On one end, you've got really strong systemic games like *XCOM* that rely on you to create the emotional connection, and on the other end you have explicitly told stories like *The Last of Us*, which was masterfully crafted. *The Last of Us* was a high watermark for me because every death felt justifiable, just because of how well they integrated the themes of the game and the mechanics of the game. It was like, "Yeah, I will kill to save this girl who holds the key to saving the human race." It's an incredible combination of personal relationships and global significance, and it's a very hard line to walk. Very few games have done that.

The Last of Us hits these really special plot points at the same time for everybody. It's a third-person action-adventure game that's "grounded"— that means that if a normal fifty-five-year-old man wouldn't be able to do something, then this character wouldn't be able to do it. Frequently, you find Joel boosting Ellie—the young girl—up to a high ledge and then Ellie drops down a rope or a ladder for him to climb up. This is a pattern that's repeated until the very end of the game, when it hits you with a twist. Joel boosts Ellie up, and she cries out—at first you think she's in pain, she's been attacked, she's calling out your name. You quickly find an alternate route, and after a few harried seconds of chasing her down, you find her in the second story of a room petting the head of a giraffe. It's the most unexpected and moving twist in a game ever, and it's about being alive. The giraffe moves away, and the player goes around the corner to see a vista shot of a whole herd of giraffes that escaped from a zoo and are living calm, peaceful lives in the remains of a ruined university. It gives me hope for games, and their relationship with death, that the most emotionally affecting moment we've seen is the awe that a young girl experiences at seeing something alive.

In a totally open-world game, though, all narrative bets are off. I was actually just playing *Fallout 4* yesterday, and I was liberating one of the farms. I had done this quest for a farmer. Some raiders stole his sword, and I had to go to an ironworks and kill a bunch of these guys to get his sword back. They were all very clearly bad guys: They were actually really weird—they worshipped the forge, and he had a son who had gotten sucked into this cult or something. So I had this choice: Do I persuade the son to come back or not? I didn't have enough charisma to do it, so I had to kill the son and then go back and lie to the farmer and give him his sword back. That completed the story. But what was really interesting about it was that the first time I played it, I had finished the whole thing and was talking to the farmer, and midway through our conversation, a bloatfly spawned out of nowhere and started attacking us both and broke up the conversation. All of a sudden I'm trying to kill this bloatfly in the middle of an emotional conversation with this farmer whose son I had just killed.

It was an emotionally affecting moment in *Fallout* for me, but it was disrupted by the fact that it's an insane, open-world game where anything can happen at any time.

WEIRD TERMINOLOGY

We've got all kinds of weird terminology that has popped up around death in video games. An example is the "kill trade"—what this usually refers to is that two people in a multiplayer match fire at roughly the same time and kill each other simultaneously. It's typically a pejorative and indicative of the system functioning improperly.

Another curious shorthand that exists in video games is "suicide." Obviously, in real life, suicide is a choice that a human makes—but we've abstracted it to represent all accidental deaths. Like, if I walk backward into a fiery pit, then I have committed suicide according to the game, despite the fact that I merely exited the game world by mistake.

It can also represent a choice to intentionally restart—you can often choose "suicide" on a menu somewhere, and your character will die and you can "respawn." Players make this choice so that they can change the weapons or setup that they have, or they can restart in a better physical position in the world. Electronic Arts' *Battlefield* series actually made a very subtle change to their game from *Battlefield 3* to *Battlefield 4*—they changed the "suicide" option to read as "redeploy." Same function, but it was out of respect to people that might have had or were dealing with issues of suicide. The word can trigger thoughts, and they didn't want to have to force their players to deal with emotional trauma when making a tactical choice.

COPS PULLING THEIR GUNS ON CIVILIANS

We had this experience working on *Battlefield Hardline* where we went into it thinking we were going to make *Bad Boys* meets *Battlefield*, which is a game that makes sense. Those are themes that match up. But for a variety of behind-the-scenes reasons, we were forced in the direction of, "It's a game about cops, and we're looking at *End of Watch* and *Drive* as our inspirations." That doesn't match up very well with military-style warfare.

About six months before the game was released, Ferguson happened, and we saw a militarized police force confronting impoverished civilians on the streets of America. We're like, "We have a problem here. This is no joke." So myself and the producer who I worked with on my level—I did the first level of the game, which takes place in a Miami 'hood —we tried to take out the kind of brutality and violence that you would naturally put into a *Battlefield* game and replace it with something a little more subtle. We had to retrofit it, and this level had to operate around teaching the player how to play the game.

If you're dealing with other human beings, and having to kill them is part of your gameplay, you should have a justification for that. You look at a game like *Battlefield 1*, which deals with World War I, and the justification is there. It's two state-sponsored armies at war. They're sworn enemies. But cops pulling their guns on civilians is a much more subtle, much more nuanced kind of thing.

It's tough. What we're talking about is probably the most controversial aspect of modern games. I'm speaking about this as a gamer and as a game developer, and my views obviously don't represent the greater game-development community at large or any of the companies I've worked for. This is just me talking. But we definitely think about it. I mean, some game developers don't give a shit. In a game like *Doom*, it doesn't make any sense for them to care about violence. They chose a great setting for their game, where none of that ever clashes because you're never really killing human beings, and you're in space. The Rockstar guys, they don't care at all. I know people who have worked with them, and it just doesn't matter to them. *Grand Theft Auto* sells really well, and some of the stuff in their games is really genuine, and some of it's really comical. The best games are the ones that have a consistent tone, and the mechanics and the theme agree really well. They're masters at taking tropes and turning them into satire and never really taking them too seriously, but also making it fun. That's why people love their games so much.

BECAUSE WE MAKE IT THAT WAY

Why is it so satisfying to kill people in games? It's because we make it that way.

I don't believe that people see a visual depiction of death or violence and that inspires them to go out and create more death in the real world. If you see a grisly image and you're attracted to that, you're already attracted to it. It's a psychological thing. But where people become actually violent in the real world are in competitive environments. Failure to succeed is perceived as a threat, and I will tell you 100 percent that game developers exploit that psychology to the maximum.

The reward system is based on decades of initially intuitive understanding of psychology and how human beings work, and now game developers connect players' actions with psychological research about why people act the way they act in games. The reason that games make people violent is because of competition, which exploits our core psychology. I remember hearing a story of a Korean gamer in a gaming cafe who lost at some multiplayer game, and he knew where the person was who killed him, and he went to that game cafe and beat the shit out of the kid in the bathroom. I imagine the violent kid also probably had some emotional issues, too, but that's your lizard-brain coming in and saying, "That person is a threat to me, and I'm going to physically assault them." Game developers are 100 percent aware of that. They're 100 percent aware of how you feel when you level up in *Call of Duty*, when you get a kill streak.

Take a *Call of Duty* match and watch it over and over again and just think about every single element. Every detail is thought out. The sound that the bullet makes, the little X that appears, and the icons that the players can use to decorate their little profiles: All of those things are really specifically chosen to exploit the deep competitive nature that humans—and especially men—have.

There's definitely this sort of toxic masculinity at the core of a lot of first-person shooters that is self-perpetuating. It drives a lot of women out of those competitive online, multiplayer shooter-type games. That would be a controversial statement on a gaming message board, but it is a fucking fact. If my wife were to play *Call of Duty* online and self-identify as a woman, it'd be over. They'll call her fat or say, "You're a slut," whatever. When a woman is more successful than men who are playing a game, especially in an anonymous environment, they revert to the mean stuff very quickly.

The best day of my life was when I figured out how to mute everyone that wasn't a friend on Xbox. I was playing *Battlefield 3*, and some guy was just screaming at me by name to get out of a doorway, and I'm like, *This is not a healthy environment. This is toxic masculinity in my face.*

This is a big area of concern for game companies, and I know that some teams are coming up with different solutions to make the gaming environment less threatening. Right now, though, it's rough.

TO SELL AN IDEA, YOU
HAVE TO BELIEVE IN IT

Homefront was a super hard game to make. This was like six or seven years ago, before the concept of theme was something that I was really thinking about. For whatever reason, the game really lodged in the public's consciousness and became the go-to game to criticize. I still remember the interview that kicked it all off because it was me and another guy, and the interviewer was extremely adversarial toward us. He wrote a scathing, very critical article about the game, which he hadn't played, and it just set the tone. Then the marketing didn't really help that much.

Originally it was going to be a game where China invaded the US. That makes some sense, right? You can see China having a radical change in government and then deciding to invade the United States of America and starting a war of some kind. That, combined with the peak oil crisis— which is what the backbone of the game is about—that makes sense. But at one point marketing freaked out, and they were like, "Oh, but then we can't sell the game in China." Someone in corporate, who wasn't part of the team, decided it should be North Korea. Everybody on the team was like, "That's insane." I would believe Burkina Faso before I would believe North Korea. But it had to be North Korea because that's what corporate decided on.

That was actually my job, writing the backstory of how North Korea could invade the United States of America in twenty-six years, based on where we were at that time. It was a weird exercise. I actually ended up talking to an ex-CIA guy who helped write this backstory with me. I wrote a bunch of newspaper articles that you can pick up in the game, and they explain the exact events that led you to this moment in time. It was weird having to do that and to believe in it. Part of it is like, to sell an idea, you have to believe in it. I had to make myself believe in this idea that I thought was completely absurd.

There's some pretty grim stuff in that game that I'm personally responsible for. I don't know how I feel about it in retrospect. The sequence the game opens with is: You're taking this bus ride. You get captured by the North Koreans, and you're taken on a prison bus to an internment camp, and you ride past these vignettes of people being torn out of their houses. One of the most controversial things for the team, which I was personally responsible for putting in the game, was a child witnessing his parents getting shot in front of him by the North Korean soldiers. The internal reaction to that was extremely divisive. When we were showing it to the marketing team, there were people who were like, "You can't have this in the game." There were two women who were mothers who were particularly upset. At the time I thought that was good, that it was a sign that the game was working.

In retrospect, I think I regret putting that in. Even though the goal of it was to make the enemy faceless and evil, I just don't think the world is better off for that imagery existing in it.

I WOULD QUESTION MY WHOLE CAREER

When I've worked on these games, I've always put aside any kind of moral objection I might have to representing violence in video games. I don't know if that's cowardice on my part or what, but I like a paycheck and I like making games. And first-person shooters are the kind of games that people like.

When something like the mass shooting at the Pulse nightclub in Orlando happens, though, there's that moment where you're like, *Please, please don't let this person have been a fan of my game.* There's that moment where you're like, *Oh my god, if it turns out that it was* Battlefield Hardline *that was his favorite game, and that's all he wanted to do was play that game* . . .

I can't imagine what it must have been like for a guy like John Carmack and the guys at id Software who created *Doom*, and then the national conversation was, "These two kids at Columbine were obsessed with the game *Doom*."* How does that make you feel? I don't know Carmack. For me, if somebody said after a shooting, "All this guy did all day long, all he wanted to do was play *Battlefield*," yeah, I would question my whole career. It would be very, very challenging to deal with. As a developer, that's one of those things where you have to ask yourself whether or not it's worth it.

Any time there's a shooting, people bring up video games as a part of the conversation. Right now, they're blaming radical Islam because that's the easy low-hanging fruit right now. But if it wasn't Islam, it would have been video games.

I was accused of being part of the military-industrial complex once, on a message board, while I was working on *Homefront*. That was a first for me. I think the apogee of that relationship was when *Medal of Honor:*

---

* Two high school seniors in Columbine, Colorado, killed twelve of their classmates and one teacher in 1999. The killers were both fans of multiple id Software games, including *Doom* and *Wolfenstein 3D*.

Warfighter was working with gun manufacturers to advertise their guns on the game's website. There was a huge outcry over that.

I think that kind of taught everybody a lesson. But there's no conspiracy. It's just that everybody wants to make money, and guns are big business. Games with guns, games with killing—it's just business. Of course, somebody on the inside of conspiracy theory would say that, right?

VIRTUAL REALITY

I have the Oculus Rift virtual reality headset. There's this little thing for it called "Dreamdeck"—it's just three or four little vignettes. One of them fades in, and you're in a black room, and there's a *T. rex* right in front of you. I've shown people this demo. One of the girls I showed it to was screaming and trying to cover her eyes with the VR headset on. This is real to people. It's so presence-inducing. Where that can go is potentially very chilling, and it's going to be a whole new set of responsibilities for game developers to deal with.

I happen to know that the first thing one company is working on is a gun that feels real to hold. There is a prominent company that's making a gun that has recoil built into it, and it has perfect tracking. You can only speculate on the impact that's going to have on people because real VR is extremely presence-inducing. It's going to change people. It's going to change the sense of presence versus that abstraction of looking at a monitor. It's a very, very different thing.

Games are the Trojan horse of VR, but VR has potential beyond what we can think of right now, especially to deal with post-traumatic stress disorder. I think that VR is going to be one of the things that helps people cope with psychological issues. I'm hoping we're going to see things like Rosetta Stone software for PTSD, where it's a program that's scientifically proven to help veterans or victims of domestic violence to move forward at their own pace and deal with tragedies in their lives. I think that's one of the powers VR is going to eventually end up having. Being able to cope with death is a very real possibility, beyond just talking to a psychologist. Having experiences tailored to moving you through the stages of grief and moving on. There are astounding opportunities there.

This comes at a time, too, when in the next two or three years, it's going to become really, really easy to do facial capture. To be able to preserve your loved ones cheaply and simply after just taking a couple of pictures of that person's face—just being able to be in the same room with them again in VR after they've died? Your mind wanders thinking about the effect that would have on people. Your grandmother dies, and you want to see her again, and you *can* see her. Maybe she's sitting in a rocking chair, and you've taken the facial scan and applied it to the body of a more generic character, and it's kind of like seeing her again and reminiscing on the person she was and thinking about her. People will probably get a little obsessed with it and get lost in it. Maybe you get addicted to seeing your lost love one. But the technology is going to be there for people in a couple years.

WE ARE ANIMALS

The term *game* broadens every year. A lot of people wouldn't have considered *Gone Home* to be a game five or six years ago. You wouldn't have even thought to have made it. As the definition of *game* blurs into interactive experience, which blurs into tools that can help people cope, I think we'll see more of that. I really think games can have some transcendent power to help people deal with real-world death—and I hope games stop being games and become just part of the fabric of our lives.

Of course, we'll all be playing *Mortal Kombat* until we're ninety and we keel over. We'll all be yelling "Fatality!" I don't see that stuff going anywhere because it's entertaining to a lot of people, and that's all right. There's nothing wrong with being entertained. It's just when entertainment allows people to take their preexisting pathologies and magnify them and multiply them and express them in the real world.

That's the stuff that we really have to work out when it comes to death and video games. It's a cultural thing, and it also relates to guns and how we approach guns in our culture. We are animals. That's a very real fact that we have to deal with: We're trying to fight against ourselves and our nature.

CONDUCTED JUNE 14, 2016

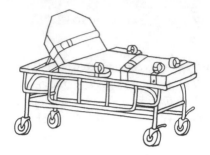

FRANK THOMPSON

FORMER DEATH ROW WARDEN

Frank Thompson makes a hell of a first impression. The seventy-three-year-old former superintendent of the Oregon State Penitentiary in Salem is tall, broad-shouldered, and pulls his gray hair back into a ponytail. What's most striking, though, is Thompson's intense focus. His very presence encourages those in his company to get to the point as quickly as possible.

Lately, Thompson's focus is singular: He wants to end the death penalty in his home state of Oregon. Since retiring from his work in corrections—where he spearheaded the rewriting of the state's capital punishment protocol and oversaw its only two modern executions—he has relentlessly pursued that goal via speaking appearances, meetings, fundraisers, and letters to politicians and newspapers. These days, he has little time for anything else. He often worried aloud about whether or not this interview would be worth the effort.

Thompson doesn't really express much trauma over having overseen two electrocutions. He is happily married, at ease with himself, and proud of his career in corrections. His argument against capital punishment doesn't focus particularly on the strain it puts on those who participate in executions. He just strongly believes that the death penalty is bad public policy.

We met three times over nine months before Thompson agreed to be included in this book, and whenever I got off topic, his gaze tightened. "If there's a flaw in my personality," he told me, "it's that I like being in control of things." Thompson exerts that control effortlessly.

I'M NOT A BLEEDING-HEART LIBERAL

You are talking to a death-penalty abolitionist who was the lead in conducting the only two executions in the state of Oregon in the last fifty-two years.

I have not always been against the death penalty. In fact, I grew up in a community of blacks, many of whom supported the death penalty because the death penalty was seen as being the just desserts for certain types of crimes. When you consider a crime as hideous as the premeditated rape or killing of children or babies—I have long felt that when you commit these kinds of crimes that you have given up the right to have an advocate at the table about whether or not you should live, and whatever the society metes out for your behavior, you're at the mercy of that society.

There came a point in my life where a very close friend, a police officer named John Hussey—we graduated from police academy together—was abducted and killed. I can remember hoping that the guy who killed him would be executed. Not too long after that, in the same city, my cousin, a state trooper by the name of Louis Perry Bryant, was abducted and killed, and I felt justice had been served when his killer was executed.

I accepted capital punishment as being a proper sanction, even though it was a part of a flawed criminal justice system. All of our systems are flawed, and I'm the kind of person that believes that if a system is, on balance, necessary, you try to improve it from within, but you don't throw the baby out with the bathwater. So I tolerated it.

I was in law enforcement and in the military. Both of those are very conservative organizations. Both are driven, in part, by accepting the need to kill under certain circumstances. I'm not a bleeding-heart liberal. If somebody's kicking at my door, and I reasonably feel that if I don't do something right now, he's going to kill me and my family, he may not see the sunrise, okay? Sometimes you gotta do what you gotta do.

The question is, what are you accomplishing by killing somebody? When you take a life, and it cannot be reasonably shown to have had a demonstrably positive outcome or made the community safer, then it's immoral. Then it's wrong to require and expect people to kill folks. It's bad public policy.

Many people will say it's a deterrent, but if the death penalty deterred anybody, do you think we'd be having all of these mass shootings right now? The majority of people on death row aren't committed to a cause like these people. They commit crimes in the heat of passion, or they're in some kind of demented state of mind. You take demented state of mind, heat of passion, and people committed to a cause—that's the majority of your people on death row, and executions can't deter any of those.

I KNEW THAT THERE
WAS THIS EVIL OUT THERE

I grew up in the segregated South. Didn't really pay much attention to its being segregated because my black experience met all of my needs. I had a wholesome family, and my mother and my father were together all of their lives. Christian family, both my parents were educated, and they were public school teachers.

Our grandparents were first-generation descendants of ex-slaves. But I doubt if you'll find anybody my age who had parents who talked about what they gleaned about the experiences of slavery and its impacts from their parents. They just didn't talk about it. That might have been because, for them, they were living the legacies of slavery, and reliving the past offered little in coping with the future. In some ways I'm a little disappointed, because that history is a part of who I am. In my parents I had people who knew ex-slaves, their grandparents. That's a big chunk of this nation's history, and folks just didn't talk about it.

I was educated in a black school system in Little Rock, and it was not as good as the system that the white kids would go to, but it was sound. It was one of the better schools. I wanted for nothing. Living in a segregated environment didn't really negatively impact my ego or sense of worth because all of my basic needs were being met. I knew that there was this evil out there that someday needed to be reckoned with, but I was patient enough to wait until the fifties, sixties, and seventies came along, which became other chapters in my life.

I guess for most purposes we were middle, lower-middle class, at least. For blacks, I guess we might have been upper-middle class. It was a fairly unremarkable upbringing when you compare it to the rest of black society, but very remarkable in terms of wholesomeness, love, being protected, and giving me a sense of worth and pride as an individual.

When you go to a segregated school system all your life, that's overt racism. But I didn't really run into a lot of overt racism from individuals until later, when I got to college. It was going on all around me, but I was always big enough that nobody really had the guts to come up to me personally and affront me on an overt basis. Was it happening to other kids in my community? Of course. I lived in an environment where I really didn't let it get to me. I didn't let it affect my psyche or my ego.

I DON'T HAVE ANY WAR STORIES

I went into college to be a doctor and flunked chemistry my first semester. That put the quietus on the medical career. When I started at the University of Arkansas in Fayetteville, blacks were not allowed to live in the dormitories on campus. I lived in the basement of a white family's house about a mile from campus. Northwest Arkansas gets extremely hot and extremely cold, so that was really tough walking back and forth to school, carrying those books. Not having all of the other accommodations that students normally have—easy access to the library, easy access to recreational and social facilities, living in the basement—it was fairly austere.

The civil rights movement had already started. Martin Luther King was quite active, and there were sit-ins going on in the South. I became involved in demonstrations there on campus. Lots of marching, and a couple times we took over buildings. We took over the journalism building one day, then we went over to the president's office and we sat in there. We really put our energy into trying to get minority representation in all of the key areas where decisions were being made about our lives. We tried to get student representatives in student government, and I think we expedited the commitment of the university to hire black faculty, which was significant. It was important for us to see staff and faculty members who looked like us. We were successful in getting the swimming pool, restaurants, and theaters integrated. Those activities really consumed me more than my studies did. I became sort of disenchanted with school. When I left in college in '63, the dormitories still had not been integrated.

I was fed up with school, and I didn't want to go back home. At the time they were still drafting, and if I wasn't in college, then my number to be drafted was not too far away. I thought, rather than doing two years, I'll go ahead and do three. I went into the military, and went to Korea. I was a military policeman. My experience there was fairly unremarkable. I don't have any war stories to tell—and I'm glad. Vietnam was getting on the news during those days, but what many people don't realize is that a lot of stuff was still going on in Korea at the time.

I had allowed for the possibility that I might've made a career in the military, and I think I could have done pretty well. But I got into the military during the thick of things in Vietnam, and I thought, *I don't want any of that.* I didn't agree with the war. So I got out.

When I came back to the same school in 1966, the dorms were integrated, and there were more black students on campus. Civil rights demonstrations were still very frequent across the country, so I became involved in activism again. I got my undergraduate degree in social work, then went to law school. I wound up serving as associate dean of students at the university. I was a criminal investigator for the police department there. I became executive director for the Economic Opportunity Agency in Fayetteville, and later I became director of the Little Rock Job Corps Center.

SOCIETY'S GARBAGE CANS

There was a public announcement advertising for a corrections personnel administrator for the state, and I went down and interviewed. By that time, I had been the executive director of two agencies, and I had been an associate dean on a college level. So my experiences made me very competitive.

They hired me as the personnel manager for the State of Arkansas Corrections Department. That was the beginning of my career in corrections. I knew then that that's where I was gonna be for the rest of my career. After serving as personnel administrator for three or four years, I went in to the director and said, "Hey, look, I'm older than most of you, and I want to be a warden. The next time you get a chance, I want you to put me on track to becoming one."

A year later, he called me in. I was thinking maybe he was going to let me be an assistant warden. But he said, "Frank, how would you like to be a warden?" Man, I almost crapped in my pants. I knew I could do it. He said that not only was he offering me an opportunity to be a warden, he was going to put me in charge of the construction of a brand-new prison. Now that's huge.

I later found out that one of the reasons he offered me that opportunity is that nobody wanted to go down there. It was down in the delta—Dermott, Arkansas. It was mosquito infested. But it was a stepping stone for me to the rest of my career. I took it. The prison was built, we took on inmates, and that's the beginning of my career in corrections.

Corrections was, in many ways, an expression of everything that was wrong with our society, and I felt that every bad system needed good people in it. I thought I had a grasp on one of the truths about what was wrong with the country, and that was the societal handling and treatment of the minority poor. Prisons are really a microcosm of everything that's wrong with a society. It's like the garbage can: If you want to really know something about a person's lifestyle or that family, you go through their garbage and see what they throw away. You can learn a lot. Prisons are society's garbage cans.

I had relatives who had done time. I didn't like the way prisons were being run. I had an idea about a better way of running them. Prisons are quasi-military. I liked the structure and environment. I like getting up in the morning with an idea, putting it to paper, calling a group of people around, having them chew on it—not telling them what to do but letting them know where I'd like to go—and telling them that I want them to help me get there. One of the most rewarding things I think I can experience is to go in with a new idea and have people who support you and believe in you bite into it, take it on, and make it happen.

Coming up in the environment I came up in, almost all of the systems needed to be changed; the political arena, the economy, the school systems. As a black, I felt that all of the systems needed to go through a revamping. I guess I was, in the grand scheme of things, trying to find out: Where did my talents and my skills and my passions fit?

I believe in getting into a situation and becoming a part of it and understanding it. If there's nothing to bite into or change today, don't worry about it. Don't be frustrated. Just be patient. I do believe that I carry that with me a barometer of what's fair and not fair, and what's just and not just, that some people I have worked with didn't carry. I trusted my gut in those regards. I didn't go in and say, "I want to change the educational system in prison." Or, "I want to change the work programming in prisons." Sometimes people become mission-driven, and they piss everybody off, and their mission may be ill-conceived. I wanted to get into the prison system and understand it, and earn respect, gain a position of leadership where I could begin influencing things in a positive direction with my own staff, without dictating from the beginning.

LIKE THE GLADIATORS BACK IN THE DAY

I came into the prison system when some of the last vestiges of what Arkansas prisons were like in the past still existed. There was an era in Arkansas where inmates were being abused, and some of these abusive practices were dying out at the time I became a warden. When I started, they still had an activity—as a part of the annual rodeo schedule—where they would tie a bag of money between the horns of a bull and turn the inmates loose. If an inmate could grab the money between the horns of the bull, they could keep that money. That was just for the male inmates. Then they would grease a pig and tie a bag of money on the pig, and turn female inmates loose to get the money—in an arena like the gladiators back in the day. Of course, the inmates were usually black. By the time I left the Arkansas prison system, it had moved forward to where these type of these activities had been discontinued. There was a time when the Arkansas prison system was nothing to brag about.

I spent five years as a warden at that institution, then I came out here for twenty years. I had always wanted to live in Oregon. Back in the military, when I was stationed in California, I used to drive back and forth from California to Seattle, and I learned to love Route 101 up into Oregon. I just always thought that if there was heaven on earth, part of it was in the Pacific Northwest. A couple of headhunters gave me an application for a job in Oregon, and the rest is history.

I'VE ALWAYS KNOWN THAT I WAS A GOOD SOLDIER

When I first came here, my first day was at Oregon State Pen here in Salem. That's where death row was. I became the superintendent there, and that's where I was when the executions took place, and where I was when I had the administrative responsibility for capital punishment.

I can remember when I was applying for the job, they pointedly asked me, "Frank, you know the job that you're applying for calls for the execution of people. If you become the warden, if you become the superintendent, do you think you can handle it?"

I've always known that I was a good soldier. Of course I didn't want to do it, but there was nothing that said to me that I couldn't do the job.

I said, "Of course." But I knew I was coming to Oregon. Man, they hadn't executed anyone in about thirty years. Nobody really thought we would have to execute anyone. I thought, *I might make it out of here without having to do it.* Well, within my first two years, one of the inmates volunteered his execution. He gave up his appeals.

I am familiar with the reasons that people commit suicide, but I still don't understand it. Somewhere on the continuum of life, a person on death row who volunteers to die is not too unlike a person who decides to commit suicide by cop.

There are people on death row who actually become new people, spiritually. They look at their life differently. The same things that motivated them and that they put value in at that point in their life are different from what got them in trouble in the first place, and they accept the fact that they have so severely transgressed the expectations of society that they don't have a place out there. They don't have any other place but to be on the row, and they don't wanna be in that hole anymore.

One guy who volunteered for the death penalty said he was just "tired of being around these other no-good dudes" on death row. The idea of being on death row for the rest of his life, with a bunch of people like that, was too much for him. He knew he was going to die on death row, so why wait? It was a very practical thing for him. There are guys who just get tired.

It's hard for me to understand that because I've never been a person who was so sick and so debilitated and so dependent on the rest of the world for my next breath and my next meal that I felt like I didn't want to live. But if I am deathly ill, and there is no hope for my recovery, that seems different from suicide. It's sort of a hospice kind of thing, where I can accept my demise without any fear. In that sense, I guess it makes sense for a person who has been sentenced to death, who feels there's no hope of ever getting off of death row, and death row is just such a negative existence that they feel they are in a sort of emotional hospice. It's a prolonged process. It's just a torturous, emotional death. I worked in that world long enough to where, on some level, that makes sense to me.

WHAT IF THE SUCKER GOES SOUTH?

If Oregon had had an execution protocol when I took the job, being the kind of person I am, I probably would have come in and done it without questioning it. Since there was nobody, and I put emphasis on *nobody*, in the state who knew anything about executing anybody—it became my job to rewrite, or coordinate the rewriting, of the entire execution protocol.

The US Supreme Court required that all executions in the country stop until the state was able to come up with a constitutional approach to executing people. Incrementally, the states started bringing their systems in. Lethal injection had become the gold standard in terms of constitutionality—capital punishment in Oregon had previously been by gas.

The law had changed, but the facilities and the tools and the equipment—none of that had been retrofitted. I had to help rewrite the policies to match the laws and then retrofit our institution. I had to construct the execution room, work with the Department of Justice in rewriting the policies and procedures consistent with standard lethal-injection protocols, and then train my staff to those new procedures.

This was the first time in thirty-two years we were gonna be killing somebody, right? And I had to kill them with a process that had never been tried before in Oregon. Usually when you go into a new undertaking, you've got veteran people around who can say, "Okay, man, here's what we're doing. And we've found out that you don't do this and you don't do that." I didn't have a soul at my disposal, and I answered directly to the governor. On top of that, I was the first black person ever to run Oregon State Penitentiary. What if the sucker goes south? What if I mess around and leave an important "t" uncrossed and fail to dot an important "i," and it was an oversight on my part?

THE WORLD IS NOT GOING TO BE BETTER OFF

I pulled my team together, we pulled our process together, and we started practicing, practicing, practicing. One of the best inoculations to anxiety and fear is training. I had been preparing and revising and writing and training and talking to staff and visiting other states almost to the point of exhaustion, so that when the time came, being the soldier that I am, it was more "Let's get this done, get it done humanely, and get it behind us," rather than it being this ominous threat hanging over my head.

I don't remember being overwhelmed with the whole notion that I was having to participate in the taking of a life. That notion just permeated everything that I did. When I was getting the gurney and when I was with my staff, who were setting up the IVs, and when I was being trained on how to administer the lethal injection—because I had to train somebody else how to do it—all of that created in me a sort of commitment to getting the job done that helped me with what was actually going on.

During one of our training sessions, I realized that we were going to take the life of a person, and that the very next day, the world would not be any better off. That realization became the genesis of my questioning. When I went in the room that night of the first execution, if somebody had asked me if I believed in capital punishment, I would have answered no. I was a supporter of the death penalty when I accepted the job. But in the process of preparing for it, I'm standing there looking at my staff, and I'm thinking to myself, *You know, when we are finished with this execution, we're gonna be going back to business as usual, and the world is not going to be any better off.* I began to think about it that night, about where did I really, really stand on the issue of the death penalty. It's not that I tossed and turned. My whole process was one of serious contemplation. It was a fairly sober, heavy deliberation about just what is this that I'm involved in.

At some point I began to feel more paternalistic toward my staff than I felt like a leader. Paternalistic because I realized that I was leading all of these men and women into new territory, and they were totally dependent upon me to get them through this. I didn't want any casualties. I wanted the only casualty to be this inmate. I don't want anybody having nervous breakdowns.

I don't know how it began to hit me, and I can't really describe how, but I found this burning desire to quit dodging the question of how I truly felt about the death penalty. Fairly quickly, I couldn't deny the question of, "How can you live with yourself, training decent men and women on how to take the life of a human being in the name of a public policy that cannot be shown to work?" Now, I didn't say that it *can't* work. But if you hold it up to evidence-based scrutiny for positive outcomes, it couldn't produce positive outcomes that it makes society safer. Circumspectly, sound public administration theorists and practitioners will tell you that if you have an expensive public policy that you cannot show to be effective, you have to start looking for something that you can *show* works.

Here I am, about to execute someone, and I'm thinking to myself, *This doesn't make any sense.* I felt the need to talk to my staff about how I felt. A leader has to be believable. If a leader is believable, your staff, your followers, can even tolerate your mistakes because they know you're human. I'm just not good at speaking one way and believing and acting another. I went back and told them, "You know, we're in the middle of this, but I want to let you know that, if you all are wondering where my heart is in this whole process, I'm against the death penalty. But I don't want you to lose any confidence. Generals have been known to lead in the fighting of wars, but report to the president, 'Hey, this war is not getting us where we need to be.'"

I talked to my staff—beautiful people—and they knew I was bound to that position. Every one of them stood by me because they believed in what we were doing. We knew that the whole state was watching us.

THE PROCESS

The execution room and where the inmate resided were essentially one large room with a cell that was sectioned off from the gurney room, where he ultimately was going to meet his demise. The inmate would be taken down to that cell either twenty-four or forty-eight hours prior to the execution.

You have to assign someone to monitor the inmate, watch the inmate 24/7, and make sure that he doesn't kill himself. There's an irony in watching an inmate to be sure he doesn't kill himself so that you can kill him later on. He's under twenty-four-hour surveillance, he gets the same meal that all other inmates get, and you try to be as accommodating as possible because you realize this is a very tough situation. You try to get the inmate, within policy, whatever they need.

Meanwhile, the larger execution room is empty except for the gurney on which the inmate is going to be placed. There are a couple of stands next to the gurney that accept the tubes coming out of two holes in the wall, which assist in feeding the line down where the staff would be inserting the IVs. When it's time for the inmate to be executed, you have what you call a tie-down team that goes into the cell where the inmate is and asks him, "Are you ready?" You hear of rare cases where the inmate is clawing and kicking and protesting, but that almost never occurs.

You take the inmate in, and usually it's a fairly straightforward, calm process. You put the inmate on the gurney, the tie-down team secures the inmate to the gurney: ankles, knee area, upper thigh, waist, chest, wrists, and a strap across the forehead. Once he's tied down, a security person goes in and checks to make sure it's secure. Once he looks at me, I give the nod through the one-way pane behind which stands the executioner. I look toward the executioner and give the nod, and he begins the process of administering the drugs.

Then our job is to watch the inmate to be sure that everything is going along according to plan. He has a heart monitor attached to him. You're standing with a medical professional who assists in reading the heart monitor, and after the inmate stops breathing and the heart monitor flatlines, you go in and you lift the eyelid of the inmate to see if there is any consciousness. It's almost impossible for a conscious person not have some kind of quiver or flicking of the eye if you touch it. What you need to see is an absolute absence of response when you move that eyelid.

You don't get the response, and the physician tells you that he's passed. With that being said, I go out and meet with the press, and I talk to the press about the time that the inmate was declared dead, and describe generally whether or not it went according to plan, whether or not there were any issues. In the two experiences that I had, there were no issues, so it was pretty straightforward. I was fortunate.

IN SOME SENSE I WAS HELPING HIM GET WHAT HE WANTED

I'm not really sure why society is so interested in "How were you feeling when you executed the inmates?"—more than "Where were you morally and ethically?" and "Where was your level of guilt or the lack of guilt?" Those are the most important things. Anyone can get afraid. You get afraid going across a bridge. You get afraid of dogs. Many fears are without basis—and many fears are due to a poor perception of reality.

The emotions I was going through came from being involved in something as daunting and serious as an execution, and it's not having any socially redeeming outcome. That was morally heavy to me. Very heavy.

The man we were going to execute had volunteered. He wasn't fighting it. He was asking for the process to be humane and constitutional, and in some sense I was helping him get what he wanted. I didn't want him suffering, I didn't want him lingering there unduly.

It really isn't until you've been through it ten or fifteen times that it becomes emotionally just burdensome. I think if I had continued to have to do that and couldn't find any rhyme and reason and logic or a socially redeeming outcome, it could have begun to work on me. To some extent, taking the abolitionist route shortly after having been involved in the two executions, that has been sort of therapeutic for me. I don't think my advocacy would be as effective and potent had I not had that experience. The experience was in some ways utilitarian. It helps to be an advocate for repeal who's been there and done that.

HOW ABOUT YOU HANG IN THERE

The responsibility is hugely emotional. It's a heavy responsibility that exacts an emotional toll on the person who's responsible. I think we classify emotionalism as being something that happens uncontrollably. Well, there was some of that, but those persons weren't any more emotionally involved, as far as I'm concerned, than I was. My level of responsibility was consuming. There were those who, after having gone through the two executions, said that they could not do it anymore, that they would prefer changing their jobs and do something else. We had psychological mental health professionals make themselves available to our staff. In fact, the first two or three meetings were essentially required, and if the staff felt the need to follow up with that kind of service, then we would make sure that they had it.

My staff was a great bunch of people. Fortunately, we only had to do it twice. Some of the real, real terrible kinds of emotional experiences that people are known to have come out of places like Texas, Florida, and Alabama, where people have been doing it for years, over and over and over again.

In my thirty-plus years of running penitentiaries and being in corrections, the time I spent conducting executions isn't even a flicker in time. Having to conduct an execution doesn't characterize everything that goes on in corrections. Should a police officer quit the police force if somebody on that force abuses his authority and kills an innocent person? How about you hang in there, and because of that experience that you had, you take it and try to make the system better. You talk to someone. You go to someone that can make a difference. I believe you uphold the law, and if you find something wrong in its application, you're not a bad person—you upheld the law. But if you're upholding it and you don't feel that it's right—and you say nothing and do nothing—that's where your responsibility to society really manifests itself.

THE NECK OF THE WOODS I GOT LOST IN

I've become increasingly aware that poor people are disproportionately chosen to be executed in this country, and in certain parts of the country, it's poor black people. I had become increasingly aware of that for some years before I dropped my support of the death penalty, but when you're a person who came from segregated schools and not being able to live in the dormitories in college, you understand why some systems may yet have those archaic and outdated protocols, and you equip yourself with patience.

I knew what it was to be treated differently because of my skin color, and those experiences gave me a framework of learning how to cope and deal with it, as long as I could find benchmarks of success. To me, this was just the neck of the woods I got lost in. I had to find my way out, and as long as I had a means of finding my way out, I was ready to deal with it. Getting out was always good enough of a motivation. So I came out to Oregon. I think I've been blessed and reached a reasonable degree of success in this area.

We're reaching the times when it's not that surprising anymore for a minority to do well. I mean, look at Obama. Who would've ever thought that would happen? Because you are a minority, you have unique challenges that are more specifically related to your race than you might otherwise. But I truly don't believe that anybody on the face of the earth does so without facing challenges of some sort.

I am a professional who happens to be black. I'm not a black professional. My life experiences come together on a day-by-day, circumstance-by-circumstance basis. If I approach things as a black man, I'll get a black response, when probably I just need to be getting a response out of life that has to do with being a human being. Sometimes, that calls for becoming an activist, and if the circumstance requires me to become an activist, I will. I am extremely pragmatic.

I'D BE CRAZY IF I WEREN'T OPTIMISTIC

Eventually I changed institutions. If another execution had taken place, I would not have been the one to conduct it. I remained in the prison system—at one time, I had the administration of eleven of Oregon's thirteen prisons—and had made up my mind that I wasn't going go public with my opposition to the death penalty until I retired, which I did in 2010.

When the governor announced that he was putting a moratorium on the death penalty, I was very happy. I had already come out of the closet, so to speak, when he made the announcement. I had written a letter to his office letting him know that I was going to become active, and I had let Oregonians for Alternatives to the Death Penalty know that I wanted to become a part of their organization. But I learned of the actual moratorium in the media like everyone else.

I joined Oregonians Against the Death Penalty in 2011. It's a group of professional people from all walks of life: human services, ministers, lawyers, businesspersons, artists, academics. They're very civic-minded, conscientious, caring people.

In college, my activism was more spontaneous—demonstrating, marching. We engaged with people on the street and students. Today, I deal with civic leaders, administrators. It seems that we can get more done because of our maturity in life and our jobs. We can talk to heads of organizations. We know people of means who can make contributions. When you're young, you haven't cultured those kinds of relationships.

Oregon has gotten rid of the death penalty three times since it's become a state. If you think about it, as long as we've been a state—I mean, two executions in fifty years now? Oregon doesn't really have a capital punishment practice. If the state were to execute somebody tomorrow, and say you've executed three people in fifty years, you still ought to put Oregon in the capital-punishment category reluctantly.

I'd be crazy if I weren't optimistic about abolition. If I were in Texas I'd be a little less optimistic, but here I think it's quite probable. It's time for Oregon to end the death penalty. It's just time. The problem we have here is that capital punishment is a part of the constitution, so it's difficult for legislators to legislate it away. They can put it on the ballot, but what scares me is that it is such an emotional thing. If this was on a ballot in Oregon a day after a mass shooting, it could be such an emotional thing. I mean, I'd hate for integration to be put on the ballot in some parts of the country, where you have urban unrest. We're going to be going for an initiative, and what we're really struggling for now is to raise the awareness and educate people that evidence-based outcomes should be the mantra for evaluating any public policy. That shouldn't be a hard thing here. Capital punishment generates such an emotional reaction, and people often take a position on it without really thinking.

If we do get it overturned, I have a little apprehension about that because I need a cause and a reason to get up in the morning. I'm not real sure what I'll do next.

THERE IS A UNIVERSAL PATTERN

I'm seventy-three years old, and I cannot remember when I have not been a religious person who believed in there being a God and there being an afterlife. The longer I live, the more I believe in that. Now, most of the various spiritual disciplines, in some ways, fail to answer all of the questions that one's own mortality presents to you. That's just the way life is. But there's one thing for sure: Life is going to end for all of us. Every human being who has contemplated their own mortality will meet their own demise.

Those two certainties ought to come together to cause a reasonable person to allow for the probability that those aren't the only certainties in the universe. There's no arguing that there was a beginning of your life, and there's no argument that there's going to be an end, and this whole process repeats itself over and over above our control unless we try to somehow interrupt it. There is a whole universe of facts that mankind can't contemplate or appreciate. Then how can mankind be so pompous as to declare the nonexistence of God? The more mankind comes to know and understand, the more mankind becomes aware and appreciates just how little is actually known and appreciated. I would submit to you that God exists in a realm that mankind is incapable of comprehending.

There is a universal pattern. There are those who would subscribe to the fact that the Big Bang started it all. I accept the Big Bang theory, but the Big Bang theory for me is nothing more than an expression of there being an intelligent designing capacity to the universe—and I call that God. There are too many people who feel like allowing for there to be a God is abandoning common sense, logic, and scientific appreciation.

As long as I live the kind of life that I think is moral and sensitive to the well-being of my fellow man, I don't fear my death. I don't want to linger here on earth to where I can't get up to go piss when I want to, and to where I can't tell a person "Thank you for turning me over," and I'm writhing in pain. I don't want that. I want my last days to be those where I look back and say, "You know, you made some mistakes, Frank—and some of them were fairly stupid and reckless—but by and large, you've been a pretty good old dude." If I can look back and feel that God is pleased with the life I have tried to live, then I don't have a problem. I'm not fearful.

\\

CONDUCTED JUNE 30, 2016

ACKNOWLEDGMENTS

Emily Cable kept me fed and housed for the eighteen moody months I worked on this project, and for some crazy reason she married me in the middle of it. Her inspiring mantra, "You just gotta do it, man," got me through many a long day.

This project would not have materialized without a leap of faith from Daniel Harmon and the unwavering support of my dear friend Adam Grano. Thank you both. I also had amazing sidekicks in my editorial assistants, Kate Wilson and Julia Mucha, who tackled endless hours of transcription and gave me invaluable feedback on the project. Elizabeth Kurata also helped with transcription, and is cool. I had additional assistance from my longtime editor and mentor Mark Baumgarten, my inspiring friend Liz Crain, and the unbeatable Bay Area trifecta of Clara Sankey, Andi Winnette, and Laura Howard. The Jarman and Cable families were also both endlessly supportive and encouraging. There are too many Portland-area supporters to thank, but most of the people I love are between Sauvie Island and the Terwilliger Curves; between Pittock Mansion and Mt. Hood. Hang in there, guys.

Above all, I'd like to thank all the tough, smart, hilarious women who have always been my mentors, my confidants, my best friends, and my heroes. You taught me how to be myself, kept me from losing my mind, and more often than not, kept me employed. Most importantly, where this book is concerned, you taught me how to communicate honestly and openly. I owe you everything, and when I pay it all back, I swear I'll do better than seventy-nine cents on the dollar.

ADDITIONAL THANKS

Courtney Campbell, Kelly Clarke, Wynde Dyer, Father Noel, Eden Dawn, Kyle Morton, David Huddle, Willy Vlautin, Tom Bissell, Will Weimers, Michael Heald, Emily Cooke, Jim Sandberg, Henry Huntington, Amy Dials, Amy Sly, Brian Mumford, Ben Hubbird, Rich Kahan, Dave Goshien, Joe Ring, Ally-Jane Grossan, Fiona McCann, Karolina Waclawiak, Ross Simonini, Sam Riley, Laura Gibson, Holly Munoz, Aku Ammah-Tagoe, Isaac Fitzgerald, Jordan Karnes, Daniel Levin-Becker, Devan Cook, Amy McCullough, Jared & Brianne Mees, Aaron Mesh, Annie Wyman, Carrie Clements, Carson Ellis, Neko Case, Jonah & Gabi, Helen & Garrett, Kathryn Borel, Vendela Vida, Grady Herndon, Jay Horton, Nilina Mason-Campbell, Matt Singer, Katrina Nattress, Jason Simms, Michael Byrne, Jessi Brandhagen, Rachel Taylor Brown, Chris Lydgate, Zach Dundas, Michael Mannheimer

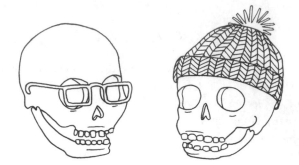

ABOUT THE AUTHOR

Casey Jarman is a writer, editor, and illustrator based in Portland, Oregon. He graduated from the University of Oregon with a journalism degree in 2004. He lives with his wife and two cats, and works out of a small office in the train station downtown. Casey has written—mostly about music and film—for *Nylon*, *Huck*, and *Portland Monthly*. He has served as music editor at *Willamette Week*, and as managing editor at the *Believer*, where he remains a contributing editor. In 2013, he co-founded Party Damage Records, which has released fifteen albums to date. He plays too many video games, collects too many books and records, and he has a love for obsolete technology that borders on creepy.

ABOUT THE ILLUSTRATOR

Brooke Weeber is a Portland-based artist. She received her BFA in painting from the University of Oregon in 2003 before moving to the east coast, where she picked up another degree from the French Culinary Institute of New York. After working for four years as a high-end cake decorator in New York City, she re-rooted herself in Portland, Oregon, in 2009. She sells prints and greeting cards featuring her art at local boutique shops and around the world. When she's not making art, Brooke camps, climbs, and generally explores the wilderness of the Northwest with friends and with her dog, Huxley.